KT-405-924

THE AA GUIDE TO
The Lake District

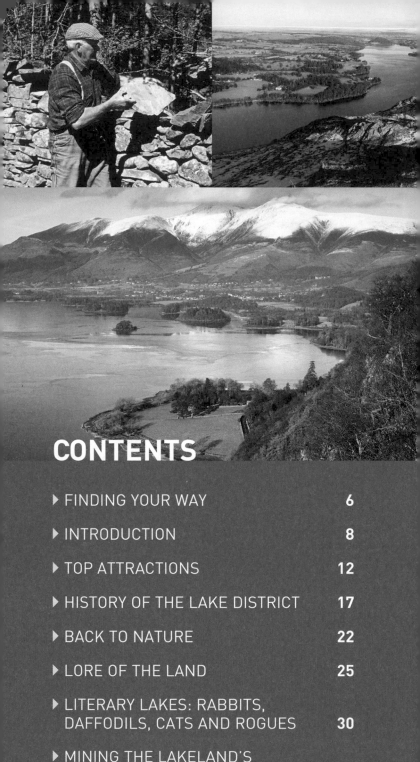

CONTENTS

▶ Finding your way

Use the maps below together with the atlas section and the town plans throughout the guide to explore the Lake District. The A–Z section lists the best of the region, followed by recommended attractions, activities and places to eat or drink. The Places Nearby section then lists other points of interest within a short travelling distance to help you explore a little further.

Many of the restaurants that we've included carry an AA Rosette rating, which recognises cooking at different levels nationwide, from the very best in the local area to the very best in the UK. Pubs have been selected for their great atmosphere and good food. You can find more Rosette-rated places to eat at theAA.com.

We're guessing you probably have your accommodation sorted already, but for those who like to play it by ear, we've recommended a few campsites to help you out (see page 50). Caravan and campsites carry the AA's Pennant rating, with the very best receiving the coveted gold Pennant award. If your tastes run more to luxury then theAA.com also lists AA-rated hotels and B&Bs.

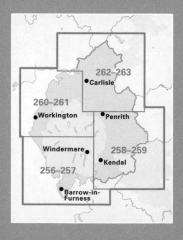

INTRODUCTION

Close your eyes and try to imagine a landscape so excruciatingly picturesque that it takes your breath away. Now visualise yourself standing on a high fell top, looking out over a lush green valley with sunlight shimmering on the surface of the lake running along its length.

You see a shadow on the water, as an osprey swoops from the sky and snatches a plump fish in its talons before soaring skywards again. If you can visualise that you're halfway there but, in reality, the Lake District is far more beautiful than anything you could possibly imagine.

The Lake District is part of the County of Cumbria, an area stretching from the Scottish Border in the north to Lancashire and North Yorkshire in the south – from the Irish Sea in the west to Northumberland and County Durham in the east. It's a mountainous region containing the highest peaks in England, two National Parks and Hadrian's Wall, a World Heritage Site.

Cumbria has the second lowest population of any of the English counties yet the Lake District is the most populated of all the National Parks. Even so, the 41,000 people who live

there make little impact. It is largely rural with only one city and only five towns with a population of more than 20,000, so there is plenty of space for visitors.

There are lots of reasons for visiting the Lake District. You may be interested in its historic sites, outdoor areas or tourist attractions. Or you may simply be looking to get away from it all, a place where you can hide away in a remote cottage with a pile of books, a bottle or three of wine and a roaring log fire. If you are keen on archaeology then there are enough ancient sites and remains to spend the rest of your life poking around, and still not cover a fraction of them.

Naturally, it's the best place in England for hill walking with so many routes to choose from. Peace and quiet is popular and, contrary to popular belief, always easy to find. Even at the height of summer, with congested roads and hordes bustling round the main beauty spots, it is still possible to find solitude. On the Northern Fells, in an area known as the Back o' Skiddaw, you can spend days walking and not meet another soul. These fells lie north of Blencathra and Skiddaw, separated from them by a marshy area shown on maps as Skiddaw Forrest – although you'd be hard pushed to find much in the way of trees there. Beyond the highest point, Knott is a wonderful circular walk that goes through Trusmadoor – a mountain pass between Meal Fell and the amusingly named Great Cockup – before flanking Little Cockup to return to the road. Spend an afternoon there and you might start to believe that you are the last person left on Earth.

Then there's the area's reputation for fine food and drink. Nothing tastes quite as good as a few slices of freshly cut Cumberland ham. Another mouth-watering experience is Tattie Pot, a rich, lamb-based stew, which is greatly enhanced by the addition of black pudding.

Cumbria has been described as a 'foodie heaven' with good reason. You'll easily find locally grown and produced delicacies, such as Cumberland sausage, Herdwick mutton, the famous Kendal Mint Cake and Grasmere Gingerbread as well as many different products made from damsons, which have been grown in Westmorland since the early 18th century.

There's a very popular food festival held in Cockermouth every September and that's the best place to sample and buy Cumbrian fare. At other times, you can arrange your own tours around the various artisan producers. Or, if you prefer a more hands-on approach to food, you can sign up for a variety of courses where you can learn to cook, bake, cure hams, preserve food in traditional ways or even acquire the skills and knowledge needed to forage for food in the wild.

If you would prefer an activity holiday then look no further. It's hardly surprising that fell walking is one of the most popular outdoor activities in the Lakes, or that there are abundant opportunities for sailing, kayaking, canoeing, waterboarding, windsurfing and water-skiing.

Why not try your hand at quad bike riding, abseiling, scrambling, rock climbing, caving, aquaseiling or even ghyll and gorge scrambling – that's if you don't mind getting wet. There are opportunities to try skydiving, paragliding or learning to fly a fixed-wing aircraft and glider. Or you could try outdoor survival skills, and learn to cook with a Kellie Kettle, trap animals and build a survival shelter. And don't forget that this is also an amazing place to go cycle touring or mountain biking.

▶ Ashness Bridge, Skiddaw Mountain in background
◀ Derwent Water (previous page)

TOP ATTRACTIONS

▲ Derwent Water

Derwent Water (page 118) is over a mile wide, making it the Lake District's widest lake. It also has a number of charming islands, and some amazing waterfalls on its eastern side. The lake and its surrounds are accessible by ferries, running from seven landing stages, making this an ideal area for climbing, walking, sight-seeing and relaxing.

▼ Cumberland Pencil Museum

Bizarre yet fascinating, this unusual museum (page 163) looks at the history and technology of the humble pencil, which was, apparently, first made locally in the 16th century. (Graphite was discovered in nearby Borrowdale.) Ideal for kids, with an on-site giant, puzzle trails, and other exciting stuff.

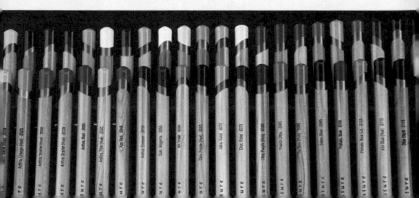

◄ Theatre by the Lake

Described as 'the most beautifully located and friendly theatre in Britain' (page 164), this venue is just a short stroll from Derwent Water. The 400-seat main house and 100-seat studio host up to nine productions a year. There are also a variety of festivals, visiting companies and musicians, and the theatre is open all year.

▶ Brantwood

Brantwood (page 106) is one of the most beautiful houses in the Lake District. It was home to writer, artist and thinker, John Ruskin, from 1871 until his death in 1900. There is a museum on Ruskin, and the estate's grounds are also well worth a visit. Ancient woodland, lakeshore meadows, open fell and eight landscaped gardens.

◄ Brockhole

Brockhole (page 246) is set in 32 acres of grounds on the shore of Windermere. Opened in 1969, it was England's first National Park Visitor Centre. You'll find all the info on the Lake District you could want, as well as details on lake cruises and canoe hire. There's an adventure playground, indoor play area and extensive events programme including exhibitions.

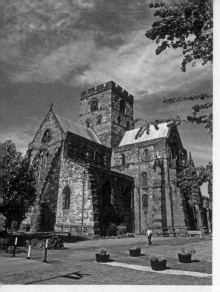

◄ Carlisle Cathedral

Carlisle Cathedral (page 91) was founded in 1122 as a priory, but became a cathedral in 1132 and has held a daily service for almost 900 years. It has a magnificent high ceiling, with a beautiful blue background and gold painted stars; stained-glass windows dating from the 14th to the 20th centuries, and a 16th-century Brougham Tryptich altarpiece made in Amsterdam.

► Honister Slate Mine

Honister (page 72) is the last working slate mine in England. You can explore the caverns hacked out by Victorian miners, learn the history of the famous Honister green slate, find out how to rive slates and see local skills in action. The tour is both underground and overground and involves some clambering.

◄ Rydal Mount

Rydal Mount (page 206) was poet William Wordsworth's home from 1813 until his death in 1850. He lived here with his wife, three children, his sister and his sister-in-law; and wrote more than half of his published poetry here. The house was originally a farm, built in 1550, and enlarged about the middle of the 18th century. The garden here is still much as he left it.

▲ The World of Beatrix Potter

The World of Beatrix Potter (page 245) is just like stepping into the books and meeting old friends. The exhibition features 3D scenes from Potter's tales, complete with sounds and smells which transport you to the bustle of Mrs Tiggy-Winkle's kitchen and help you savour the ripe tomatoes in Mr McGregor's greenhouse. Walk through Jemima's woodland glade, the Peter Rabbit Garden, and see the gooseberry bush where Peter got caught in a net. There's also an interactive timeline, which tells the author's life story.

▼ Hill Top

This small 17th-century house (page 193) is where Beatrix Potter wrote many of her famous children's stories. It's just as she left it, and in each room you can recognise something that appears in one of her books. Her will decreed that Hill Top should remain exactly as she had known it, and it is chock full of Beatrix Potter memorabilia, including her original drawings.

◀ Lake Windermere

Windermere (page 240) is England's longest lake, and it's very easy to get on to, either by hiring a dinghy, or on a cruise via Waterhead and Lakeside. Belle Isle, the largest of the lake's islands, still has the romantic round house built there in 1774. There's plenty of lakeside walking on the western shore, much of which belongs to the National Trust.

▶ South Lakes Wild Animal Park

You can hand feed giraffes, penguins and kangaroos or get up close to rhinos, tigers, bears, hippos, monkeys, vultures and lemurs at South Lakes (page 115). There are aerial walkways and viewpoints, a gift shop and restaurant, all overlooking a recreated African Savannah.

◀ Muncaster Castle

The view from the terrace of Muncaster Castle (page 190) is quite something, but there's much more to this charming Victorian castle. Lord Muncaster remodelled both the medieval remains and the 18th-century house to create a castle complete with towers, carved chimneypieces, an octagonal library and a collection of silverware.

HISTORY OF
THE LAKE DISTRICT

Prior to 1974, Cumbria didn't exist. That is, in the political sense; the land and everything it contains, of course, has been around much longer – several millennia in fact.

Politicians created this 'new' place with an Act of Parliament, which took the ancient counties of Westmorland, Cumberland, Carlisle, North Lonsdale, Lancashire North of the Sands and part of the West Riding of Yorkshire, and stuck them all together. However, it's good to know that this ceremonial name changing had little effect on the locals and you'll still hear them using the old names and find newspapers with such subversive titles as the *Westmorland Gazette* and the *Cumberland and Westmorland Herald*.

So much for Cumbria's recent history but if you were to go back to the very early Stone Age, you would find a large community of people living and working here. They've left few signs but if you wander about the southern slope of Pike O' Stickle in Langdale and look for the small cave near the summit you'll be exploring one of the most important stone axe factories in Europe.

▲ Castlerigg stone circle

Life advanced slowly through the Mesolithic period before entering the Neolithic or New Stone Age. However, by the early Bronze Age (4,500–1,500 BC) folk were getting the hang of building stone circles, lots of them. About 25 per cent of all the stone circles in England are here. From the spectacular and easily accessible – such as Castlerigg (see page 101) and Long Meg and her Daughters (see page 138) – to the obscure, remote and partially buried remains that you're likely only to spot while exploring the remote moorland on foot.

The builders of these ancient monuments made and worked with bronze, turning it into axes, spearheads and luxury goods. They developed trading networks, via the main valleys, plains and along the coast, which connected the various settlements. Unfortunately, only a few isolated examples of their bronze works have been found in the area.

Next the Celts arrived and with them the Iron Age. The Celts were a tribal people and it was the Carvetii tribe who settled in North Cumbria. They lived in roundhouses, enclosed by a ditch and bank or, in some cases, a dry-stone wall. They probably spoke a version of *Brythonic*, the great-great-grandfather of modern Welsh. Ancient names, such as Blencathra, hold echoes from that time. Go tramping across the fields and fells and you'll find plenty of evidence of settlements, field systems and their network of hill forts. Those at Swarthy Hill and Carrock Fell have been dated to around 500 BC.

Around AD 43, the Romans – intent on world domination – arrived in England. But it took them the next 30 years to sort out the troublesome southerners and make it to the Lakes. The impact of these invading legions is still highly visible in the region in the roads and forts they left behind. For example, the Stangate was an ancient road that was built to link forts in modern-day Carlisle with Corebridge in Northumberland.

However, the Romans never really got to grips with the tribes north of the Solway, so Emperor Hadrian had a huge wall built to keep them out – and you'll find the longest visible stretch of it in Cumbria. You can trace the line of the Roman road from Brough (see page 78) – via the fort of *Galave* at Ambleside (see page 55) – to Ravenglass (see page 200), where you'll find the tallest surviving Roman structure in the UK. The bathhouse that served the nearby fort of *Glannaventa*, dates from the second century. If you drive up the narrow, twisting road that climbs the impossibly steep Hardknott Pass (see page 144), you'll find the extensive remains of another fort founded by Hadrian and see the outline of the commandant's house, parade grounds, bathhouse and barracks.

The Romans hung around for several centuries but by AD 410 they'd gone home and Britain entered the Dark Ages – so-called because few records remain, yet a number of myths and legends date from this time. One such tale is that King Arthur, for example, actually roamed around Cumbria and not Cornwall, as historians would have you believe. Arthur's father, Uther Pendragon, allegedly lived in a castle in the Eden Valley. In his book, *The Quest for Merlin*, Tolstoy firmly places the tribe of Arthur in modern northwest England/southwest Scotland.

Warlords quickly filled the power vacuum left by the Romans and while they were busy doing what warlords the world over do, Christianity arrived. St Patrick may be the patron saint of Ireland, but before he went there to interfere with the snake population, he lived in Cumbria. He was probably born near Ravenglass or somewhere on the Solway. St Ninian was another local holy chap who crossed the Solway, and introduced Christianity to the Scots. St Mungo, alias St Kentigern, was another. He headed north into Strathclyde to do a spot of missionary work but they threw him out. Fortunately, he was a persistent soul and went back to eventually found a little place called Glasgow.

▼ Hardknott Roman Fort, Hardknott Pass

By the seventh century, it was the turn of the Anglo Saxons to invade and they set about Anglicising the Celts with a spot of applied genocide, ably assisted in their gruesome mission by the Black Death. Meanwhile, royal patronage considerably boosted the power of the church when, in 685, a bishop called Cuthbert was given 'Cartmel and all the Britons therein'.

As the power of the bishops increased and their estates expanded, they built fabulous abbeys, monasteries and churches. Life was good, if you were a bishop. Until, of course, the pesky Vikings came along and spoiled everything. Unlike the royals, the bishops' ineffective military meant they were unable to defend their estates against the invading hordes.

Next came the Norsemen who, no respecter of the locals, raped, pillaged and laid the countryside to waste, reducing Carlisle to rubble. They had so much fun they decided to stay in the region for a while. Today, many descriptive names, introduced by the Norsemen – including dale, howe, thwaite, fell and the famous Herdwick sheep – are still in common usage.

Cumbria also shares a border with Scotland and there are periods in its history when it was part of Scotland. The Normans took it from the Scots in 1072 and built Carlisle Castle to stop them from taking it back again. Despite this, the Scots returned in 1136 and stayed until they were kicked out again in 1157.

Many of Cumbria's square stone towers, or peles, date from the 15th and 16th centuries when they were built to defend the local landowners against the border reivers, who made frequent raids – carrying off livestock and any human beings they thought worthy of a ransom. Raids went in the opposite direction too and you'll find a similar network of towers on the Scottish side of the border.

Cumbria is rich in minerals, and they've been mined here since the 12th century. This activity peaked during the Industrial Revolution, when new communication networks were needed to transport minerals, raw materials and goods manufactured in the Cumbrian factories and mills. As a result, three canals were built at Kendal (see page 154), Ulverston (see page 225) and Carlisle (see page 88). Then the railways came and the canals declined. In turn, the motorcar brought about the decline of the railways but by then the era of the tourist had dawned.

The Romantic poet William Wordsworth was instrumental in encouraging the upper classes and literati to visit by writing his *Guide to the Lakes* in 1835, even though he was against the general masses spoiling his Lakeland idyll. Later, Wainwright's *Pictorial Guides to the Lakeland Fells* encouraged increasing numbers to visit as fell walking became fashionable. The railways also enabled rich industrialists from Lancashire to reach the lakes easily, and so they built their great mansions round Windermere (see page 193).

It wasn't long, however, before the continually rising visitor numbers started to have an adverse effect on the environment and so the Lake District National Park was formed in 1951. Its aim was to preserve the countryside from commercial and residential expansion. Tourism continued to increase with the building of the M6, which allowed easier access to the northwest. Nowadays the old narrow roads within the national park get congested during peak periods.

Until the end of 20th century, Cumbria had an industrial base that included shipbuilding, gypsum, bakeries and nuclear power. Calder Hall at Sellafield was the world's first commercial nuclear power station. Closed in 2004, the site is now used to reprocess spent nuclear fuel from around the world. The Sellafield Visitor Centre was once a major attraction, drawing 1,000 visitors a day but its popularity declined and it is now a conference centre.

Now, in the 21st century, agriculture and forestry are all major industries and, more recently, renewable energy and water have also started playing their parts in boosting the local economy. Tourism, however, remains the Lakeland's most vital industry and every year thousands of visitors flock here to walk, to take in the magnificent scenery or to simply enjoy the fine air, good food and convivial company.

BACK TO NATURE

Did you know that the collective noun for a group of toads is a knot? Or that those wonderful, furry, flying, mammals called bats are each capable of devouring over 3,000 midges in a single night?

With so few people actually living in this largely rural area, there's plenty of room for a huge variety of creatures. This is the best place to visit if you want to get up close to nature or see creatures you won't see in other parts of the country.

You'll also stand a good chance of spotting Britain's indigenous red squirrel here. While they have been all but wiped out in southern Britain owing to the advance of the North American tree rats (grey squirrels), red squirrels are still hanging on in the Lake District where they make their homes in the abundant conifer woods. Seek them out in the woodland round Thirlmere (see page 219).

Another rare sight is the osprey. With a wingspan of up to 5.5 feet, this massive raptor is very popular owing to its spectacular hunting techniques. Swooping down to the water's surface with talons outstretched and wings swept back, it snatches an unlucky fish from under the surface before taking off again. Once a common sight in Britain, ospreys were hunted nearly to extinction

◀ Rare red squirrel ▲ Osprey

by 1916. A breeding pair returned to Scotland in 1954 and with conservation protection their population has grown. They reappeared in England in 2001 when a pair nested in the Lake District. They spend the winter months in Africa so you'll only see them here between early spring and mid-autumn. Osprey nest in pine forests near lakes and rivers where they can find food. If you head to the osprey observation point (see page 232), a ten-minute walk uphill from the Mirehouse car park, north of Keswick , you'll enjoy a wonderful view over Bassenthwaite Lake. You'll need to hang about a while to catch a glimpse of one though. If you don't fancy the trek or can't manage it, the Whinlatter Forest Visitor Centre (see page 232) has a video link to an osprey's nest.

Natterjack toads are probably the noisiest of the amphibians and during their mating season can be heard for miles. You can tell them apart from the common toad by a yellow line which runs down the middle of their backs and their shorter legs make them appear to run rather than hop.

Although this is not the most northerly colony (that's on the Scottish side of the Solway) Cumbria has two of the country's largest colonies in England and about 65 per cent of the total natterjack toad population. During the breeding season from April to June, the National Trust Nature Reserve at Sandscale Haws near Barrow in Furness runs guided tours.

Like natterjack toads, bats are nocturnal and the best way to see them is on an organised tour. Eight distinct species can be found in Cumbria including the pipistrelle, Soprano pipistrelle, Daubenton's, Brown long-eared, Brands's, Natterer's, Whiskered and Noctule. The National Trust run organised bat walks at Fell Foot Park, Newby Bridge, Windermere, at Acorn Bank, Temple Sowerby near Penrith and at Sizergh Castle south of Kendal (visit nationaltrust.org.uk for details).

Cumbria is home to some pretty rare butterflies too. Bring a field guide with you and see how many you can spot. The National Nature Reserve at Finglandrigg Wood (see page 95) on the Solway Plain is a large area of semi-natural woodland where you'll sight some toppers – including the marsh fritillary. This butterfly was extinct in Cumbria by 2005 but was reintroduced in 2007 and is doing very well. Mid-May through to the first half of June is when you should look for it. You may also come across the purple hairstreak, pearl-bordered fritillary and ringlet butterflies during the summer, as well as the forester and silver hook moth. This reserve also contains peat bog, heathland and rough pasture providing homes for shy creatures such as the otter and badger, roe deer, brown hare and tiny wood mouse. Keen twitchers can spot over 40 species of birds, including long-tailed tits, tawny owls, buzzards, reed buntings, grasshopper warblers, garden warblers and willow tits.

A rare gem of an insect canalso be found here. The mining bee is a solitary beastie unlike the sociable honey or bumblebees. The female lays her eggs in a series of underground chambers along with some nectar and pollen. This keeps the larvae going until they become adults and head for the surface in the spring. Don't worry about getting stung as these bees are not at all aggressive.

The reserve is well served with interpretation boards covering the history and the wildlife of this spectacular landscape and how it is managed.

▼ Tawny mining bee

LORE OF THE LAND

In the wild, dramatic landscape of the Lake District, it was believed that the caverns and fissures in the rocks were the entrances to fairyland, while elves dwelt in the hills and inhabited burial mounds where they feasted at night. An old tale tells of a man who was thrust off his horse by the elves and, had he not had a Bible in his pocket for protection, would have been dragged into their den, never to be seen again. Travellers also traditionally carried iron or steel crosses and rosaries as charms against the evil powers of fairies, and made sure that they crossed over running water to dispel the fairy influences. Elves, it was thought, could also use minute arrows or 'elf shot', given to them by the fairies, to kill cattle in the dead of night.

Massive in the memory

Giants loom extra large in Lakeland lore and evidence of their presence is all around, from the tumulus at Standing Stones in Cumbria – marking the grave of a giant killed in battle – to Kentmere Hall built with the aid of the Troutbeck Giant – a man of

huge strength and appetites who, unaided, lifted a beam that had defied the muscle of ten ordinary mortals. Most spectacular of all is the Giant's Grave in a Penrith churchyard, a pair of 11-foot-tall mutilated stone crosses and four hog-back stones – said to symbolise wild boar killed in nearby Inglewood Forest – and a cross known as the Giant's Thumb.

What's intriguing is that the grave, said to be the resting place of Sir Hugh (or Ewain) Cesario, may commemorate two heroes conjoined in folk memory – Owain, son of Urien of Rheged from the late sixth century, and 10th or 11th century King Owain of Strathclyde. Near Edenhall, a pair of Giants' Caves, or Isis Parlis, sited on the face of a perpendicular rock, were the refuge of Sir Hugh – and the alleged abode of the Giant Isis who seized men and cattle, then drew them into his den to devour them.

Lakeland spirits

Today, you can waterski across Lake Windermere, but in the past you would have always needed a ferryman to row you over. Legend has it that one stormy night, the ferryman was called from Rawlinson's Nab on the eastern bank, but returned from his mission alone and 'ghastly and dumb with horror' having been summoned by a mysterious spirit – the Crier of Claife. A few days later the ferryman died and for weeks afterwards shouts and yells could be heard from the Nab, particularly when storms were raging. People were so afraid that a monk was called to confine the troublesome ghost to a quarry on Claife Heights above the lake. He's believed to be there still, wailing with the wind.

Haunting Thirlmere Lake is a black dog, seen swimming across the lake in a ghostly replay of the marriage of a murdered bride, half-strangled and then thrown into the water to drown. Armboth House, where the wedding was to have taken place, is now beneath the waters of the reservoir created in 1894. But it's said that on the anniversary of the tragedy, which happens to be Hallowe'en, the wedding feast is laid out and the sounds of church bells, eerie music and breaking plates echoes up from the deep.

Nature lore

Trees in the Lake District have special powers. Owing to its ability to overcome the malign influence of witches and evil spirits, sprigs of rowan (mountain ash) were hung in shippons and stables to protect valuable animals, and in dairies to make butter solidify or 'come'. In order to see the 'dead light' or spirit form of someone who had recently passed away, a branch of yew was cut with a large V-shaped notch in one end then lowered to the ground, while its bearer knelt with his right eye closed and peered through the V.

Individual trees stand out too. At Satterthwaite a massive oak tree was regularly decorated with rags and crockery on Maundy Thursday in a ceremony inherited from pagan tree worship, while at Hesket-in-the Forest and near Anthorn hawthorn trees mark out the locations of ancient courts. To commemorate the death of a hound named Hercules, who expired after chasing a stag from Whinfell to Redkirks in Scotland and back again, the Hartshorn Tree on the Clifford Estate was decorated with the stag's horns. Equally legendary were the Capon Trees, like the one now marked with a memorial near Brampton. Lovers kept their trysts beneath the Brampton Tree until in 1746, when six Jacobite rebels were hanged from it, then drawn and quartered – transforming the tree to a place of dread haunting. Many a Brampton mother has threatened naughty children with punishment by the Capon Tree Boggles.

Beneath the branches of the oak trees that they held sacred, Lakeland Druids lived and worked their charms with the help of mistletoe gathered from nearby. At the centre of Castlerigg Stone Circle – a place of pagan worship – it's said that the beautiful virgin Ella, her neck garlanded with oak leaves, was sacrificed as a sop to the 'Great Spirit'. But although she was set on fire after the Arch Druid rubbed two pieces of wood together in strong sunlight, she was miraculously saved by the sudden upsurge of floodwaters.

Witches and wizards

Cumbria's famous witches include Mary Baynes, whose cottage reeked of brimstone – the 'Devil's perfume' – and who cursed a man who was later blinded in an accident. Like other witches, she could, at will, turn herself into a hare. The Eskdale Witch could do the same, and could only be killed with a silver bullet.

For extreme spookiness, few places beat the old coffin path in Wasdale over which bodies were carried by pony and cart to St Catherine's Church in Eskdale. One day, when a young man's body was being taken on its final journey, the pony bolted and both horse and corpse disappeared. A few months later, the same thing happened with the body of the man's mother. The villagers ran after the pony and found it – and the young man's coffin but not the mother's. Today it's said that the ghost of a horse can still be seen galloping over the moor at night, pulling a coffin behind it.

Cumbria lays claim to wizards too. Michael Scot, who lived in the 13th century, is said to have built a church in a single night; thrown rocks on to Carrock Fell, and turned a coven of witches to stone, thereby creating Long Meg stone circle, as a punishment for

▲ Rowan tree

dancing on a Sunday. He could summon demons and command the sea. He cured the illnesses of the Holy Roman Emperor, and measured the distance to the stars.

A matter of luck

Even if fitted with the latest electronic security devices, many prestigious Lake District homes are still 'protected' by drinking vessels known as 'Lucks'. Most famous is the Luck of Edenhall, near Langworthy, a glass beaker enamelled and gilded in green, red and white, and allegedly left by the fairies after they had been sorely interrupted by human intrusions while drinking. 'If that glass should break or fall/Farewell the luck of Edenhall', sang the fairies as they departed and, although the house was demolished, the glass – which was almost certainly brought from Syria at the time of the first Crusade in the 13th century – is preserved today in the V&A in London.

At Haresceugh Castle near Renwick, the Luck, now vanished, was a silver-rimmed wooden bowl, imbued with the power of a guardian spirit. Different again is the Luck of Burrell Green, a brass dish with a central spiral-shaped boss in the form of a rose, and assigned occult powers. In 1417, so the story goes, at the wedding between a daughter of the resident Lamb family and a king of Mardale, a servant was sent to the well for water. As he did so, hobgoblins appeared saying 'bring us food and wine and we will bless the wedding'. The servant did as he was told and was given the dish as a reward.

The idea that luck can change hands is still prevalent among Lake District farmers. When cattle are sold, the vendor traditionally gives back a portion of the money received to the purchaser. If this is not done, the animals will fail to thrive and could even die. On receipt of a knife, scissors or other cutting tool as a gift, then a penny is given in exchange, the coin symbolising the fact that the gift will not sever the friendship.

LITERARY LAKES: RABBITS, DAFFODILS, CATS AND ROGUE

A walk in the Lake District inspired one of the best-known poems in the English language. William Wordsworth and his sister, Dorothy, were returning to their home in Grasmere (see page 133) when, according to Dorothy, they 'saw a few daffodils close to the water side... as we went along there were more & yet more & at last under the boughs of the trees, we saw that there was a long belt of them along the shore, about the breadth of a country turnpike road.' Much later William sat down and wrote:

> *I wandered lonely as a cloud,*
> *That floats on high o'er vales and hills,*
> *When all at once I saw a crowd,*
> *A host, of golden daffodils;*
> *Beside the lake, beneath the trees,*
> *Fluttering and dancing in the breeze.*

◀ Lake Coniston and the Old Man of Coniston

If you visit in spring, you can still walk around Ullswater to Rydal Bay (see page 222) and see the bright yellow blooms.

Although the first English writer to mention the Lake District was Thomas Gray in 1769, its literary associations really began with Wordsworth. You can visit the large Georgian townhouse in Cockermouth (see page 102), where Wordsworth was born in 1770. He lived his entire life in the Lakes, moving first to Hawkshead to attend school, then travelling through Europe for a spell before taking up residence with his sister at Dove Cottage in Grasmere.

Other poet friends came to live nearby. Robert Southey who would later become Poet Laureate and Samuel Taylor Coleridge. They became known as the Lakes Poets. Wordsworth, his sister and family moved to Rydal Mount near Ambleside in 1813 and this is where he died on 23 April 1859. He was buried at the Church of St Oswald, Grasmere (see page 134).

Some of the best-known children's books have strong Lake District connections too.

You may not come across Postman Pat and Jess, his black and white cat, on your travels round the sparsely populated valley of Longsleddale near Kendal but that is the setting of ficticious 'Greendale'. John Cunnliffe, the creator of the *Postman Pat* children's books, lived in Kendal. Pat's Post Office was based on the one at 10 Greenside in Kendal, near where Cunnlife lived. Sadly the Kendal Post Office closed in 1993.

Beatrix Potter's delightful *The Tale of Peter Rabbit* and other stories may have had their genesis in Scotland but the success of that book and a small legacy enabled her to buy Hill Top at Near Sawrey (see page 193) where she moved in 1905.

Potter's charming fictional characters Jemima Puddleduck and Tom Kitten sprang from her experiences of living and farming there. As well as writing and illustrating, she became an acknowledged breeder of Herdwicks, the very hardy breed of fell sheep indigenous to the Lake District. She also bought up neighbouring farms and land in an attempt to preserve traditional fell farming. When Potter died, she left most of her estate to the National Trust. Today you can visit her farm at Hill Top, ramble across large parts of the countryside and view her illustrations at the Beatrix Potter Gallery (see page 147) located in her husband's former law offices in Hawkshead.

When you outgrew Peter Rabbit you may have enjoyed *Swallows and Amazons* and later followed Rogue Herries as he tramped the Lakeland fells. You can relive your childhood by joining the Swallows, or the Amazons, in their adventures. The stories involve

▶ Borrowdale

a lot of sailing and while the author, Arthur Ransome, set them in actual Lake District locations he moved things round a bit. The Lake described is Windermere (see page 240) but the land around about is actually Coniston (see page 105). A 1974 film, available on DVD, used Ransome's actual locations.

In 1924, Hugh Walpole bought Brackenburn, a traditional Cumbrian stone cottage on the west bank of Derwent Water. The views across the water to Skiddaw, and Castlerigg Fell were the inspiration for his series *The Herries Chronicles*. They're fiction but the landscape and buildings are real.

On a windy night in 1730 Francis 'Rogue' Herries brings his family to their ancestral home in remote Borrowdale:

'Under the black hills it seemed so very small, and in the white moonlight so cold and desolate... there were two little attic windows like eyebrows...'

The Hazelbank Hotel occupies the very spot where Walpole created this home of the 'Rogue' and the birthplace of his daughter Judith Paris. Take the bridleway from Rosthwaite, past the hotel and over the fells to the picturesque hamlet of Watendlath and seek out Judith Paris's House. A plaque on the corner is a clue.

You can see a lot of grand Lake District scenery by visiting the locations in *The Herries Chronicles*. Read the books and study maps, or cut corners by watching *Herries Lakeland – The World of Hugh Walpole and the Herries Chronicles*.

▼ Derwent Water

MINING THE LAKELAND'S RICH INDUSTRIAL HERITAGE

Seeing so many mountains and valleys with vast expanses of water and just a few, scattered, small towns, you could be forgiven for assuming that the Industrial Revolution bypassed the Lake District. However, you soon find lots of evidence to the contrary if you gently scrape the surface. While this area may not have been crammed full of the smoke and the fire-belching 'dark satanic mills', which characterised much of Lancashire and The Black Country, it did play its part.

Cumbria is blessed with lots of natural resources including minerals, rocks, slate and limestone. Add lots of water, a coastline, river estuaries, mountains and dense woodland and you have the raw materials that sustained the industrialised society of the 18th and 19th centuries.

The origins of Cumbrian industry go much further back though. During the neolithic, this was a major centre for making stone axes. When the Romans arrived they burned lime to provide building mortar. Later, during the Agrarian Revolution, lime was used to make the soil less acidic. Large-scale commercial kilns produced the lime but many farmers and builders built their own,

smaller kilns. Look for the remains of one on the pier at Whitehaven harbour. Walk the fells and the valleys and you'll soon come across more. At Greenside Lime Kiln in Kendal there's a large-scale commercial kiln with interpretation boards that tell you everything you need to know about the lime burning industry.

Cumbria is one of the most extensively mined areas in England and you'll find old workings throughout the county. Evidence of mining exists as far back as the 12th century, and no doubt was carried out by the Romans before that. Through the ages men have burrowed deep underground to extract lead, coal, copper, zinc, tungsten, barite, graphite and iron ore. Cumbria had, until recently, the last working iron ore mine in Europe. The Florence Mine closed in 2007 when it was no longer viable to keep pumping out the water. Its Heritage Centre closed at the same time but there are many similar sites that tell the story of mining in Cumbria.

On Whinlatter Pass, above Braithwaite, you'll find Force Crag, the last working metal mine in the region. It operated from 1839 to 1991, producing lead, zinc and barites. The buildings are early 20th century but it's the only site still containing most of its processing equipment. The National Trust runs periodic guided tours, which must be booked in advance.

At the top of the steep and narrow Honister Pass, connecting Borrowdale and Buttermere, is Honister Slate Mine (see page 72), which is still working and produces Westmorland green slate – it is a fascinating place to visit as you can see the slate being mined and worked. If you want a more detailed insight into this industry then sign up for their Industrial Heritage tour.

Borrowdale (see page 71) is also the place where graphite was first discovered in the 16th century, the only deposit of solid graphite ever found in such a quantity. At first shepherds used it to mark their sheep, then the government took over and used it to line cannonball moulds. Later, in nearby Keswick, it was used to make the first pencils. They are still made there and the original factory now houses the Cumberland Pencil Museum (see page 163), which is more interesting than it sounds.

You'll find the last traces of a vanished copper mining industry up a mile-long unsurfaced track behind Coniston village. Most of the mine buildings in Coppermines Valley have now been converted into holiday homes and a Youth Hostel but you may still come across shaft entrances. Don't under any circumstances venture inside. Many are highly unstable, some with rotten wooden floors, which you could fall through into the deep voids below. You'll get more enjoyment from your visit here if you check out the mining display in The Ruskin Museum (see page 107) in Coniston beforehand.

Locally mined ore was processed at Duddon Iron Works, near Broughton-in-Furness. What's left is one of the most complete charcoal-fired blast furnaces in Britain and a must-see. It opened in 1736 and produced iron for 130 years. Water powered, the bellows and locally produced charcoal fuelled the furnace. The remains have been partially restored and the interpretation boards provide a good overview of iron production.

Charcoal burners working in the Cumbrian woods were responsible for producing the fuel for this mighty furnace. Foresters ensured that there would be a constant supply of wood to feed the mills, which produced the bobbins essential to the Lancashire spinning and weaving mills. Stott Park Bobbin Mill (see page 177) was making quarter of a million of bobbins every week at its peak. It's one of the finest surviving examples and the mill's new exhibition covers the production from tree to bobbin on the original belt-driven machinery.

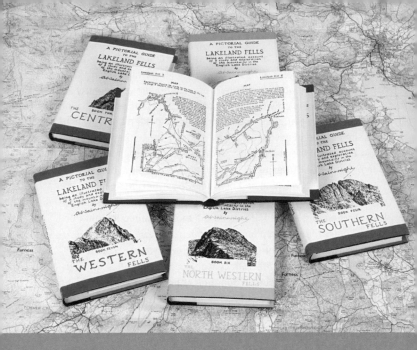

ALFRED WAINWRIGHT'S LOVE LETTERS TO THE LANDSCAPE

There is a wonderful series of small, handwritten and illustrated books by Alfred Wainwright, which have been aptly described as 'love letters to the landscape'. There are seven of them, each with the title *A Pictorial Guide to the Lakeland Fells*. Published between 1955 and 1966, they have been described by the author Mark Richards as being '… on a par with the songs of Lennon and McCartney, both innovative in their time and now classics of their genre.'

With the aid of these guides, you can explore the fells and remote places of Lakeland in the company of one who knew them best. They are the *de facto* reference manuals to 214 fells but can be read as much as a philosophical work than a series of dry instructions. Each guide contains observations, history, advice, opinions and some of the author's dry humour, such as the comment on his final resting place, 'And if you, dear reader, should get a bit of grit in your boot as you are crossing Haystacks in the years to come, please treat it with respect. It might be me.'

Even if you don't use them as guides you will want to own them. Mark Richards who has 'adored their tiniest detail since first discovering them at the age of 12', confesses to never having used them on the fells.

Alfred Wainwright is known to millions, but how did he come to write these little books and why are they still so popular?

Wainwright was born into a poor Lancashire family in 1907. He left school when he was 13 but, having done well, secured an office job with Blackburn Borough Engineers department. He studied hard at night school and eventually gained a qualification in accountancy, advancing his career in local government. Outside of work he had three main interests – walking, drawing and supporting Blackburn Rovers.

When Wainwright was 23, he went on a walking holiday to the Lake District and fell in love. Eleven years later he moved to the Lakes, got a job in the Borough Treasurer's Office in Kendal, eventually becoming Borough treasurer. He spent the rest of his life in the Lakes.

He had a very unhappy marriage and it was probably seeking escape from the problems at home that drove him to spend all his spare time walking on the fells, or in his small study working on his books.

He started the first book, *The Eastern Fells*, in November 1952 and it was completed by Christmas 1954. In its conclusion he wrote that other than climbing he would be 'happy to sit idly and dream of them...' However, he also realised that he should put something back so started to write about them, and to draw pictures. He went on walking trips at weekends, writing notes, sketching and taking photographs. Then he painstakingly prepared the pen-and-ink drawings and wrote the text in his neat handwriting. One page was an evening's work and it took him 13 long years to complete all seven books. In the final volume he concludes, 'When I came down from Starling Dodd... I had just succeeded in obtaining a complete view from the summit before the mist descended.' He'd been trying to get this view for weeks but managed just before the end of the summer bus service. He didn't drive and failure would have put the book back a year.

Wainwright self-published his first volume; it's a facsimile of the manuscript but his handwriting is so neat it looks typeset. Further volumes were produced by various publishers and are now available from Frances Lincoln. Obviously, if you plan to use Wainwright's guides for walking you'll also need an up-to-date OS Outdoor Leisure map.

In the 1970s, Wainwright's friend and fellow outdoor writer Mark Richards 'spent many weekends in his company, watching him craft his final guidebooks.' It was that close contact and influence that led Richards to produce *The Lakeland Fellranger* series. Published by Cicerone, these guides contain Harvey specialist walking maps but are illustrated by Mark's pen-and-ink drawings.

Wainwright divorced his first wife, Ruth, in 1967 and married the much younger Betty McNally, his walking companion, with whom he'd been having an affair. When he died on the 20 January 1991, Betty, following his wishes, scattered his ashes on his favourite fell.

'All I ask for, at the end, is a last long resting place by the side of Innominate Tarn, on Haystacks, where the water gently laps the gravelly shore and the heather blooms and Pillar and Gable keep unfailing watch. A quiet place, a lonely place. I shall go to it, for the last time, and be carried: someone who knew me all my life will take me there and empty me out of a little box and leave me there alone.'

In Buttermere Church there's a monument to the memory of this remarkable man and you'll find more information about the great man's life and works at Kendal Museum (see page 157) in Kendal.

▼ The summit of Haystacks

LOCAL SPECIALITIES

Cumbria is foodie heaven and many of the delicacies you'll find here are based on traditional, often secret, recipes that have been carefully handed down through the generations.

Cumbrian people are fortunate in having plenty of good quality local ingredients with which to work including meat from Herdwick sheep and hand-reared pigs and produce from well-husbanded dairy cattle. Add to that, wild game from the moors and forests and locally caught trout and salmon, char, shrimp and herring, and it's hardly surprising that Cumbria produces some mouth-watering dishes.

One of the most distinctive of all the Cumbrian delicacies is the long, flat, coiled, sausage. It's made from pork, chopped not minced, so it's chunkier than standard sausages. It now has protected geographical status, so you know anything labelled 'Traditional Cumberland sausage' was made here. Buy them from a local butcher and you can guarantee that the sausages on your plate won't contain any preservatives or artificial colouring.

Cumberland hams are dry cured in salt for a month and sometimes also rubbed with brown sugar. Then they are washed, dried and hung in a cool place for a few months to finish. You'll need to soak the ham overnight to remove a lot of the salt content before boiling it. It's mouth-wateringly delicious when sliced and served with pickle, fresh bread and salad. Or try it with the Cumberland sauce that's made from redcurrant jelly mixed with mustard, ginger, port and the juices of oranges and lemons. The sauce is also the perfect accompaniment for lamb and other meat dishes.

Stews and hotpots used to be staple food for most working people and you'll still find regional variations throughout Britain, from Irish stew to Lancashire Hotpot and Scottish Stovies. In Cumbria the finest dish of them all is Cumberland Tattie Pot. It's made from diced lamb with layers of carrots, swede and black pudding, topped with sliced potatoes, then baked in the oven until the meat is tender and juicy. Pickled red cabbage is a great accompaniment.

Then there's cottage pie. Similar to Tattie Pot, but with mushrooms and tomatoes instead of black pudding, it is stewed then topped with mashed potatoes and cheese. If you've read this far, your mouth is probably watering, and you'll find these dishes served in village pubs and small, family, restaurants throughout the Lake District.

Another Lakeland speciality is the delightful flavoured bread called A Whig which you'll come across in artisan bakers and village stores. There are different variations depending on the particular village. In Hawkhead they favour adding caraway seeds.

Grasmere Gingerbread is another Lakeland treat and can only be bought from one shop and, yes, you've guessed, The Gingerbread Shop (see page 134) in Grasmere. The shop's bakery is housed in the old village school and the gingerbread is still made from a secret recipe devised by Sarah Nelson, who died in 1904. You'll find it very different from most other gingerbreads. Cartmel Sticky Toffee Pudding, while originating in the village of the same name in the south Lakes, however, is widely available throughout the county as well as in Cartmel Village Shop.

If you get a chance, do sample Cumberland Nicky Rum. It's a flan made from rum, ginger, dates, molasses and

▼ Herdwick sheep

various spices. The pudding originated in Whitehaven, which was once England's second biggest port. During the time of the East Indies trading routes, these ingredients were among the cargoes unloaded here and small quantities were 'acquired' by returning seamen to take home to their wives.

Hilary and Tensing ate Kendal Mint Cake on the summit of Everest in 1953, and it's still made in Kendal by three different companies. However, its creation was apparently an accident. A confectioner, while making a batch of clear mint, had a lapse of concentration and the product ended up cloudy. But it tasted nice and so Mint Cake was born. It is widely sold in camping shops throughout the Lake District.

Having eaten your way through some of this stuff,

you'll be looking for something to wash it down with and there are lots of local beers to fit the bill. Keswick Brewery is a small, recently established craft brewer producing a variety of very tasty ales and beers. Jennings Brewery in Cockermouth (see page 102) was established in 1828 but is now part of a much larger brewing empire. However, it still makes exceedingly fine ales using pure Lakeland water. You can also seek out the many microbreweries that have sprung up over the last few years.

In more remote Ennerdale there's the excellent Ennerdale Brewery at Corasdale Farm and Old Hall Brewery is south of Hawkshead. There are many more. Some offer guided tasting tours and most have on-site shops.

▼ Jennings Brewery, Cockermouth

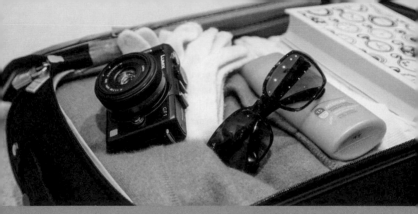

BEFORE YOU GO

THINGS TO READ

There are a few books you might like to start reading to whet your appetite before you pack your case and head off to the Lake District.

Hugh Walpole's *Herries Chronicles* (1930–33) would be a very good first choice (see also page 32), and if you don't want to read the entire series start with *Rogue Herries*, which has excellent descriptions of Borrowdale.

Surprisingly few crime novels have been set in the Lakes. Or so, novelist Martin Edwards discovered when he started looking at Cumbria as the backdrop for his novels, and so set his two main characters, DCI Hannah Scarlet, of the Cumbria Constabulary Cold Case Team and the historian Daniel Kind in the county. Try the first novel in the series, *The Coffin Trail* (2005) and you'll probably want to read the rest.

The true story of local lass Mary Robinson (1778–1837), known as the Maid of Buttermere is one which Wordsworth and Melvyn Bragg used in different ways. The poet mentions her in *The Prelude* (1850) while Bragg turned the tale into a novel (*The Maid of Buttermere*, 1987). Bragg was born and raised in the region and has written other books which are set here. *The Cumbrian Trilogy* (1969–80) is based mostly on Wigton and follows the lives of a family from the 1920s through to the 1970s. They may be works of fiction but *The Hired Man* (1969), *A Place in England* (1970) and *Kingdom Come* (1980) are all firmly rooted in the landscape and the history of the Lake District.

Ernest Hemingway featured the region in his novella *The Torrents of Spring* (1926), and Ian McEwan in his Booker Prize winning *Amsterdam* (1998). *The Plague Dogs* (1977), by Richard Adams, has lots of excellent and very accurate descriptions of the countryside, while Hunter Davies' *Wainwright: the*

▲ Bags packed, ready to go

Biography (2007) is a must read if you are interested in fell walking. Davies' biography, *William Wordsworth* (2009), deals with the poet's relationship with his sister, his marriage and his affair with a French girl that produced a child. Davies has also written several non-fiction books that are now over 30 years old but still worth reading. *A Walk along the Wall* (2000) and *A Walk Around The Lakes* (2000) are invaluable resources of information if you plan on walking here or along Britain's most important Roman monument, Hadrian's Wall. For a more-up-to date walking guide you can't beat *50 Walks in the Lake District* (2013) by AA Publishing.

THINGS TO WATCH

You shouldn't be surprised to learn that the Lake District is a major star of television and film. The great director, Alfred Hitchcock, used Langdale Chase Hotel near Windermere as his location for *The Paradine Case* (1947). And, although it sits at 1,000 feet above sea level, the market town of Alston (see page 54) was transformed into the fishing village of Bruntmarsh for the ITV dramatisation of *Oliver Twist* (1999).

Fictional Belgian detective, Hercule Poirot, moved with his characteristic 'rapid mincing gait' along the cobbled streets of Kirkby Lonsdale's (see page 169) Main Street and Market Square in the TV episode *Double Sin* (1990). But the rather elegant Art Deco hotel featured in the sereis is actually the Midland Hotel in Morecambe, just over the Cumbrian border in Lancashire. In October 2013, Kirkby Lonsdale was again transformed to play the part of early 19th-century Launceston for a BBC adaptation of Daphne Du Maurier's smuggling tale, *Jamaica Inn* (2013).

The BBC also made two series of *Wainwright Walks* (2007), with Julia Bradbury following many of the writer's walks. But it's the scenery that the steals the show. Both series are regularly broadcast on a number of satellite channels.

Lots of films have Lake District locations or are based on Lakeland stories. Ennerdale (see page 124) is instantly recognisable in the final scenes of Danny Boyle's, post apocalyptic horror, *28 Days Later* (2002), and the final scenes of Harold Pinter's interpretation of John Fowles' novel *The French Lieutenant's Woman* (1981) were shot around Windermere.

Pandaemonium (2000) is also worth watching as it tells the story of the early years of the Lakeland poets, William Wordsworth and Samuel Taylor Coleridge.

Although *Miss Potter* (2006) was mainly filmed in Italy and the Peak District, it's nevertheless a smashing introduction to Beatrix Potter's years in the Lake District.

Probably the best Lake District film of them all is *Withnail and I* (1987), a black comedy set in the 1960s. When the protagonists escape from London to Uncle Monty's cottage in the countryside it's the landscape round Shap and Bampton that you're seeing. Sleddale Hall, near Shap's Wet Sleddale Reservoir was used as the cottage. You'll find the telephone box that Withnail uses to phone his agent on the main road in Bampton, and the bridge – where he and Marwood go fishing – at the bottom of the hill from Sleddale Hall.

THINGS TO KNOW

Cumbria has the longest lake in England (Windermere), the deepest, (Wastwater), but confusingly only one real lake. Other than Bassenthwaite Lake the rest are all meres or waters.

You'll find England's smallest church, St Olaf's, at Wasdale Head, Europe's second smallest cathedral in Carlisle (see page 88), and England's highest peak, Scafell Pike, which reaches 3,210 feet.

In an area noted for its steep mountain passes, it's really not surprising that the Lake District has England's steepest road. Hardknott Pass (see page 144) has an overall gradient of 1 in 3 but parts of it are 1 in 2.5. It is also narrow and twisting, so don't try towing a caravan up or down here. It's so steep you might feel that your car is toppling backwards.

Ulverston (see page 225) was the birthplace of omedian Stan Laurel, the sport of pole vaulting and the cradle of the Quaker movement – their first headquarters were at Swarthmoor Hall (see page 225).

In the Pennine Hills, Alston Moor (see page 54) claims to be the highest market town in England. Keswick has the world's longest pencil (over 26 feet) and Hadrian's Wall is Britain's most important Roman monument. Long Meg (see page 138) is the second largest stone circle in Europe, and at Muncaster Castle (see page 190) you'll find one of the finest collections of captive owls in the world.

The most scenic railway line in Britain has to be the 72-mile stretch of the Settle–Carlisle line (see page 88), which runs through the Eden Valley and over the Pennines into the Yorkshire Dales. And, finally, a 2013 YouGov survey gave the accolade of 'Britain's Best Road' to the A591 between Windermere and Keswick.

THINGS TO PACK

OK, now you've made the decision to head to the Lake District. Do you go prepared and loaded for Arctic conditions or travel exceedingly light?

Which option you choose will depend on a number of factors, such as the time of year, what you want to do and your personal preferences. Even in the summer months you'll need wet-weather gear, unless you're very lucky, as well as sandals, sunscreen and swimwear. In winter, take plenty of warm clothing. Here's a few suggestions.

Fell walkers will need a good pair of walking boots, a small rucksack, layers of clothing – to regulate body temperature – and a waterproof outer shell. You'll also need a compass and the relevant OS Outdoor Leisure maps. You could take a GPS but don't rely on it for navigating. Batteries flatten and equipment malfunctions in more remote areas and could leave you stranded. Pack spare clothing, a flask for hot drinks, water bottle, enough food to keep you going – and don't forget the obligatory Kendal Mint Cake. You'll also need a decent walking guide so you might want to take a copy of the AA's *50 Walks in The Lake District*.

If you prefer water sports then you'll want a neoprene wetsuit. Even in the summer the water is perishingly cold. Do take a camera or video and don't forget to pack the charger. The scenery is so spectacular that you'll want to have lots of images to help you remember your trip.

Everyday clothes should be casual but comfortable. Swimwear, shirts, tops and shorts for during the day in summer, with long sleeves and trousers at night. There are some fancy restaurants in the Lakes so you might want to think about taking something that will you can dress up a bit if necessary.

You'll need a warm jumper or fleece in the evening, even in

▼ Scafell Pike

the summer. In winter, you'll probably want to keep one on during the day too.

There are plenty of clothing stores in the Lake District. Keswick, in particular, is a shopper's paradise as its many outdoor equipment shops seem to have permanent sales. If your idea of a grand holiday in the Lakes is just to go clothes shopping then the bare essentials are all you'll need. Don't forget your credit card.

BASIC INFORMATION

Before rushing headlong towards the Lake District spare a few minutes to read this section – your wealth and sanity may depend on it. Here are a few suggestions to keep you out of trouble, help preserve your bank balance and make the most of your trip.

Don't use a satnav

The very first thing you should know about visiting Cumbria is that in these parts, your satnav is not your friend. Lakeland has several, breathtakingly gorgeous but exceedingly steep, narrow, winding mountain roads that are a tad challenging. If you're not used to driving on roads like this, then you don't want your first experience of them to possibly be on a dark, wild, rainy night, trying to find your accommodation. If you are pulling a caravan as well, then you could be in trouble.

One local business went as far as to say that if potential visitors used a satnav to find them they would, 'end up on top of a fell', while another reported that most of their satnav-igating customers ended up at a remote farmhouse.

If you must use your satnav, then don't rely on it. Plan your routes on a map sticking to main roads and then programme the beast to stick to them. But don't avoid the Hardknott and Wrynose passes altogether or you'll be missing out on a great free Cumbrian attraction. You should try them during the day, however, when you can at least see what you're getting in to.

Think about when you want to visit

You may not have any choice about when to take your holidays but if you do, think first about why you want to come to the Lake District. During the summer months the main beauty spots and attractions get very crowded and the roads leading to them become congested. If you're heading out onto the fells it's not so bad but you'll still come across a crowd of other walkers. Going off-season you'll find the Lakes much quieter and over the winter months the fell walking is superb – particularly on a crisp, frosty day with a clear blue sky. The downside is that many of the attractions will have shut up shop until the spring.

Think picnic

If you hate waiting in a queue for a table or can't afford to eat out all the time consider buying some of the fresh Cumbrian goodies that are on sale everywhere. Freshly baked artisan bread, a slice or three of Cumberland ham, some local cheeses, farmhouse pickles and a bottle of locally brewed beer is all you'll need. Then have yourself a picnic on the fells, by a lake of even in your car, if it's raining.

Things to do with kids when it's raining

Nothing can ruin a family holiday quite as effectively as a few days of incessant rain. And, yes, it has been known to happen in the Lake District – even in August. Add a car full of bored restless children and your sanity might well be on a shaky peg indeed. Bundling them into paid attractions is a surefire way of burning a week's budget in a couple of days. There's the admission fee, a small gift from the shop ('Aw, pleeeease, can I just have a pencil or a rubber'), then lunch or afternoon tea. Even your bank manager will be weeping.

One solution might be to take out a family membership to the National Trust and use it to gain admittance to all of their properties whenever you want. Even when it's wet the children will have a great time sailing on the restored Victorian steam yacht *Gondola* on Coniston Water, or visiting Wordsworth's Birthplace in Cockermouth, Beatrix Potter's farmhouse or Sizergh Castle.

Many brownie points will be earned if you take them on the Lakeside Railway from Haverthwaite to Windermere. It's a short route, but the train is exceedingly slow. You might also want to visit the Aquarium of the Lakes before the return journey. The Beatrix Potter Experience is also a great treat, particularly if it's on a day when they are serving Peter Rabbit Teas – and they'll get fed as well. Rheged near Penrith, as well as being indoors, has an Imax cinema and a shop selling paper and art materials – perfect for keeping fidgety fingers busy.

▼ Peter Rabbit at the Beatrix Potter Experience

FESTIVALS & EVENTS

From the sensible to the downright bizarre, Cumbria has lots of festivals and events. Here's a selection of the best.

FEBRUARY

▶ **Keswick Film Festival**
Held in several venues including the Alhambra Cinema, Theatre on the Lakes and the Imax at Rheged.

MARCH

▶ **Words by The Water**
Celebrating books and words, this festival is held over ten days in Keswick.

APRIL

▶ **Bowness Bay Blues**
Held in a picturesque setting on the eastern shore of Lake Windermere, this event specialises in acoustic music and rhythm and blues.

MID-APRIL TO AUGUST

▶ **Peter Rabbit Tea Parties**
A great event for kids at The World of Beatrix Potter in Bowness on Windermere. The tea parties start with a rather splendid lunch of sensible edibles but follow with lots of cake. Beatrix Potter reads *The Tale of Peter Rabbit* then the kids get a small gift and a balloon. The ticket also includes entry to The World of Beatrix Potter, where you'll find the rabbit in question and more of Potter's characters including Mrs Tiggy-Winkle.

MAY

▶ **Cockermouth Georgian Fair**
Sedan Chair Races, Morris dancers, old-style fairground attractions, live period music and tumblers and jugglers feature at this popular event.

▶ **Ireby Festival**
The small, rural village runs a superb music festival featuring guests such as Eddi Reader and Kate Rusby.

▶ **Stepping Stones**
Folkies will love this small folk music festival launched by Steeleye Span's, Maddy Prior 2012, held in the grounds of Kirklinton Hall near Longtown.

JUNE

▶ **Appleby Horse Fair**
One of the longest running Cumbrian events is Appleby Horse Fair, which has been held in Appleby since 1685 when it was granted a Royal Charter by James II. This is a major tourist attraction for the town.

▶ **Dentdale Music and Beer Festival**
A chance to try 25 real ales.

▶ **Whitehaven Festival**
Harbour renovations mean that this festival won't run in 2014 but will resume in 2015. Established in 1998, the event is

hugely popular and offers a mix of live music, street theatre, visiting ships, air displays and street markets.

JULY

▶ **The Cumbria Steam Gathering**
Held at Cark Airfield in Flookburgh, near Grange-over-Sands, you can wander around a huge variety of steam engines, vintage commercial vehicles and classic cars, military vehicles, cars, motorbikes and bicycles.

▶ **Elephant Festival**
Kids will be delighted by this event, which takes place in the small town of Tebay. Everybody makes their own Elephant, which are and you'll find them displayed all over town.

▶ **Grass Roots Festival**
This three-day festival was established in 2006 to promote musicians and raise funds for Cumbria's Air Ambulance and the town's Mountain Rescue Team.

▶ **Maryport Blues Festival**
This well-established weekend event takes place in Maryport, the most southern town on the Solway Firth.

AUGUST

▶ **Kendal Calling**
A mixture of traditional rural entertainment, contemporary music and art in Lowther Castle Gardens, this is a small intimate event with a limited number of tickets. But with eight stages there's still enough variety to satisfy most people.

▶ **Lake District Summer Music Festival**
If your taste in music veers more towards the classical then this annual festival in Kendal will appeal.

▶ **Solfest**
If you want to take your children to a music festival then your first choice should be Solfest. This popular, eclectic gathering started in 2003. The emphasis is on providing a safe, family-friendly atmosphere with superb music. It's run as a not-for-profit venture by volunteers. The festival isn't running in 2014, but will make a triumphant return in 2015.

SEPTEMBER

▶ **Taste Cumbria Food Festival**
The county's best produce.

▶ **Egremont Crab Apple Fair**
This is the oldest fair in the world and offers a host of attractions, including the annual 'gurning' competition. Aspatria resident, Tommy Mattinson has won it 15 years in a row and is in the *Guinness Book of Records* as the World Champion. His father was ten times winner before him.

NOVEMBER

▶ **The World's Biggest Liar Competition**
This competition is held each year at the Bridge Inn, Santon Bridge (see page 203). It's a memorial to a Wasdale Publican called Will Ritson who was famed for his tall tales. The 2013 winner, 25-year-old Jack Harvey from Whitehaven, beat off 11 other contenders with his story that Cumbrians are, genetically, two per cent badger. Runner up was the Right Hon. Septicas Peabody who claimed that a fish and chip shop had been opened on the summit of Scafell Pike. Poor Johnny Liar, who had previously won the title seven times, was this time relegated to third place.

CAMPSITES

For more information on these and other campsites, visit theaa.com/self-catering-and-campsites

Woodclose Caravan Park
►►►►►
woodclosepark.com
High Casterton, Kirkby Lonsdale, LA6 2SE | 015242 71597 | Open Mar–Oct
Woodclose is set in idyllic countryside within the beautiful Lune Valley. Ideal for a 'back to nature' kind of experience, with riverside walks, woodland walks, top notch amenities blocks and a 'Wigwam' pod village. Wildlife abounds.

Skelwith Fold Caravan Park
►►►►►
skelwith.com
Ambleside, LA22 0HX
015394 32277 | Open Mar–15 Nov
In the grounds of a former mansion, Skelwith Fold is in a beautiful setting. A real plus is the five-acre family recreation area, which has spectacular views of Loughrigg Fell.

Wild Rose Park ►►►►►
wildrose.co.uk
Ormside, Appleby-in-Westmorland, CA16 6EJ | 017683 51077

Open all year (restricted Nov–Mar shop closed, restaurant restricted service, pool closed 6 Sep–27 May)
Situated in the Eden Valley, this large, leisure group-run park offers superb facilities including four wooden wigwams for hire. Traditional stone walls and the planting of lots of indigenous trees help it to blend into the environment, and wildlife is actively encouraged. New for 2014 is a stylish reception with adjacent internet café.

South End Caravan Park ►►►
walneyislandcaravanpark.co.uk
Walney Island, Barrow-in-Furness, LA14 3YQ | 01229 472823 & 471556 | Open Mar–Oct (restricted Mar–Easter & Oct pool closed)
A friendly family-owned park next to the sea and close to a nature reserve, on the southern end of Walney Island. It offers an extensive range of quality amenities including an adult lounge, and high standards of cleanliness and maintenance. There is a bowling green, and a snooker table is also available.

Dandy Dinmont Caravan & Camping Park ►►►

www.caravan-camping-carlisle.itgo.com

Blackford, Carlisle, CA6 4EA

01228 674611 | Open Mar–Oct

The grass pitches are immaculate, and there are larger hardstandings for motor homes. This park attracts mainly adults; cycling and ball games are not allowed.

Lakeland Leisure Park

haven.com/lakeland

Moor Ln, Flookburgh, LA11 7LT

0871 231 0883 | Open mid Mar–end Oct (restricted opening mid Mar–May & Sep–Oct, reduced activities, outdoor pool closed)

This flat, grassy site is ideal for families. The touring area is quietly situated away from the main amenities, but the swimming pools, all-weather bowling green and evening entertainment are just a short stroll away. A new lake featuring water sports amenities opened in 2013.

Castlerigg Hall Caravan & Camping Park ►►►►►

castlerigg.co.uk

Castlerigg Hall, Keswick, CA12 4TE | 017687 74499

Open mid Mar–7 Nov

Old farm buildings have been converted into excellent toilets with private washing cubicles and a family bathroom, reception and a well-equipped shop. There's also a kitchen/dining area for campers, and a restaurant/takeaway.

Lowther Holiday Park ►►►►►

lowther-holidaypark.co.uk

Eamont Bridge, Penrith, CA10 2JB

01768 863631 | Open mid Mar–mid Nov

Lowther Holiday Park is a secluded natural woodland site with lovely riverside walks. The park is home to a rare colony of red squirrels, and trout fishing is available on the two-mile stretch of the River Lowther that runs through the park.

Troutbeck Camping and Caravanning Club Site ►►►►►

Hutton Moor End, Troutbeck, CA11 0SX | 017687 79149

Open 9 Mar–11 Nov & 26 Dec–2 Jan

Between Penrith and Keswick, this quiet, well-managed campsite offers two immaculate touring areas and a maturing lower field with stunning views of the surrounding fells. The log cabin reception/shop stocks local and organic produce.

Park Cliffe Camping & Caravan Estate ►►►►►

www.parkcliffe.co.uk

Birks Rd, Tower Wood, Windermere, LA23 3PG | 015395 31344

Open Mar–9 Nov (restricted opening weekends & school hols facilities open fully)

A lovely hillside park set in 25 secluded acres. The camping area is sloping and uneven in places, but well drained and sheltered; some pitches have spectacular views. The park is well equipped for families, and an attractive bar and brasserie restaurant serves quality food.

A–Z of
The Lake District

VISIT THE MUSEUMS | GET OUTDOORS | EXPLORE BY BIKE | GO BACK IN TIME | TAKE A TRAIN RIDE | MEET THE WILDLIFE | TAKE IN SOME HISTORY | HIT THE BEACH | EAT AND DRINK | GET INDUSTRIAL | VISIT THE GALLERIES | GO CANOEING | TRY HORSE-RIDING | PLACES NEARBY | CATCH A PERFORMANCE | GO ROUND THE GARDENS | TAKE A BOAT TRIP

▶ Alston Moor

An isolated North Pennine town, Alston Moor is set in the middle of spectacular moorland. With its cobbled streets, ancient buildings and railway station, it seems that little has changed in the last 100 years. The C2C cycle path and the Pennine Way long-distance path intersect here. The surrounding moorlands, rivers and woods are home to a rich variety of wildlife.

VISIT THE GALLERY
Gossipgate Gallery
The Butts, Alston | 01434 381806
Open daily 10–6 (last entry 5.30pm)
This the place to go if you want to buy an original painting, sculpture or jewellery by local artists or just to browse and enjoy looking at the artwork. You can have a cup of tea and a cake too.

WALK THE NORTH PENNINES
Pull on your hiking boots and head out into the rugged landscape of the North Pennines to discover the region's unusual but characteristic rock formations, peat bogs, moorland and waterfalls. If you are a nature lover, take to the moors to see black grouse, golden plover, merlin and many more rare bird species; or stroll through woodlands where red squirrel and deer still roam.
You will pass by rivers alive with otters, herons, salmon and brown trout. There are several short walks around the town, like the one out from the Gossipgate Bridge to the Seven Sisters waterfall; or for something more adventurous, you can walk part of the historic Pennine Way.

TAKE A TRAIN RIDE
South Tynedale Railway
south-tynedale-railway.org.uk
The Railway Station, Hexham Road, CA9 3JB | 01434 381696
If you love railways, and particularly steam trains, take a trip on this narrow-gauge railway through the beautiful South Tyne Valley. The line runs between Alston and Lintley via Kirkhaugh. The timetable and the type of locomotive vary according to the season. Check online or by phone before you visit to find out which trains are running and when. In general, trains run daily during the summer and weekends only at other times. In December, there are regular Santa specials and the trains may be off completely in January and February. But it is always worth checking with the website for special events.

PLAY A ROUND
Alston Moor Golf Club
alstonmoorgolfclub.org.uk
The Hermitage, Middleton in Teesdale Road, CA9 3DB
01434 381675 | Open all year daily
This is the highest golf course in England and has stunning views of the North Pennines.

Visitors are welcome at very modest rates. The clubhouse opens only at weekends..

EAT AND DRINK
Lovelady Shield Country House Hotel ⊛⊛
lovelady.co.uk
CA9 3LF | 01434 381203
Set among three acres of lush gardens with the River Nent running past, this gorgeous country house has rooms of generous Georgian proportions. The dining room is suitably elegant with its pastel hues, and service from the friendly team is just the ticket. Food is served in the elegant dining room where the menus follow the seasons, using local produce as far as possible.

▶ Ambleside

Right at the top of Lake Windermere, Ambleside is a perfect base for touring the central Lakes, with Grasmere and the Langdale valleys just a short drive away. Like many Lake District towns, it seems that every other shop sells walking boots and outdoor clothing.

The Romans built a fort they called *Galava* close to where the rivers Brathay and Rothay combine and flow into Windermere. Now called Waterhead, the remains of the fort are still visible; while in the Armitt Museum you can see many of the artefacts unearthed here over the years. A few hundred years after the Romans, the Vikings overran the area, supposedly bringing with them the hardy local Herdwick sheep. Although Ambleside won its market charter in 1650, it still remained fairly isolated and remote from the rest of Britain. However, this all began to change during Queen Victoria's reign as the industrial revolution brought charcoal production and woollen mills, and at the same time the town gained fame and prosperity through the steady growth of tourism.

Traditional Lakeland sports are held at Ambleside on the Thursday before the first Monday in August. Events on display include fell racing, hound trails, and Cumberland and Westmorland wrestling.

TAKE IN SOME HISTORY
Bridge House
Rydal Road, LA22 9AN
The best-known and most photographed building in Ambleside is also the smallest. It won't take long to look it over but you definitely don't want to miss it. It is 300 years old, built on a little bridge across the beck of Stock Ghyll, and thought to have been an apple store for Ambleside House. Supposedly a family with six children once lived in this small space, but now it must be one of the tiniest National Trust shops in the land.

VISIT THE MUSEUM
The Armitt Collection
armitt.com
The Armitt Museum & Library,
Rydal Road, LA22 9BL
015394 31212 | Open Mon–Sat
10–5 (last entry 4.30pm). Closed
24–26 Dec
If you want to get an overview of
Lake District history, this
fascinating and entertaining
collection celebrates the land
and the people, spanning 2,000
years from the Roman
occupation to the 20th century.
There are facts, artefacts,
historic photographs and
renowned works by the area's
better-known former
inhabitants such as Beatrix
Potter, Kurt Schwitters and
John Ruskin, as well as
displays about the daily lives of
Ambleside's hard-working
townspeople in past times. The
collection includes most of
Beatrix Potter's scientific
illustrations as well as pictures
by artists such as William
Green and J B Pyne. Originally

founded as a library by the
Armitt sisters in 1909, it still
has over 11,000 books in its
reference library.

SEE A LOCAL CHURCH
St Mary the Virgin
Vicarage Road, LA22 9DH
Designed by Sir George Gilbert
Scott and built between 1850
and 1854, this large, early
Gothic-style church is worth a
visit to see the many stained-
glass windows – particularly,
the Children's Windows
designed by Henry Holiday, in
commemoration of the 1870
Education Act. The 26-foot long
Rushbearing Mural is perhaps
the highlight of the church. It
was painted in 1944 by Gordon
Ransom and depicts the
Rushbearing Ceremony, which
still takes place on the first
Saturday in June, when the old
rushes on the church floor are
thrown out and replaced with
new ones. The mural includes
more than 60 figures
representing local people.

GET ON THE WATER
Waterhead
Just a short walk from the
centre of Ambleside is the lake
at Waterhead. Just imagine
Bowness Bay in miniature, with
a short stretch of beach, rowing
boats for hire and ever-hungry
ducks, and you've got the
picture. You can board the
steamers *Swan*, *Tern* and *Teal*
here on their round-the-lake
cruises. Just cruise round the
lake or get off at Wray Castle
and take the gentle lakeside

▼ Bridge House, Ambleside

▲ Stock Ghyll Force, Ambleside

walk to Ferry House and then continue round the lake by boat to Ambleside. A walk in the opposite direction, following Stock Ghyll through lovely woodland, will bring you to the entrancing Stock Ghyll Force waterfall. 'Force' is a corruption of 'foss', the old Norse word for waterfall. Or combine a cruise with a visit to the Motor Museum (see page 63) or the Aquarium (see page 176).

EXPLORE BY BIKE

Ghyllside Cycles

ghyllside.co.uk

The Slack, LA22 9DQ

015394 33592

If you fancy a spin on the open road, you can hire everything you need here, from bikes to helmets, and a puncture repair kit just in case. There are bikes of all sizes and tagalongs for children. The friendly and knowledgeable staff will advise you on the best options for your family, including routes to suit your abilities.

EAT AND DRINK

The Apple Pie Eating House and Bakery

applepieambleside.co.uk
Rydal Road, LA22 9AN
015394 33679

As well as their famous (and eponymous) apple pie, you could try the Lakeland gingerbread or a Bath bun here. With views over Bridge House and the hills, it's the ideal spot to enjoy the delicious treats, baked dishes or just a cappuccino.

The Britannia Inn

thebritanniainn.com
Elterwater, LA22 9HP
015394 37210

With slate walls several feet thick, a series of small, cosy rooms with low-beamed oak ceilings, winter coal fires and a fine selection of ales, this is the ideal place to get warm and comfy after a day on the hills. Built as a farmhouse and cobblers, this whitewashed free house in the Langdale Valley is nearly 500-years old and became an inn some 200 years ago. There is always a good offering of ales but during the two-week beer festival in mid-November, even more beers are laid on, some quite unusual. The inn offers a wide choice of fresh, home-cooked food. Dine alfresco in the garden and take in the views of the village and tarns.

Drunken Duck Inn ◉◉

drunkenduckinn.co.uk
Barngates, LA22 0NG
015394 36347

The story of the name alone is worth a visit to this 17th-century inn. A Victorian landlady found her ducks seemingly dead in the road. Unaware that they were merely sozzled from drinking beer, which had leaked into their feed, she started plucking them for the pot. When they started to recover, legend has it, that full of remorse, she knitted them waistcoats to wear until their feathers grew back. They still brew beer here next door at Barngates Brewery, using water drawn from the fells. Enjoy a pint of Cracker Ale or Chesters Strong & Ugly in the oak-floored bar, its old oak beams hung with Kentish hops, and oak settles covered with local Herdwick wool. Sketches, prints, a black slate bar, fox masks and enamel signs all add to the atmosphere, along with candlelight and a log fire. Typical lunchtime fare is soup, salads, sandwiches and chips or a hearty dish of steak or lamb, ordered at the bar. Dinner menus are more formal, with imaginative food.

Golden Rule

goldenrule-ambleside.co.uk
Smithy Brow, LA22 9AS
015394 32257

This is a haven of good craic in front of real log fires, popular with locals and visitors alike. Beers are from Robinsons and, although the food is limited, the welcome is warm. If you're in need of some R&R, this is the perfect place, as you won't find any big screens, background music or games here.

Wateredge Inn

wateredgeinn.co.uk
Waterhead Bay, LA22 0EP
015394 32332

The Wateredge Inn was converted to a bar and restaurant from two 17th-century fishermen's cottages with large gardens, so there's plenty of seating running down to the lakeshore. The same family has run the inn for nearly 30 years. The lunch menu offers sandwiches, salads, pub classics and slates – platters of smoked fish, charcuterie or cheese and antipasti, while the dinner menu has a wider choice of equally good food. Specials and a children's menu are also available.

Waterhead Hotel ◉

englishlakes.co.uk
Lake Road, LA22 0ER
015394 32566

The Waterhead is a townhouse hotel near Ambleside, overlooking Lake Windermere. You won't be able to forget the town's most famous residents, as readings from the works of Beatrix Potter are thoughtfully piped into the lavatories. You can order hearty lunches of soup, sandwiches or sharing platters at the bar. The bar menu is available all day until 7pm and there is a children's menu. From 7pm onwards there is an opportunity for more sophisticated dining from the restaurant menu.

▶ Appleby-in-Westmorland

Appleby sits in a loop of the tree-lined River Eden, with its Norman castle standing protectively above. Although much of Appleby Castle dates from the 17th century, when it was restored by the redoubtable Lady Anne Clifford, it still has an impressive 11th-century keep. Once the county town of Westmorland, with a royal charter dating from 1174, it has a typical medieval layout, with the castle at the top of the hill and the church at the bottom.

At either end of its main street, Boroughgate, one of the widest in England and also one of the finest, the High Cross and the Low Cross mark what were once the boundaries of Appleby market. The attractive almshouses, known as Lady Anne's Hospital, are still maintained by a trust fund set up by Lady Anne Clifford to provide homes for 13 widows. Lady Anne is buried in Appleby, in St Lawrence's Church, which also has one of the oldest working church organs in the country.

TAKE IN SOME HISTORY
Appleby Castle

applebycastle.co.uk

CA16 6XH | To book a tour telephone the tourist information office in Appleby (017683 51177)

This is one of the oldest and most interesting castles in Cumbria (now open again after being closed for over a decade). You need to book a castle tour in advance and they are limited to 12 visitors at a time, but you will get the undivided attention of your guide. The keep is over 900 years old and there would have been wooden keeps and forts here even before that, going back to Roman times. The stories of Lady Anne Clifford – in her own words – are fascinating. You can see her chair, her bed and her accounts; climb the spiral staircase to the top of the tower and hear all about the ghosts.

SEE A LOCAL CHURCH
Church of St Lawrence

Low Wiend, CA16 6XG

Although it might be said to be a bit of a hotchpotch of styles, this building is still impressive. The oldest part of the church is 12th century, the porch is early 14th century but the arch, with its impressive dogtooth moulding, was built 100 years earlier. The interior is largely in the Decorated style. Enter through the imposing arch of the Gothic-style cloisters and don't miss the Clifford Chapel with its fascinating memorials to the formidable Lady Anne Clifford and her mother. You can also see the oldest (c.1542) working church organ in Britain, which was transported here from Carlisle Cathedral in 1683. The organ case woodwork dates from the 1540s, 1680s and 1830s.

▼ Appleby Castle

TAKE A TRAIN RIDE
Settle-Carlisle Railway
settle-carlisle.co.uk
Appleby Station | Check the website
for tickets and timetables

Whether you love trains, just love travelling through beautiful countryside or if you have children who haven't experienced train travel, go for a ride on the highest railway line in England. Trains leave every two hours and the 40-minute trip from Appleby to Ribblehead will take you through the wild and remote countryside of Wensleydale, over spectacular viaducts and into Yorkshire at Ribblehead. You can download audio guides from the website and there are often volunteer guides on the trains. At Ribblehead there is a visitor centre for the line as well as views of the massive 24-arch Ribblehead viaduct and, of course, a gift shop and a tea room.

EXPLORE THE TOWN
You can easily explore the town and its surroundings either by picking up one of the self-guided walking leaflets at the Tourist Information Centre or going on one of the guided walks, which start from the Cloisters every Tuesday at around 11am, except in the winter months. Whatever your level of fitness you will find a walk to suit – from an easy stroll around the historic centre to tackling part of the long-distance Cumberland Way, which ends here.

5 castles

- Appleby Castle
  page 60
- Pendragon Castle
  page 172
- Muncaster Castle
  page 190
- Penrith Castle
  page 196
- Brough Castle
  page 78

PLAY A ROUND
Appleby Golf Club
applebygolfclub.co.uk
Brackenber Moor, CA16 6LP
017683 51432

Remotely situated, this heather and moorland course welcomes visitors and often has special offers for groups out of season. If you are a keen golfer you will particularly enjoy several long par 4 holes. Add the superb views of the Pennines and the Lakeland hills and even Mark Twain might have enjoyed a round of golf here.

EAT AND DRINK
Appleby Manor Country House Hotel ⊛
applebymanor.co.uk
Roman Road, CA16 6JB
017683 51571

All the public rooms, including the oak-panelled restaurant and the conservatory extension, have amazing views over Appleby Castle and the Eden Valley towards the fells of the Lake District. Dinner is traditional and makes good use of local ingredients. Lancashire hotpot or bubble-and-squeak appear on the menu but there are also more exotic touches, such as shrimp foam with seared scallops and pea puree, and there is a wide selection for vegetarians. During the day you can have snacks and afternoon teas in the patio area.

The Royal Oak Appleby
www.royaloakappleby.co.uk
Bongate, CA16 6UN | 017683 51463
You'll get good pub grub here and your dog, your children and your muddy boots will be welcome too. Parts of the inn date back to 1100, with 17th-century additions. Enjoy your visit with a pint of Hawkshead in front of an open fire in the oak-panelled lounge. There are fish and chips, steak and curry nights, and they serve pensioners' lunches on weekdays.

Tufton Arms Hotel
tuftonarmshotel.co.uk
Market Square, CA16 6XA
017683 51593
If you are interested in interior design, it's worth visiting this 16th-century inn, now Grade II listed, just to see what owner Teresa Milsom has done with the place. The inn was rebuilt in Victorian times with tall ceilings and now its attractive wallpapers, engravings and prints, heavy drapes and period furniture all harmonise with contemporary fabrics, soft tones and modern lighting. The beer is good too. On hand pump in the bar are Cumberland Corby and the house beer, Tufton Arms Ale. The Conservatory Restaurant overlooks a cobbled mews courtyard, where a serious wine list complements the excellent food.

▶ **PLACES NEARBY**
St Margaret and St James Church
Long Marton, CA16 6JP
Long Marton is just three miles north of Appleby on the B6542. The church is Grade I listed and predates the Norman Conquest. The tower was added around the 12th century and, although it has been much altered and restored over the centuries, the original Saxon stone carvings and Norman additions are well worth a visit.

▶ Askam-in-Furness
Askam-in-Furness is a Victorian town, which grew up around the iron ore industry. Few signs now remain of its industrial past, apart from the street names such as Steel Street and Furnace Street. The Iron ore ran out in 1918 and the industrial buildings were gone by 1933. There is still a railway station in the town.

GET OUTDOORS
The Duddon Estuary

There are great views from the long beach across the Irish Sea and the old slag heaps are a haven for wildlife. In particular, there's a colony of rare natterjack toads; even if you don't see one, you can't miss their very loud mating calls between the end of April and July. The beach is a Site of Special Scientific Interest (SSSI).

Askam Pier

The pier, built out of slag from the ironworks, is quite a sight, stretching right out into the sea.

PLAY A ROUND
Dunnerholme Golf Club

atantalus.com/dunnerholme
Duddon Rd, LA16 7AW
01229 462675

You will love the stunning views of the Cumbrian Mountains and Duddon Estuary from this course. Uniquely it has 10 holes, but 18 tees, so that you repeat the holes from a different perspective. There are two streams, providing water hazards on the 1st, 2nd, 3rd and 9th holes. You won't often see a green on a huge rock; but here the green at the 6th is atop Dunnerholme Rock, an enormous limestone outcrop jutting right out into the estuary.

EAT AND DRINK
Taste of India

82 Duke Street, LA16 7AD
01229 468986

This Indian restaurant is a real hidden gem and it's well worth travelling some distance to in order to enjoy the well-cooked authentic dishes served here. The service is excellent and there are lots of quiet little corners to sit and enjoy an intimate dinner. It's moderately priced too.

▶ Backbarrow

Backbarrow lies on the River Leven just south of Windermere. In the past there were corn mills on the river, an iron furnace and a dye works, but now people visit for the views of the river, the walking and the motor museum.

VISIT THE MUSEUM
Lakeland Motor Museum

lakelandmotormuseum.co.uk
Old Blue Mill, LA12 8TA
015395 30400 | Open daily 10–5.30

This is the perfect wet weather day out in the Lake District. Whether you are particularly interested in cars or not, the whole family will find plenty to interest them here. As well as the 30,000 exhibits, there is a range of motoring memorabilia, bringing back a bygone age in petrol pumps, adverts and ornaments. For adults, this will bring back memories from your childhood or of your first car, while children will find the quaint old cars fascinating.

There are pedal cars – every boy's most memorable Christmas present – and at the opposite extreme, the story of Donald Campbell's daring exploits in *Bluebird*. This British speed record breaker broke eight absolute world speed records in the 1950s and 1960s, and remains the only person to set both world land and water speed records in the same year (1964). But even if you are completely unmoved by cars in any shape or form, there are bicycles and motorbikes, replica shops, fashions and the story of the Women's Land Army. The one thing you can be sure of is that you'll never get round everything.

GET ON THE WATER

Sail down to Lakeside from either Bowness (see page 240) or Ambleside (see page 55), then jump on the connecting bus and head off to the Lakeland Motor Museum (see page 63). Alternatively, start and finish at the Lakeland Motor Museum and spend some time mooching around the shops in Bowness in between. The service operates daily in summer and winter at weekends.

EAT AND DRINK
Café Ambio
lakelandmotormuseum.co.uk
Old Blue Mill, LA12 8TA
015395 30448
The museum cafe at the Lakeland Motor Museum is a lovely airy space with views to the river and the trains. The food is good and fresh, and the service fast and friendly. Couldn't do better really.

▶ Barrow-in-Furness

Even the most loyal of locals would hesitate to describe Barrow as beautiful. Until the mid-19th century there was just a tiny fishing village here, on the tip of the Furness Peninsula. What made it grow at an astonishing rate were the iron- and steel-making industries, closely followed, logically, by the construction of ships. The shipbuilding company of Vickers became almost synonymous with Barrow and, even today, long after the great days of British shipbuilding have gone, the docks and shipyards are an impressive sight.

TAKE IN SOME HISTORY
Furness Abbey
www.english-heritage.org.uk
LA13 0PJ | 01229 823420
Open Apr–Sep Thu–Mon 10–5, Oct–Mar Sat–Sun 10–4
The majestic red sandstone remains of this beautiful 12th-century abbey lie in a peaceful valley, which poet William Wordsworth called the 'vale of nightshade'. View the fine stone carvings and visit the exhibition to find out more about the powerful religious community that was once based

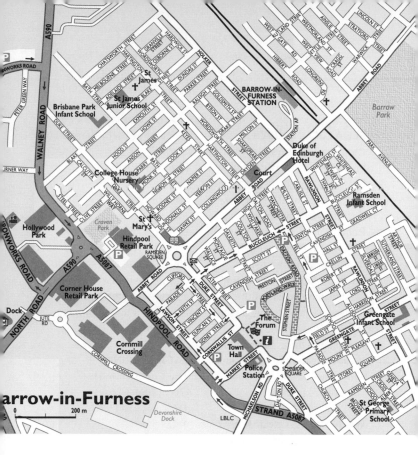

Barrow-in-Furness

0   200 m

here. You can get some idea of
the size of the community from
the monks' dormitory, which is
200 feet long.

VISIT THE MUSEUM
Dock Museum
www.dockmuseum.org.uk
North Road, LA14 2PW
01229 876400
Open all year Wed–Sun 11–4
You'll get a fascinating overview
of shipbuilding, past and
present, at this fantastic little
museum. Sitting astride a deep
dry dock, the exhibition tells
how, in the space of a
generation, Barrow became a
major force in maritime
engineering. Barrow's past,
however, concerns much more
than ships. You'll find exhibits
telling tales of the Vikings, the
Romans and even the story of
the oldest known northerner
from 10,000 years ago.

GET OUTDOORS
**National Trust Nature Reserve
at Sandscale Haws**
Barrow-in-Furness, LA14 4QJ
The estuary of the River Duddon
is just four miles north of
Barrow-in-Furness. Its sandy
grassland dunes are home to a
variety of wildlife including
migratory birds such as Red
Knot, Common redshank and
Pintail. You'll also find some
interesting flora including the

rare Dune Helleborine. Look out for natterjack toads – one fifth of the entire UK population lives here.

SEE A LOCAL CHURCH
Church of St Mary
Duke Street, LA14 3QU | Open daily
St Mary's was the first Catholic church to be built in Barrow. Designed by Edward Welby Pugin in 1866, building was completed in 1888 with its landmark tower and spire. Edward's father, A W N Pugin, who designed parts of the Houses of Parliament, was a leading figure in the Gothic Revival and the arcaded interior is richly decorated in that style with carvings and different-coloured marbles.

WALK THE CISTERCIAN WAY
Enjoy the sands of the Furness Peninsula, the wildlife and the abbey by following part of this 33-mile walk from Grange-over-Sands to Roe Island. It is an ancient trail, now way marked, that crosses the low limestone fells on the shores of Morecambe Bay and the sands of the Furness and Cartmel peninsulas. If you are feeling energetic the trail takes about two to three days to complete.

CATCH A PERFORMANCE
Forum 28 Theatre and Arts Centre
theforumbarrow.co.uk
28 Duke Street, LA14 1HH
01229 820000
Have a look at the varied activities and performances in this small theatre. There are exhibitions, lectures, workshops and all sorts of performances from dance to amateur dramatics as well as concerts by performers on tour.

PLAY A ROUND
Barrow Golf Club
barrowgolfclub.co.uk
Rakesmoor Lane, Hawcoat,
LA14 4QB | 01229 825444
Open Mon–Sat ex BHs
This pleasant course is laid out on two levels of meadowland, with views of the nearby Lakeland fells and west to the Irish Sea.

EAT AND DRINK
The Chetwynde Hotel
chetwyndehotel.co.uk
Abbey Road, LA13 9JS
01229 811011
If you're in search of the perfect place for a romantic meal or special occasion, this might be just the venue. You can start with an aperitif in the lounge or on the patio, and then enjoy a candlelit meal in the restaurant. The food is a very successful fusion of British and Mediterranean styles, and the staff are friendly and efficient.

Duke of Edinburgh Hotel
dukeofedinburghhotel.co.uk
Abbey Road, LA14 5QR
01229 821039
This busy venue has a warm and welcoming public bar with two open fires. The food is good, with simple favourites, such as pizza, burgers or deli, to a range of main courses and

children's menu. If you like to sample good cask ales, they serve a range of beers, including four guest beers. Head downstairs to the Vaults Live Music bar for live music three nights a week. Thursday Jazz Night is free of charge but there is a small door charge on Friday and Saturday.

The Furness Railway
76–80 Abbey Road, LA14 5UB
01229 820818
Originally a Victorian co-op department store, this building has a beautiful wood and glass frontage. It's a Wetherspoons pub so you know what you are getting – a cheap and cheerful pub grub and drinks in pleasant surroundings.

▶ Bassenthwaite Lake

Owned by the National Park, only quiet activities are permitted on the lake. It is important as a home for a rare fish, the Vendace, as well as for wintering wildfowl, and is designated as a Site of Special Scientific Interest and a National Nature Reserve. It is an inspiring setting, with Skiddaw (3,054 feet, 931m) rising in the east and it certainly inspired Tennyson, who described, in his poem *Morte d'Arthur*, the dying King Arthur being carried across the waters of the lake on a barge, thus making Bassenthwaite Lake the last resting place of Excalibur. Take some time to pop into the pre-Norman Church of St Bega. There must have been a problem with lengthy sermons here because there is a wrought iron hourglass used for timing them, although there is no information about what happened if the sands ran out. St Bega's Church inspired the opening lines of Tennyson's *Morte D'Arthur*, which he wrote while staying at Mirehouse (see page 67) in 1835.

> *...to a chapel nigh the field,*
> *A broken chancel with a broken cross,*
> *That stood on a dark straight of barren land.*

Just a short distance from the shores of the lake is Bassenthwaite, an archetypal English village with its green and pub at the heart of community life. It is primarily an agricultural community with limited, but nevertheless charming, amenities.

TAKE IN SOME HISTORY
Mirehouse and Gardens
mirehouse.com
Keswick, CA12 4QE | 017687 72287
House open: 30 Mar–Oct Wed, Sat–

Sun, (also Fri in Aug) 1.30–4.30; gardens, lakeside walk and tea room open: 30 Mar–Oct daily 10–5
Beside the A591 are the grounds of this 17th-century

▲ Skiddaw, Bassenthwaite Lake

house, leading down to the eastern shores of the lake. Mirehouse was first built for the eighth Earl of Derby in 1666 and sold by him to the Greggs 22 years later. Since then, it has been in the same family. It was left in 1802 by the last of the Greggs to John Spedding of Armathwaite Hall, who sat at the same school desk as William Wordsworth. You can easily spend a whole day here enjoying the heather maze, a rhododendron tunnel and poetry walk for children and grown-ups alike. There are four adventure playgrounds in the gardens, which stretch from Dodd Wood to Bassenthwaite Lake. You can wander through the wildflower meadow and the walled garden, or explore the house with its fine furniture, literary portraits and manuscripts reflecting the family friendships with Tennyson, Wordsworth, artist Francis Bacon and many more. Or take the waymarked walk to enjoy the lakeside scenery.

MEET THE ANIMALS
Lake District Wildlife Park
lakedistrictwildlifepark.co.uk
Coalbeck Farm, CA12 4RD
017687 76239 | Open daily 10–5.30 (or dusk)
Enjoy a fun and educational day out amid breathtaking scenery,

EAT AND DRINK

Armathwaite Hall Country House & Spa ◉
armathwaite-hall.com
CA12 4RE | 017687 76551
Don't head here in your muddy boots after a day on the hills; this is a place to savour for a special occasion. In a magnificent building, hung with creepers, the Lake View Restaurant is a lovely high-ceilinged room with oak panelling, decorated in rich golds and reds and with comfortable chairs at formally set tables. The dress code is smart, no jeans and no trainers. The food is a mix of traditional and contemporary, British with a touch of French.

The Old Sawmill Tearoom
Mirehouse, Under Skiddaw, CA12 4QE | 017687 74317
At the foot of Dodd, just off the A591 and handy for both Mirehouse and the osprey observation points in Dodd Wood, this lovely woodland tea room serves hot and cold snacks, as well as homemade cakes and scones.

The Pheasant ◉
www.the-pheasant.co.uk
CA13 9YE | 017687 76234
At the foot of the Sale Fell and close to Bassenthwaite Lake, this 17th-century former coaching inn is surrounded by lovely gardens. You can almost sense the history the moment you walk through the door. One of the regulars here was the legendary foxhunter John Peel,

at this award-winning wildlife park. From antelopes to zebras, you can see over 100 species from every corner of the world, ranging from cheeky mandrills and meerkats to endangered species, such as gibbons and Asian fishing cats.

GO FISHING

Bassenthwaite Lake
Permits available from Keswick TIC (Moot Hall, Keswick, Cumbria, CA12 5JR | 017687 75738; keswick.org) or The Pheasant (017687 76234; www.the-pheasant.co.uk) You will find mainly pike here although there are also roach, perch and eels, and there is some salmon fishing at the outflow by Ouse Bridge.

whose 'view halloo would awaken the dead' – according to the song, *D'ye Ken John Peel*. In the bar, with its panelled walls and oak settles, hang paintings by Cumbrian artist and former customer Edward H Thompson. Here, you'll find fine ales such as Coniston Bluebird or Hawkshead Red, and an extensive selection of malt whiskies. The food has gained a much coveted AA Rosette, and meals are served in the restaurant, bistro, bar and lounges overlooking the gardens. You can choose from light lunches, three-course dinners and afternoon teas.

▶ Birdoswald Roman Fort

Birdoswald, CA8 7DD | 016977 47602 | Open Apr–Oct daily, Nov–Mar, Sat–Sun

The perfect place for a family day out, Birdoswald Roman Fort is set above the dramatic Irthing Gorge, with a picnic area now looking out over it. The remote five-acre remains of the Roman fort and settlement at Birdoswald is the most interesting spot in this western expanse of Hadrian's Wall. It was built in about AD 125 when its Roman name was *Banna*, and at its busiest would have housed up to 500 foot soldiers. They were there to protect the wall and, in particular, the bridge across the River Irthing, from the Scots. The part of the wall that runs eastwards from Birdoswald towards Harrow's Scar is the longest visible remaining stretch. You can explore the perimeter wall of the fort with its entrance gates and part of one turret, while the interactive visitor centre brings to life a vivid picture of Birdoswald in Roman times. Excavations have unearthed the granaries, added in about AD 200, and other finds have included an Arm Purse, containing 28 silver coins, and some delicate gold jewellery now on display in Carlisle's Tullie House Museum (see page 92).

▶ Blackwell, the Arts & Crafts House

blackwell.org.uk

Bowness-on-Windermere, LA23 3JT | 015394 46139 | Open 18 Jan–Dec daily 10.30–5 (Closes at 4 Nov–Feb)

This is likely to be one the most impressive houses you will ever see. Designed by the architect Mackay Hugh Baillie Scott and completed in 1900, Blackwell still retains almost all of its original details in pristine condition. It is undoubtedly one of the most important examples of an Arts and Crafts house in Britain and after a restoration project, costing a staggering £3.25 million, it was opened to the public in 2001. William Morris and John Ruskin both influenced Baillie Scott and the Arts and Crafts' rural motifs are evident everywhere – in the stained-glass windows, tiles and decorative friezes of wild flowers, berries and animals. In room after room you'll find delightful details and interplays of light, all with the majestic backdrop of lake and distant fells. The White Drawing Room is considered to be one of the finest interiors of its period. The overall impression of the interior is strikingly modern, spacious and minimalist.

Blackwell is also an important exhibition space for innovative ceramics, textiles, jewellery and furniture by contemporary artists.

EAT AND DRINK

Belted Will
www.beltedwill.co.uk
Hallbankgate, CA8 2NJ
016977 46236
You'll find this typical village pub serves a very decent pint, alongside simple but well-delivered food. The very friendly service includes pick-ups and drop-offs if you are walking. The 'Will' in question was Lord William Howard from nearby Naworth Castle, a feudal baron in the time of the reivers.

Pheasant Inn
pheasantinncumwhitton.co.uk
Cumwhitton, CA4 9EX
01228 560102
The Pheasant dates from the 17th century and has built an enviable reputation, both for the quality of its food and of its cask ales, which are drawn from a range of local breweries and from further afield.

▶ Borrowdale

The so-called Jaws of Borrowdale, where the high crags on either side of the valley almost meet, squeeze the road – the B5289 – and the River Derwent together in the tight space. The road then swings round to the west, through the village of Seatoller, to climb through the equally dramatic Honister Pass, which links Borrowdale with Buttermere. This wooded valley runs south from Derwent Water and splits into three valleys, Watendlath, Stonethwaite and Seathwaite.

GET INDUSTRIAL
Honister Slate Mine
see page 72

▶ Honister Slate Mine

honister-slate-mine.co.uk
Honister Pass, CA12 5XN | 01768 777230 | Open all year daily 9–5

Although slate has been used as a building material for centuries the first records of slate mining in Honister do not appear until the early 1700s. The Romantic poet, William Wordsworth, even mentions slate quarrying in his diaries. Here at Honister you can tour the last working slate mine in England and explore the caverns hacked out by Victorian miners. You can learn the history of the famous Honister green slate, find out how to rive slates and see local skills in action. Be warned: the tour includes both underground and surface sites and involves some scrambling.

▼ Honister slate mine

▲ Borrowdale from Castle Crag

GET OUTDOORS
The Bowder Stone
Signposted along a path east of the B5289 Borrowdale road, south of Grange

Why stop to look at a stone? Well, this one weighs about 2,000 tons and appears to be balanced, ready to topple over. A set of steps leads up to the top of its 36 feet, and, despite the attempts of almost everyone who visits to give it a push, it hasn't fallen yet. It was put into place by a glacier, which later melted around it.

ENTERTAIN THE FAMILY
The Fell Farm Experience
borrowdaleherdwick.co.uk
Yew Tree Farm, Rosthwaite, CA12 5XB | 017687 77675 | Check the website for opening times

Come here to experience a real working fell farm with 2,000 acres all set in the beautiful Borrowdale Valley. As well, as admiring the 1,500 sheep and 14 working sheepdogs, Joe, a third generation Fell Farmer, describes working life on the farm and how the land and flock of Herdwicks is managed. The Fell Farm Experience includes either lunch or afternoon tea as you choose (see also Eat and Drink, The Flock-In, overleaf).

GO FISHING
Watendlath Tarn and Borrowdale Fisheries
lakedistrictfishing.net
017687 77293

This beautiful little tarn, along the narrow minor road to Watendlath, off the B5289, is stocked with rainbow trout to add to the small wild brown trout. Day permit options are available from the tea rooms and farm at Watendlath.

TAKE THE ALLERDALE RAMBLE
On this 55-mile walk that runs from the Borrowdale Valley to

▲ Stone bridge in Borrowdale

Silloth on the Solway coast, you can sample just about all of the best that Lakeland has to offer in terms of scenery and walking. The route heads northwards along the western side of Borrowdale and Derwent Water to Keswick, where you can choose either to cross the foothills of Skiddaw or hike over the summit, before heading along the Derwent Valley to the ancient market town of Cockermouth. From here, you'll have an easier ramble through the pastoral land of mid-Allerdale to the coast at the historic coalport of Maryport, where walking along the flat coastline you have the benefit of extensive views across the Solway Firth to Southern Scotland.

EAT AND DRINK

Caffle House Tearoom

Watendlath, CA12 5UW

This cosy National Trust tearoom serves soup, sandwiches and homemade bakes. The location in the tiny hamlet of Watendlath, overlooking the Tarn, is very beautiful.

The Flock-In

borrowdaleherdwick.co.uk
Yew Tree Farm, Rosthwaite, CA12 5XB | 017687 77675
Rosthwaite is one of the loveliest places to walk in the Lakes and this working fell farm right in the bowl of the hills is a real gem. All the food is homemade, none more so than the delicious dishes featuring their own Herdwick lambs. The prices are exceptional and the quality of the food truly excellent.

Grange Bridge Cottage Tea Shop

Grange in Borrowdale, CA12 5UQ
017687 77201
Just a few yards from the famous double bridges and close to the river, this 400-year-old cottage is a favourite on the Borrowdale teashop trail. There's a cosy, cottage like interior but the beautiful riverside tea garden has real wow-factor, dropping steeply down to the river. Home-baked cakes, cream teas and light lunches are served all day.

The Langstrath Country Inn
thelangstrath.com
Stonethwaite, CA12 5XG
017687 77239

If you want to get slightly off the beaten track, you'll find this lovely family-run inn in the little village of Stonethwaite is just perfect. The16th-century inn, originally a miner's cottage, is located close to England's highest peak, Scafell Pike, and also sits on the coast–to–coast and Cumbrian Way walks. There are spectacular views from the restaurant, while the food is local and fresh with a range of cask conditioned beers and a thoughtful wine selection.

Leathes Head Hotel ●
leatheshead.co.uk
CA12 5UY | 017687 77247

The Leathes Head was originally built in Edwardian times for a member of a wealthy Liverpool ship-owning family. There is much that is unchanged, such as the original tiles in the entrance, which are still in pristine condition after 100 years. From the conservatory, you can enjoy views towards Keswick, Derwent Water, Cat Bells and Skiddaw while dining on traditional, country-house-hotel cooking based on plenty of locally sourced ingredients.

▶ Bowness-on-Solway

Part of the Solway Coast Area of Outstanding Natural Beauty, Bowness-on-Solway's main claim to fame is that Hadrian's Wall (see page 141) starts here. It stretches 73 miles from here to Wallsend near Newcastle, across the neck of England. If you are doing the Hadrian's Wall walk it is worth spending some time in Bowness at either the start or end of your walk. The sand dunes, salt marsh, shingle beds, and peat mosses make this a favourite spot with a number of species of birds. And there are viewpoints and laybys for spotting the waders: oystercatchers, curlew, golden and grey plover, lapwing, knot, dunlin, bar-tailed and black-tailed godwit, redshank, and turnstone – all in all, it's a twitcher's paradise.

▶ Bowness-on-Windermere
see **Windermere & Bowness-on-Windermere**, page 240

▶ Brampton

One of Cumbria's many attractive market towns, Brampton has held its charter since 1252. The cobbled square around the Moot Hall still bustles on market day each Wednesday. In 1745, Brampton was the headquarters of Bonnie Prince Charlie's army while the troops laid siege to Carlisle Castle.

TAKE IN SOME HISTORY
Lanercost Priory
lanercostpriory.org.uk
CA8 2HQ | 016977 3030 | Open
Apr–Sep daily 10–5, Oct Thu–Mon
10–4, 5 Nov–Mar Sat–Sun 10–4

This Augustinian priory, founded in the 12th century, is worth a visit for its atmospheric ruins and sense of history. Part of the medieval settlement is in use as the village hall, part is cared for by English Heritage and can be visited, part has been converted to private dwellings, and the interior of the nave is intact and still in use as a parish church. Set in a tranquil rural landscape, surrounded by fields and close to Hadrian's Wall, Lanercost is a magnificent and fascinating complex of historic buildings. It has been a place of worship for almost 850 years. But things have not always been as peaceful as they are now. Owing to its proximity to the Scottish border, the priory suffered during the Anglo-Scottish wars of the 14th century – in 1311 Robert Bruce himself raided it. The thick walls of the tower may well have been used for defence.

SEE SOME LOCAL CHURCHES
The Priory Church of St Mary Magdalene
The most important thing to see in the church is the huge, 24 feet by 4 feet embroidered woollen cloth designed by William Morris, which is now restored and hangs on the wall. Known as the Lanercost Dossal, it was embroidered by the ladies of the Parish including Mrs Bulkeley, Mrs Chapman and Mrs Dodgson, wives of past vicars. It was hung behind the altar on Easter Day 1887 and rehung after its restoration on Easter Day, 2013. There are also some fine stained-glass windows, designed by the Pre-Raphaelite artist Edward Burne-Jones and made by William Morris & Co. Look out too for the inscribed Roman centurial stone in the priory's fabric; it shows that stone used to build the original structure came from Hadrian's Wall. You can clearly see the stone, but it was incorporated into the stonework upside down.

Church of St Martin
www.stmartinsbrampton.org.uk
Front Street, CA8 1SH

A Pre-Raphaelite masterpiece and the only church designed by architect Philip Webb, the Church of St Martin is completely different in style from the elaborate Gothic style of the time, as it opens from a small entrance into a simple space of light and dazzling colour. It contains one of the finest collections of stained-glass windows in England, designed by Edward Burne-Jones and made in William Morris's studio. The east window is a blaze of colour depicting Christ the Good Shepherd and a pelican. Known as the Pelican Window, it marks the beginning of the art nouveau movement.

GO FISHING
New Mills Trout Farm
newmillstroutfarm.net
CA8 2QS | 016977 41115
Whether you are a regular fisher, would just like to try it out or have kids who would like to have a go, this is a great place to fish. You can take your own rod and buy a ticket to fish or you can hire a rod. The one-acre lake, set in lovely grounds around an old corn mill, is regularly stocked with trout. The ticket price includes keeping the first fish caught and throwing back the rest. There is special fun fishing for children and helpful members of staff are on hand with advice.

EXPLORE BY BIKE
Pedal Pushers
cyclehireinfo.com
Lonnings End, Sandy Lonning, Capontree Road, CA8 1RA
016977 42387 | Open daily 9–7
Cycles, tandems, children's bikes and child seats are all available here for hire, so there's no excuse not to get on your bike.

PLAY A ROUND
Brampton Golf Club
bramptongolfclub.com
Tarn Road, CA8 1HN
016977 2255
This is a challenging heathland course in rolling fell country. However, even if you are struggling with the course there are panoramic views of the Lake District, Pennines and southern Scotland to more than compensate.

EAT AND DRINK
Farlam Hall Hotel ◉◉
www.farlamhall.co.uk
Hallbankgate, CA8 2NG
016977 46234
This comfortable hotel is old fashioned in the sense that it is family run, with service and hospitality that feels part of a bygone age, but it has all the modern comforts you would expect. The tables are formally turned-out with gleaming crystal and silver on starched linen, but there is no starch in the delightfully relaxed service. Farlam Hall has been around since the 16th century, but it was a wealthy Victorian industrialist who created the glorious gardens and the grand interior. The dining room's floor-to-ceiling windows overlook the ornamental lake and food is classic English country-house cooking. The cheese board is particularly good with an excellent selection of well-kept English cheeses.

Blacksmiths Arms
blacksmithstalkin.co.uk
Talkin, CA8 1LE
016977 3452
An old country inn with cartwheels lined up outside, this is actually a former smithy. The food is good, based on traditional home cooking with blackboard specials every day to ring the changes. They serve real ales, two from the nicely local Geltsdale Brewery in Brampton and there's a beer garden in which to wend away summer days.

▸ PLACES NEARBY

A tiny hamlet in a remote corner of Cumbria, Bewcastle is less than seven miles from the Scottish border and just north of Hadrian's Wall.

Bewcastle Cross
bewcastle.com
CA6 6PX

One of the oldest stone crosses in Europe, this is a cross without its cross, as the top fell off and no one knows what happened to it. However, it is still a magnificent sight, standing over 13-feet high and made of yellow sandstone. Its weathered surface is patterned with early Celtic scrolls and intricate designs, and decorated with carvings first made some 1,300 years ago.

Church of St Cuthbert
CA6 6PX

The present church was rebuilt in 1792 and is a simple building with a west tower and bellcote, while inside there is a tapestry depicting St Cuthbert. Past rectors have included successful reivers, border raiders that operated along the Anglo-Scottish border from the late 13th century through to the 16th century. This may account for the local legend that only women were buried in Bewcastle – the local men were all hanged in Carlisle! Though only the east end remains, the earliest recorded church here dates from 1277, with building material being taken directly from the remains of the Roman fort previously on the site.

Bew Castle

Located within a short walk of Bewcastle, the castle was built in about 1092 on the site of a former Roman fort. The south wall is still standing, to almost its full height, but it is a castle to be appreciated for its setting rather than its state of preservation.

▸ Brough

Brough is a small town in the Eden Valley, at the foot of the North Pennines a few miles north of Kirkby Stephen. It is a twin village, and the southern part, Church Brough, has a ruined Norman castle and a Roman fort once stood here. The northern Market Brough is on a medieval road, and in the 18th and 19th centuries was an important coaching stop on the road to Scotland.

TAKE IN SOME HISTORY
Brough Castle
www.english-heritage.org.uk
CA17 4EJ | 0870 333 1181
Open Apr–Sep daily 10–5, Oct–Mar 10–4 Closed 24–26 Dec & 1 Jan

Dating from Roman times the 12th-century keep at this site replaced an earlier stronghold destroyed by the Scots in 1174. It was restored by Lady Anne Clifford in the 17th century.

▶ Brougham Castle

www.english-heritage.org.uk

CA10 2AA | 01768 862488 | Open Apr–Sep daily 10–5, Oct–Mar Sat–Sun 10–4. Closed 24–26, 31 Dec & 1 Jan

There is a lot to explore in this castle with its winding stairs and passages. A good place to start is the exhibition, which tells the story of the rich and powerful Anne Clifford, who died here in 1678, when she was almost 90 years old. As well as Brougham, she arranged the restoration of Appleby and Brough Castles, with no expense spared so that all three of her castles would be habitable.

The Great Tower was built in the 12th century of sandstone rubble, with more expensive, decorative cut stone at the corners and on windows and doors. People have added and restored the buildings over the centuries, most notably Anne Clifford. However, the Great Tower remains Brougham's most impressive feature, still standing almost to its original height. Climb to the top of the keep if you want to soak up the fabulous panoramic views over the Eden Valley.

TAKE IN SOME HISTORY
Brougham Hall
broughamhall.co.uk
CA10 2DE | 01768 868184
Open 9–6 daily. Cafe closes at 4
This inspired project, housing a range of small businesses, includes a cafe housed in a 15th-century ruin. The exterior of the hall is in a gradual process of restoration, and it is well worth a visit just to view the building. But inside you'll also find a variety of crafts including a gallery, jewellers and potters.

▼ The River Eamont and Brougham Castle

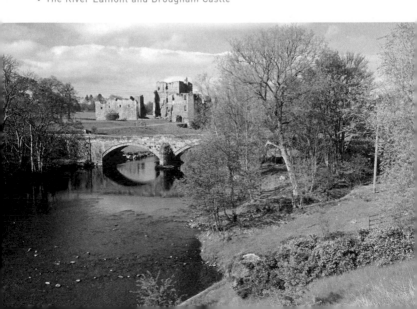

▶ Broughton-in-Furness

A lovely little town in Dunnerdale (see page 122), Broughton-in-Furness stands back from the Duddon Estuary. The market square is dominated by a huge chestnut tree and has a stepped obelisk and a pair of stone tables that were once used to sell fish caught in the River Duddon.

GO WALKING
The Lickle Valley

You will find walks to suit all ages and abilities, from gentle riverside walks and forestry rambles to more strenuous fell walks and hikes. Footpaths cross over the fells into the Duddon Valley, or up onto Stickle, Caw, White Pike and onto Coniston Old Man. Guides to walks in the Lickle Valley, Duddon Valley and Woodland Valley are available to buy at the Blacksmiths Arms (see below).

EAT AND DRINK
Blacksmiths Arms

theblacksmithsarms.com
Broughton Mills, LA20 6AX
01229 716824

This whitewashed 16th-century pub is worth a visit on its own merits but it also makes the perfect base from which to explore the secluded Lickle Valley. Originally a farmhouse and then an inn and blacksmith's, the interior is little changed, with oak-panelled corridors, slate floors, oak-beamed ceilings and log fires. The bar is reserved for drinking only, with a good choice of ales. The food is good and local and the sheltered, flower-filled patio garden is great for alfresco dining. Booking is advisable at busy times, despite its out-of-the-way location. Catch the beer festival in early October.

Broughton Village Bakery

broughtonvillagebakery.homestead.com
Princes Street, LA20 6HQ
01229 716284

This is a splendid little retreat to enjoy a tall latte or a snappy espresso. You can get a light lunch or snack or try one of the tempting home-baked cakes.

The Square Café

thesquarecafe.biz
Annan House, The Square, LA20 6JA
01229 716388

Overlooking the village square, with a few outside tables, this traditional cafe is popular with walkers, cyclists and motorcyclists. Afternoon teas with homemade scones are a favourite.

▶ PLACES NEARBY
Duddon Iron Works, near Broughton-in-Furness.

This is the restored remains of one of the most impressive, charcoal-fired Iron Works from the Industrial Revolution. It lies just North of Broughton–in–Furness on the A595. Park in the lay-by just beyond the bridge and walk from there. Open site.

▶ Buttermere & Crummock Water

These two neighbouring lakes in the Buttermere Valley, separated only by a half-mile strip of meadowland, were probably one lake originally. Buttermere is perhaps the more beautiful, although Crummock Water is twice its size with one of the most impressive waterfalls in the Lakes. Scale Force, on its western side, plunges 172 feet in to the lake.

GO WALKING

Walking is the top activity around here and there are loads of fantastic routes to choose from. The rough walk to Scale Force begins in Buttermere village through a tree-lined gorge where the Scale Beck plummets to the lake. Another path leads all the way along Crummock Water's western shore, to join up with the B5289 along the eastern shore. This road links Lorton Vale to the north of Buttermere, with the steep Honister Pass to the east before continuing on to Borrowdale. If you want a testing climb, Buttermere is surrounded by high hills, such as the 2,126-foot Fleetwith Pike, guarding the Honister Pass and the 1,959-foot Hay Stacks. Or there is an easy two-hour walk around Buttermere with superb views in all directions. To the northwest are the Derwent Fells, crossed by the Newlands and Whinlatter passes, while to the west, above Burtness Wood, stands another range of dramatic crags and fells.

▼ A view across Buttermere

Top 5 lakes

GO FISHING
Wood House
wdhse.co.uk
Crummock Water, Wood House,
Buttermere, CA13 9XA
01768 770208
You can get a fishing permit
or hire a rowing boat from
the Wood House guesthouse.

▲ The lake at Buttermere

EAT AND DRINK
Bridge Hotel
www.bridge-hotel.com
CA13 9UZ | 017687 70252
Surrounded by the Buttermere Fells, this 18th-century former coaching inn is set between Buttermere and Crummock Water with lovely walks right on the doorstep. They serve food from breakfast through to dinner to eat in or take away. If you're straight in off the hills or from walking your dog, there's the Walkers' Bar, which serves good food and real ales. But if you want to change for dinner, spruce up and have a

sophisticated four-course meal then head to the smart dining room.

Fish Hotel

fishinnbuttermere.co.uk
Buttermere, CA13 9XA
017687 70253

If you are walking, fishing or climbing, the staff at the Fish Hotel will go out of their way to provide for you. There is food available all day from breakfast to dinner and there is beer on offer from a range of local breweries. This was once the home of Mary Robinson, the legendary Maid of Buttermere, whose story was told by Mervyn Bragg in his novel of that name.

Syke Farm

Buttermere, CA13 9XA
017687 70277

Don't leave without trying the ice cream here, it's homemade with milk from the farm's resident herd of Ayrshire cattle. But this tiny tea room just below the little church is also great for homemade cakes, bakes and scones, and there's a little craft shop too.

▶ **PLACES NEARBY**

Seathwaite

From here you can get on to well-known mountains such as Scafell Pike, Great Gable and Glaramara. So not surprisingly, this little hamlet in Borrowdale is now a popular starting point for walkers. Alfred Wainwright said of it, 'Seathwaite, once in a little world of its own with few visitors, has become a pedestrian metropolis. Great days on the fells begin and end here.'

Newfield Inn

newfieldinn.co.uk
Seathwaite, LA20 6ED
01229 716208

Hugely popular with walkers and climbers, this 16th-century cottage-style pub has slate floors and the bar throngs with parched outdoor types quaffing pints of Cumberland Ale and Jennings Bitter. Served all day, food is hearty and traditional and uses local farm meats. Retreat to the garden in summer and savour cracking southern fells views, or come for the beer festival in October.

▶ Caldbeck

It's well worth a visit to this traditional fell village, preserved as a conservation area. It's not so busy as some of the better-known parts of the Lake District, but it is equally lovely. The walking and cycling routes are as likely to have ponies, sheep or ducks wandering along them as well as people. The Cald Beck provided the water for the 17th- and 18th-century woollen mills, bobbin mills, corn mills, a paper mill and a brewery. Many of the old mill buildings are still in use and it is easy to

▶ The River Caldbeck

imagine the hive of industry that existed here in the 18th century. Caldbeck is also a good stopping point if you happen to be traversing The Cumbria Way (see page 94) long-distance footpath.

TAKE IN SOME HISTORY
Priest's Mill
watermillcafe.co.uk
Priest's Mill, CA7 8DR
016974 78267 | Open Feb–Dec 9–5 daily, Jan Fri–Sun 9–4
Built by a former rector in 1702, this mill wheel has been restored to working order. There's also an 18th-century water mill, a cafe (see also Eat and Drink, The Watermill Café) and craft shops.

SEE A LOCAL CHURCH
St Kentigern's Church
CA7 3AL
You can really get a flavour of the past by visiting the churchyard of this 12th-century church. Here you can find the final resting place of the famous local huntsman, John Peel, immortalised in the song *D'Ye Ken John Peel,* and the grave of Mary Robinson Harrison, the Maid of Buttermere.

EXPLORE BY BIKE
Savvy Lake District Mountain Biking
lakedistrictmountainbiking.co.uk
Swaledale Watch, Whelpo, CA7 8HQ
08006 123 576
This is an ideal place to go if you've never tried mountain biking before. This company runs guided cycle rides every day, with discounted hire bikes if you need them. The rides can be short, medium or long or tailored to groups. If you just want to hire a bike, you can hire a mountain or road bike and everything else you need to go with it. They also organise cycling holidays, with accommodation, rides, and meals and packed lunches included.

EAT AND DRINK
Oddfellows Arms
oddfellows-caldbeck.co.uk
CA7 8EA | 016974 78227
Located opposite the church, this 17th-century coaching inn serves Jennings real ales, lunchtime snacks and simple pub grub. You can sit in the garden and admire the dramatic northern fells. The Cumbrian Way goes right past the door.

The Watermill Café
watermillcafe.co.uk
Priest's Mill, CA7 8DR
016974 78267
You can easily spend a relaxing hour or two here, eating and browsing. This beautifully restored monastic mill, overlooking the Cald Beck, has craft shops as well as the Watermill Café. Fair Trade and vegetarian options are a speciality, and on warmer days you can sit on the terrace which also overlooks the village cricket pitch.

PLACES NEARBY

Nearby Hesket Newmarket is the home of Eddie Stobart, owner of the easily-recognised haulage firm. His lorries each boast a female name painted on the front – fun for kids to look out for on car journeys. Ireby is an unspoiled village in the peaceful fells of the northern Lake District, in the area to the north of Keswick, known as 'Back of Skiddaw'. It was once a thriving market town, with the market cross, believed to date to 1200.

Overwater Hall ◉◉

overwaterhall.co.uk
Ireby, CA7 1HH | 017687 76566
Closed first 2 weeks Jan
This is a fine Georgian house with a stately facade, owned and run by the same family since 1992. Stephen and Angela are always on hand to welcome guests, to recommend undiscovered local walks and assist in any way they can. They have restored this splendidly handsome country house with its winding driveway, 18 acres of pretty gardens and woodland and created a decor which is rich with elegant, traditional charms. The dining room is formal with white linen and fresh flowers. The chef, cooks with a passion and offers a four-course traditional meal, with a fish course following the starter. There's a good deal of regional produce on the menu, and lots of flavours to be found on the plate.

The Old Crown

theoldcrownpub.co.uk
Hesket Newmarket, CA7 8JD
01697 478288
Hesket Newmarket is a pretty village just over a mile southeast of Caldbeck, and this pub is a very good reason for visiting. Owned co-operatively by the locals, the exceptionally fine ale is produced in the brewery at the back. They also serve decent pub grub and the craic is mighty.

▼ St Kentigern's Church, Caldbeck

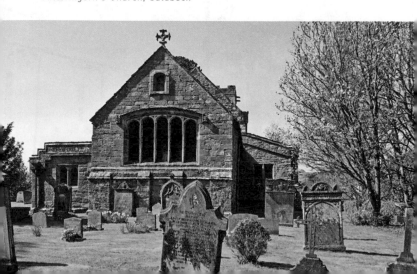

▶ Carlisle

There is plenty to see and do in Carlisle and if you are making an extended visit to Cumbria don't miss its only city. Carlisle is the main shopping centre for the English border area and much of southern Scotland. The capital of Cumbria has been an important centre of population since before the Roman occupation. You can tell that it was an important town from the size of the castle and the cathedral and the extent of the city walls – built, some 1,000 years after Hadrian's Wall, around the remains of the Roman town and fort. The 12th-century West Walls, which run behind St Cuthbert's and around the cathedral, are the best surviving examples.

So close to the border with Scotland, the Scots and the English fought over the town many times and, over the centuries, both the Scots and English held it at different periods. William II, the son of William the Conqueror, built a castle in Carlisle around 1,000 years ago, after he took the town from the Scots. It was originally wooden but soon replaced by a stone castle. It has been much attacked, but some of the 14th-century buildings remain. Carlisle is steeped in history, as you'll see from a walk around its historic centre,

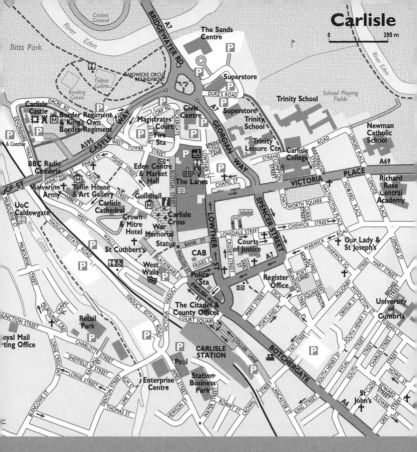

Carlisle

0 _____ 200 m

but it is also a vibrant town with all the modern shops, cafes and leisure facilities that you would expect in a city. In the wide Greenmarket you'll find street entertainers, a farmers' market and seasonal celebrations, while not far away is a modern shopping mall, the Lanes.

If you want to find out about the history of Carlisle, then visit the award-winning Tullie House Museum and Art Gallery in Castle Street with its many interactive displays. The magnificent 12th-century Carlisle Cathedral is also well worth a visit, emphasising again Carlisle's importance in medieval times. The 14th-century timber-framed Guildhall now houses the Guildhall Museum. Other notable buildings include the Citadel with its 19th-century towers dominating Henry VIII's 16th-century entrance to the city and the 18th-century Town Hall, which is now used as a visitor centre.

◀ The Citadel

TAKE IN SOME HISTORY
Carlisle Castle
www.english-heritage.org.uk
Castle Way, CA3 8UR | 01228
591922 | Open Apr–Oct daily 10–5,
Nov–Mar Sat–Sun 10–4. Check
website for school holiday times

A visit to Carlisle Castle is a
great day out for all the family.
Kids will enjoy exploring the
ramparts. Several rooms in the
gatehouse are decorated in
medieval style, while you can
explore the warren of chambers
inside the castle.

Carlisle's location, so close
to the Scottish border, ensured
its importance in history. The
first castle overlooking the
River Eden was nothing more
than a triangular area of land
encircled by a wooden fence.
William Rufus, the son of
William the Conqueror, built it
in 1092. When he was killed in
a hunting accident in the New
Forest, his brother Henry
ordered that a castle and walls
should be built to protect the
town. However, despite the new
fortifications, the castle fell to
the Scots 14 years later. It was
held by David I and Malcolm IV,
kings of Scotland, from 1136
until 1157, and was taken back
into English hands by Henry II.
Another Scottish king, William
the Lion, besieged the castle
from 1173 to 1174. Other
highlights in the castle's history
include the distinctive rounded
battlements – added much later
by Henry VIII. Mary, Queen of
Scots was imprisoned here, and
the castle was captured by
'Bonnie' Prince Charlie in 1745.
You can also find the Museum
of the Border Regiment here.

▼ Main entrance to Carlisle Castle

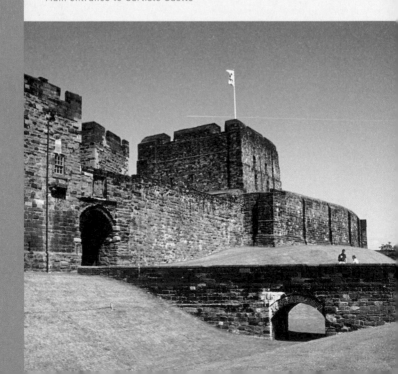

▶ Carlisle Cathedral

carlislecathedral.org.uk
Cathedral Office, Castle Street, CA3 8TZ | 01228 548071
Open Mon–Sat 7.30–6.15, Sun 7.30–5; Christmas & New Year 9.45–4

In 1122, 30 years after the castle was built, Carlisle Cathedral was founded. It was originally a priory but became a cathedral under Henry I in 1132 and has held a daily service for almost 900 years. Inside, the first thing you notice is its magnificent high ceiling, with its beautiful blue background and gold painted stars. The stained-glass windows date from the 14th to the 20th centuries – the oldest is in the East Window. Look out also for the bishop's throne or 'cathedra', the 16th-century Brougham Tryptich, a carved wooden altarpiece made in Amsterdam and two runic inscriptions carved in the 12th century. Don't forget to look up at the stone carvings atop the pillars, where the medieval masons carved their daily lives as decoration – animals, plants and the labours of the year, month by month. Don't miss seeing the buildings opposite the cathedral's main entrance too. The Fratry was a 13th-century monastic common room and now contains the cathedral library and the Prior's Kitchen Restaurant. Across from the Fratry, the 13th-century Prior's Tower was used, among other things, as a place of refuge from reivers and other Scottish raiders.

▼ Carlisle Cathedral

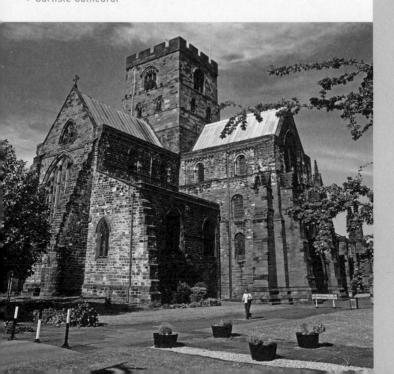

VISIT THE MUSEUMS AND GALLERIES

Border Regiment and King's Own Royal Border Regiment Museum

kingsownbordermuseum.btck.co.uk
Alma Building, The Castle, CA3 8UR
01228 532774 | Open Apr–Sep
9.30–5. Oct–Mar 10–4. Times subject
to change, check website

Trophies, models, pictures, weapons, uniforms, medals and silver tell the story of the regiments. There are many tragic and heroic stories from the wars in which the regiments have been involved. The museum has recently relocated to Carlisle Castle's Alma Building from its former home in Queen Mary's Tower.

Guildhall Museum

tulliehouse.co.uk/guildhall-museum
Green Market, Fisher Street, CA3 8JE
01228 534781 | Open Mon–Sat 9–5,
Sun 11–5 summer, 12–5 winter

One of the oldest houses in Carlisle, the Guildhall Museum is housed in a Grade I listed building, built in the 14th century. Inside, you'll find displays telling the fascinating story of the medieval guilds with different rooms reflecting the individual trades. The guilds were established for weavers, tailors, tanners, glovers, shoemakers, smiths, butchers and merchants to protect trade. The guildhall was given to the city by Richard de Redeness and used as the meeting place by the town's Trade Guilds. Four of the Guilds survive today and continue to meet annually in the building on Ascension Day.

Linton Tweeds Visitor Centre

visitcumbria.com
Shaddongate, Carlisle, CA2 5TZ
01228 527569

On a visit here, you can watch the latest designs being woven on the original old hand looms. You can even have a go yourself on another old hand loom. The family-run business is over 100 years old, and was started by William Linton in the Caldewgate area of Carlisle in 1912. William's friend, Captain Molyneaux, introduced him to a young lady known as Coco Chanel. The fashion house Chanel is still a customer today and Michelle Obama is among the many well-known people who wear these fabrics. There's also a coffee shop and a shop selling the lovely fabrics.

Tullie House Museum & Art Gallery Trust

tulliehouse.co.uk
Castle Street, CA3 8TP
01228 618718 | Open all year 10–5;
closed Sun mornings

If you want to find out about the history of Carlisle, this is the place to go. The story is told from before the Romans to the railways, via the reivers, Robert the Bruce and the Roundheads with lively displays and lots of activities, which combine education and entertainment. Children will most definitely not be bored here. You can try writing on Roman wax tablets, have a go with a crossbow, or go through a mine tunnel. The galleries include the Roman Frontier gallery and the Border Reivers gallery, with interactive displays and artefacts bringing these bloodthirsty times to life. It also has very good natural history displays and art galleries. Set in beautiful gardens, Old Tullie House is a Grade I listed building containing a nationally important collection of Pre-Raphaelite art.

ENTERTAIN THE FAMILY
Sands Centre
thesandscentre.co.uk
CA1 1JQ | 01228 625222
Call or check website for details
This is the major venue for performances of all kinds in Cumbria and beyond. Check the website for its programme, which ranges from touring shows including ballet, opera and theatre productions to big-name bands, solo performers, comedy and pantomime. The Centre also has a state-of-the-art gym, climbing wall and sports hall. You can take part in all sorts of sports and activities and they are tailored for all ages. Check the website for the holiday programme for kids, sports on offer regularly and special sessions for seniors.

SEE A LOCAL CHURCH
St Cuthbert's Church
stcuthbertscarlisle.org.uk
Blackfriars Street, West Walls,
CA3 8UF | 01228 52198
Slightly overshadowed by the cathedral, but worth a visit, is St Cuthbert's Church. Also built in the 12th century, the present buildings date from the 1700s. Its most unusual feature is a moveable pulpit, mounted on rail tracks, while the nearby tithe barn now functions as the church hall.

GO TO THE RACES
Carlisle Racecourse
carlisle-races.co.uk
Durdar Road, CA2 4TS
01228 554700
If you fancy a day at the races, check the website for fixtures. Children are generally admitted free and there are family fun days throughout the year.

▼ Underpass to the Tullie House Museum & Art Gallery

▶ The Cumbria Coastal Way

If you want to get a feel for the Cumbrian coastline then this 124-mile walk of the entire coastline, from Milnthorpe to Carlisle and on to Gretna in Scotland, is ideal. It is also quieter than many of the more central routes. The route heads out of Silverdale on Morecambe Bay, around the wide sands of the southern estuaries, through the Lake District National Park and the industrial heritage of the west coast, along the Solway Firth and by Hadrian's Wall to the River Eden and Carlisle, then across the Eden into Scotland to the official finish at the famous border town of Gretna. Allow about 10 days if you want to do the whole walk.

The Cumbria Way

This 70-mile long-distance route from Ulverston to Carlisle is the exact opposite of the Cumbria Coastal Way. It takes a straight line through the heart of the Lake District, through some of its most beautiful areas. From Ulverston the route traverses the length of Coniston, passes the lovely Tarn Hows and Rosthwaite, goes by Derwent Water to Keswick then Skiddaw and Blencathra to Caldbeck, and then on through gentler pastoral countryside to Carlisle. Unsurprisingly, this is one of the most popular long-distance paths in the country. It takes about a week to complete and there are companies that will organise the entire walk for you.

PLAY A ROUND

Eden Golf Course

edengolf.co.uk

CA6 4RA | 01228 573003

Open daily

This is a championship-length parkland course following the River Eden. There are tight tree-lined fairways and numerous natural water hazards, making it a great test of golf. The nine-hole Hadrian's course is set in natural undulating surroundings and has a contrasting style to the main 18.

EAT AND DRINK

The Basement Bar & Bistro

2 Crosby Street, CA1 1DQ

01228 596962

Just behind the main shopping area, this is a relaxed spot for a light lunch or in the evening for fantastic cocktails and imaginative food at reasonable prices. There is sometimes live music as well, which adds further to the ambience.

Crown Hotel ⊛

crownhotelwetheral.co.uk

Station Road, Wetheral, CA4 8ES

01228 561888

Just off the A69, outside Carlisle, in the peaceful village of Wetheral you'll find this attractive country hotel. You can sit in the in the comfortable, raftered conservatory restaurant and enjoy views of the gardens. The service is friendly and relaxed and the food is British with a continental twist.

Davids Restaurant
davidsrestaurant.co.uk
62 Warwick Road, CA1 1DR
01228 523578

Housed in a Victorian townhouse in the centre of the city, this restaurant is the perfect venue for a celebration or special occasion. The service here is friendly and efficient and the food is excellent. The menus are seasonal, using the best quality ingredients. They will cater to any special diets and the mid-week fixed-price menu is amazing value.

Garden Restaurant Tullie House
tulliehouse.co.uk
Castle Street, CA3 8TP
01228 618718

On the ground floor of the museum and art gallery, overlooking the quiet garden, this large refectory-style restaurant is a great meeting place and ideally situated close to Carlisle's city centre. Serving snacks and more substantial lunches, it's also family friendly.

Hell Below & Co
14–16 Devonshire Street, CA3 8LP
01228 548481

Great value for money, cheerful and good quality food – what more could you ask? Well, the atmosphere is pretty good too and the decor is fantastic – old cinema seats, red brick and chunky utilitarian tables and

stools. Whether you want to take the kids out for a pizza or go for cocktails and a meal, this place is ideal.

▶ **PLACES NEARBY**

Finglandrigg Wood on the Solway Plain
You'll find this on the B5307 about eight miles from Carlisle. There's a lay-by with a Natural England sign about a mile after Kirkbampton and as well as picnic tables you'll find waymarked paths onto the reserve. It has a wide variety of wildlife, birds, insects and plant life.

Church of St Mary
Chapel Hill Road, Wreay, CA4 0SA

If you only have time to visit one church, this is the one to see. Its dramatic and highly imaginative design is unusual and probably unique in England. Sara Losh (1785–1853), a local landowner, designed St Mary's in 1842, partly in memory to her sister and parents. Influenced by the architecture she had seen on her Grand Tour of Europe, she created a design very much at odds with the English Gothic style of the time. The church is built like a Roman basilica with a large rectangular area and a semi-circular apse. The light stone and white-painted interior walls contrast strongly in colour, shade and texture with the dark timbered roof, pews and decorative details, which are all beautifully lit. The building is alive with symbols of life and death, darkness and light. Gargoyles of fantastical creatures guard the exterior and, inside, you are nearly overwhelmed by figures – including angels, an owl, a cockerel, chrysalis and butterfly and acorns. Look for the arrow and pine cones, a memorial to Sara's friend, Major Thain, who died from an arrow wound in battle and is said to have sent her a pine cone before he died.

Plough Inn

Wreay, CA4 0RL | 01697 475770
This historic country inn has been refurbished but it still has the feel of ages past and the many lives it has touched. It serves excellent local beers, including Hesket Newmarket and Geltsdale, alongside good food prepared from locally sourced ingredients.

Solway Aviation Museum

solway-aviation-museum.co.uk
Carlisle Airport, Crosby-on-Eden
01228 573823 | Open Apr–Oct Fri–Sun and BHs 10.30–5, Nov–Mar Sat–Sun 10.30–5

There are lots of vintage aircraft on display here and if you are interested in planes you'll want to spend a good few hours here. Even if you're not a plane enthusiast, this is a highly entertaining museum for the whole family. Children will love climbing into the cockpits of some of the exhibits, in particular the stunning Vulcan bomber. Exhibits include remnants from Blue Streak, the failed missile project from nearby RAF Spadeadam, a Sikorsky helicopter and a 1930s Hawker Hart biplane.

The String of Horses Inn

stringofhorses.com
Faugh, CA8 9EG | 01228 670297
This traditional 17th-century Lakeland inn has all the regulation oak beams, wood panelling, old settles and log fires you would expect in the restaurant, where you'll also find imaginative pub food. In the bar you can sample real ales from Brampton Brewery.

▶ Cartmel

If you wonder why this tiny village in the middle of the South Lakeland District fells and countryside should have such a large and magnificent church, it is because Cartmel grew up around its famous 12th-century Augustinian priory church. Owing to it being stipulated that the local community should always have the right to worship in the Priory Church of St Mary and St Michael, it was saved when the monastery was disbanded.

Much of the stone from the monastery was re-used to build the present village and the only other relic of it that remains is the gatehouse (now a private residence in the care of the National Trust) in the little market square. The stepped market cross still stands but the markets themselves are long gone. Today, Cartmel is a pretty little village, worth exploring in its own right as well as for its gem of a church.

To the south of the village is Holker Hall (see page 152), the home of the Cavendish family; allow plenty of time for your visit because there's a lot to see.

SEE A LOCAL CHURCH

The Priory Church of St Mary and St Michael

cartmelpriory.org.uk
Priest Lane, LA11 6PU
01539 536261

This priory church will make a lasting impression on you, overshadowing the village as it does and giving an idea of how the early priories – with all their attached buildings – must have dominated their surroundings.

Founded as a priory for Augustinian canons in around 1189, the oldest parts are the chancel, transepts, the south doorway and part of the north wall of the nave, where you can see the plain and massive arches, characteristic of the period. Look for the two blocked-up doorways in the transepts, one of which once connected to the monks' dormitory. The huge east window nearly fills the east wall and some sections hold fragments of medieval glass rescued from earlier works. The south porch has the oldest glass, which dates from the 14th century and depicts angels. There is also some stunning Victorian glass, with rich colours and beautifully detailed drawings.

The Priory Church of St Mary and St Michael also served as a parish church, which saved it from outright destruction during the Dissolution of the Monasteries in the 1530s. The priory was

▼ Augustinian Priory Church, Cartmel

dissolved, and four of the monks were hanged along with 10 villagers who had supported them, but the church survived, as did the precinct gatehouse, though other domestic structures were destroyed.

The 15th-century choir stalls, each with a misericord, bear many carvings of animals, including a unicorn, mermaid, ape and peacock, as well as the Green Man. The delicate 17th-century stall backs have very fine openwork panels and slender columns topped with ornate capitals and covered in twining vines.

Make sure to notice the unique tower. Unusually the 15th-century extension was built across the original low lantern tower at a 45-degree angle. And don't miss the bullet holes still visible in the southwest door of the nave, leftovers from the 1640s, when Roundhead troops stayed in the village and stabled their horses in the church.

EAT AND DRINK

Aynsome Manor Hotel ◉

aynsomemanorhotel.co.uk
LA11 6HH | 015395 36653
Once a country residence of the Pembroke family, this is an elegant little country house at the head of the Cartmel Valley, looking southwards towards the priory, the meadows and the woods. Inside, it has an old-school feel, with starched tablecloths, silverware and gleaming glasses, deep windows and portraits in oils

gazing down from the walls. Pick any number of courses from the daily-changing menu, or go for the full five. Whatever you choose, it will be freshly prepared with imaginative combinations of flavours.

Cartmel Village Shop

cartmelvillageshop.co.uk
The Square, LA11 6QD
015395 36280
This is the home of probably the most moist and delicious sticky toffee pudding in the world!

The Cavendish Arms

thecavendisharms.co.uk
LA11 6QA | 015395 36240
A babbling stream flows past the tree-lined garden of this 450-year-old coaching inn, situated within the village walls and Cartmel's longest-surviving hostelry. Many traces of its history remain, from the mounting block outside the main door to the bar itself, which was once the stables. Low, oak-beamed ceilings, uneven floors, antique furniture and an open fire create a traditional, cosy atmosphere. As well as Cumbrian ales, the food owes much to its local origins. The menu changes every six weeks, including lunchtime sandwiches, starters and full meals.

L'Enclume ◉◉◉◉◉

lenclume.co.uk
Cavendish St, LA11 6PZ
015395 36362
The most prestigious restaurant in the region. Anyone who

follows Simon Rogan will know that he's a chef who never stands still. He's always working on the next project, whether that be a new dish, a new restaurant, growing a new kind of vegetable, experimenting with a new ingredient picked from the wild, or expanding his farm (it now spans 23 acres across five different sites). Yet, L'Enclume manages to have a pleasingly unpretentious feel, with lots of natural materials in the design – stone floors and walls and bare-wood tables – and friendly, charming and totally on-the-ball serving staff. They're all well versed in the menu, which is a good thing when you consider that a meal here is a succession of dishes all made up of multiple, often unusual, components. At the heart of everything is Rogan's true passion – super-fresh ingredients, many picked just hours ago at his organic farm nearby, or foraged from the local countryside. Livestock is also reared on the farm, and what Rogan doesn't produce himself he sources from trusted local suppliers; you can be sure that only the very best will do in his kitchen. The freshly baked breads get things off to a highly promising start, and every dish that follows bursts with fresh, powerful flavours and vibrant, natural colours, with edible flowers often used to stunning effect. (See also Rogan & Company Restaurant, page 100).

5 Cumbrian puddings

▶ **Cumberland Rum Nicky**. Try the one at **Middle Ruddings Country Inn and Restaurant** at Braithwaite (middle-ruddings.co.uk | CA12 5RY 017687 78436).

▶ **Borrowdale Sticky Banana Pudding** from **Lucy's On A Plate**, Ambleside (www.lucysofambleside.co.uk LA22 0BU| 015394 32288).

▶ **Cartmel Sticky Toffee Pudding**. Widely available but the best you'll find is from the **Cartmel Village Shop** (cartmelvillageshop.co.uk | LA11 6QB 015395 36280).

▶ **Bread and Butter Pudding**. This old favourite can be found in various guises throughout the region.

▶ **The World's Most Expensive Chocolate Pudding**. Lindeth Howe Country House Hotel (lindeth-howe.co.uk LA23 3JF | 015394 45759). It's made from four different types of Belgian chocolate, flavoured with whisky, peach and orange, layered with champagne jelly and glazed with edible gold leaf. Instead of being topped with a cherry there's a two-carat diamond and you get to wash it down with half a grand's worth of pudding wine. There's a couple of drawbacks to trying this. The first is the three weeks notice you need to give to order it. The second is the price tag – £22,000.

The Masons Arms

www.masonsarmsstrawberrybank.
com | Strawberry Bank, LA11 6NW
015395 68486

A charmingly atmospheric pub
with low, beamed ceilings, old
fireplaces and quirky furniture,
and a stunning location
overlooking the Winster Valley.
Take a seat in the busy bar,
dining rooms or heated covered
terraces and try one of the
popular dishes such as warm
pitta bread and homemade
hummus. There's plenty of
choice of full hearty courses to
follow. Wash it down with a pint
of Thwaites Wainwright or
Hawkshead Bitter.

Pig & Whistle

pigandwhistlecartmel.co.uk
Aynsome Road, LA11 6PL
015395 36482

The co-landlord here with
Penny Tapsell is Simon Rogan,
one of Britain's most
accomplished chefs. The pub
has long been his local, and he
intends it to remain just that –
a local. His short but perfectly
formed menu offers five simple
but remarkably good value-
for-money dishes. Real ale
drinkers may run into a Dizzy
Blonde in the bar – it's one of
Robinsons of Stockport's
seasonal brews.

Rogan & Company Restaurant @@@

roganandcompany.co.uk
The Square, LA11 6QD
015395 35917

If you can't get a table at
L'Enclume, Simon Rogan's

hugely celebrated restaurant
and holder of the ultimate five
AA Rosettes (see page 98),
dining at Rogan & Company is
by no means a poor substitute.
L'Enclume's little sister sits
beside the river in a lovely old
building right in the centre of
Cartmel. It's just a short stroll
away from L'Enclume, so
although you won't find the man
himself behind the stoves here
on a daily basis, you can be
assured that he's here
regularly, keeping an eye on
things and making sure head
chef Danielle Barry and her
team faithfully execute his
unique style of contemporary,
natural cooking. Staff dress
casually in long black aprons,
and bare-wood tables are

▲ Castlerigg Stone Circle

simply set with Lakeland slate tablemats and high quality glassware. Every dish is visually stunning, the ingredients as fresh as can be – little wonder when many of them have been foraged from the local countryside or gathered that morning from Rogan's own farm down the road.

▶ Castlerigg Stone Circle

www.english-heritage.org.uk

Castle Lane

Just two miles east of Keswick is one of the most dramatic and atmospheric stone circles in Britain. It dates from about 2000 BC, and, like many of these ancient stone sites, its original purpose remains unknown. There are 38 stones in the circle itself, with a further 10 in the centre, and the circle is dramatically situated – surrounded by high fells, with Helvellyn to the southeast. Made of volcanic Borrowdale rock, brought here by the glaciers of the Ice Age, the construction is actually oval in shape, 107 feet across at its widest point. The name of the stone circle means 'the fort on the ridge', though no evidence of any fort exists here.

▶ Cockermouth

For a small country market town, Cockermouth has plenty of history behind it. The most significant event as far as most of today's visitors are concerned is that William Wordsworth was born here in 1770. If you have visited Dove Cottage in Grasmere (see page 134), where the poet later lived, you will be surprised at the grandeur of his birthplace. The Georgian town house, dating from 1745, has been faithfully restored by the National Trust and furnished in mid-18th-century style, with some of Wordsworth's own personal effects.

Other famous names associated with Cockermouth include Fletcher Christian – the mutineer on *The Bounty* – Mary, Queen of Scots and Robert the Bruce.

The town now houses a printing museum, an art gallery at Castlegate House and Jennings Brewery, which dates from 1828 and offers hour-long guided tours.

TAKE IN SOME HISTORY
Wordsworth House and Garden
nationaltrust.org.uk
Main Street, CA13 9RX
01900 824805 | Open mid-Mar–2 Nov Sat–Thu 11–5 Closed Fri
William Wordsworth was born here on 7 April 1770, and his happy memories of the place had a great influence on his work. Imaginatively presented as the home of the Wordsworth family in the 1770s, the house offers a lively and interactive visit with hands-on activities and costumed living history.

VISIT THE GALLERY
Castlegate House Gallery
castlegatehouse.co.uk
CA13 9HA | 01900 822149
Open Mon, Wed–Sat 10–5, Tue & Sun by appointment only
You'll find a warm and friendly welcome here whether you go

▼ Wordsworth House

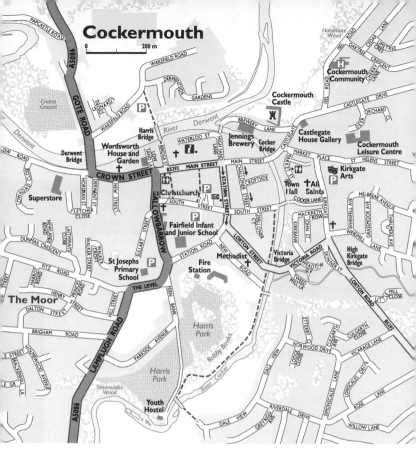

to browse or to buy. Housed in an unspoilt Georgian house, the gallery specialises in 20th-century and contemporary British art. You'll find works by internationally renowned artists – such as Sheila Fell, Percy Kelly, Carel Weight, Ken Howard and many others – as well as up-and-coming artists, particularly from the north of England and southern Scotland. There's also plenty of ceramics and pottery to see.

TOUR THE BREWERY
Jennings Brewery
jenningsbrewery.co.uk
The Castle Brewery, CA13 9NE
0845 129 7190 | Tours: Apr–Oct

5 local ales

▶ **Catbells Pale Ale**, Hesket Newmarket Brewery

▶ **Lakeland Golden**, Bitter End Brewpub, Cockermouth

▶ **Langdale**, Old Hall Brewery, Hawkshead

▶ **T'Owd Tub**, Dent Brewery, Dent

▶ **Sneck Lifter**, Jennings Brewery, Cockermouth (see below)

Mon–Sat 12 and 2, Nov–Dec, Mar
Mon–Fri 2. Closed Jan–Feb
On the brewery tour, you can see how all the beers are made and complete the tour by

sampling them. There's also an on-site shop if you would like to take some home. Jennings Brewery was originally established as a family business in 1828 and moved to its current location in 1874. It is a traditional brewer, using Lakeland water drawn from the brewery's own well.

PLAY A ROUND
Cockermouth Golf Club
cockermouthgolf.co.uk
Embleton, CA13 9SG
017687 76223 | Open all year daily
This fell course, rearranged by James Braid, has exceptional views of the Lakeland hills and valleys and the Solway Firth. There's a hard climb on the 3rd and 11th holes and the 8th, 10th and 16th are testing too.

EAT AND DRINK
Kirkstile Inn
kirkstile.com
CA13 0RU | 01900 85219
This classic Cumbrian inn stands just half a mile from the Loweswater and Crummock lakes and makes an ideal base for walking, climbing, boating and fishing. Stretching as far as the eye can see are the woods, fells and lakes. The beck below meanders under a stone bridge, oak trees fringing its banks. The whole place has a traditional, well-looked-after feel – whitewashed walls, low beams, solid polished tables, cushioned settles, a well-stoked fire and the odd horse harness remind you of times gone by. You can call in for afternoon tea, but better still would be to taste one of the Cumbrian Legendary Ales – Loweswater Gold, Grasmoor Dark Ale, Esthwaite Bitter – brewed by landlord Roger Humphreys in Esthwaite Water near Hawkshead. Traditional pub food is freshly prepared using local produce and the lunchtime menu brims with wholesome dishes intended to satisfy the heartiest appetites. If you're in need of a lighter meal, tuck into sandwiches, wraps, jacket potatoes or salads. In the evening, you'll find more varied but equally good, high quality, unpretentious food.

The Trout Hotel
trouthotel.co.uk
Crown Street, CA13 0EJ
01900 823591
There are several places to eat here – from the bar to the formal dining room – but the ambience, the service and food are good in all. The Trout is a black-and-white timbered Grade II listed hotel at the quieter end of the Georgian town centre, right next door to Wordsworth's childhood home. At the bar, there are several Jennings ales and guest ales from Corby Brewery. Throughout the menu, all the local suppliers are acknowledged, so you know exactly where the ingredients are coming from. In summer, meals and drinks can be enjoyed in the gardens overlooking the River Derwent.

▶ Coniston

If you want to get a little off the beaten track and explore a magnificent range of peaks, the little grey town of Coniston is the perfect destination. It is near the northern tip of Coniston Water and overlooked by the bulk of the Old Man of Coniston at 2,627 feet.

It was these mountains, and the mineral wealth they yielded, that created the village of Coniston. While copper had been mined in this area since the Roman occupation, the industry grew most rapidly during the 18th and 19th centuries and the village expanded accordingly. The Ruskin Museum tells the story of copper mining, slate quarrying and farming, as well as the lives of celebrities such as John Ruskin, Arthur Ransome and Donald Campbell. Don't miss Ruskin's home Brantwood on the shores of the lake; you can visit both the house and the beautiful grounds. And no visit to the Lakes is complete without a boat trip. If you have your own boat you can launch it from the public slipway (no powered craft) or you can hire a sailing dinghy or rowing boat by the hour.

Take some time to drive or walk to nearby Tarn Hows, one of the most popular beauty spots in the Lakes.

▼ Lake Coniston and the Old Man of Coniston

▶ Brantwood

brantwood.org.uk
LA21 8AD | 015394 41396
Open mid-Mar–mid-Nov daily 10.30–5, mid-Nov–mid-Mar Wed–Sun,
10.30–4

Brantwood is undoubtedly one of the most beautiful houses in the Lake District, not least owing to its situation on the eastern shore of the lake with views across Coniston Water. The atmosphere is particularly special as so many of Ruskin's possessions remain; it's as if he may return at any moment. There's a brief introductory video and then you can explore the seven historical rooms – each brimming with his furniture, art and objects. There is a small printed guide to the rooms, and volunteer stewards are on hand to answer any questions. For younger visitors, there are quizzes and activity sheets to tackle.

Even if you don't visit the house, the grounds are an attraction in their own right. Brantwood has unique mountainside gardens in a 250-acre estate with spectacular views. Half of the estate is ancient woodland with a stunning diversity of flora and fauna. Elsewhere, there are lakeshore meadows and high, open fell and eight beautifully landscaped gardens. No matter what your level of fitness, you can find a walk to suit, from low-level rambles through the garden to energetic hikes to Crag Head. A trail guide is available in the shop. If you want a real insight into the stories behind the estate and Ruskin's experiments in land management go on one of the guided walks. There are also lots of special events throughout the year. Check the website for details.

▼ Brantwood

▲ John Ruskin's bedroom, Brantwood

TAKE IN SOME HISTORY
The Ruskin Cross
St Andrew's Church, Tiberthwaite Avenue, LA21 8ED

It's worth going into St Andrew's churchyard to find the grave of John Ruskin, who died of influenza at Brantwood on 20 Jan 1900. The large, carved, green-slate cross was designed by Ruskin's friend, W G Collingwood, who was an expert on Anglo-Saxon crosses, and carved by H T Miles with symbols depicting important aspects of Ruskin's work and life. Collingwood also designed the war memorial, which stands in the churchyard. It is a 10-foot high, sandstone, Celtic Cross. If you want to find Donald Campbell's grave, you'll need to go to the New Parish Cemetery on Old Hawkshead Road behind the Crown Hotel.

VISIT THE MUSEUM
The Ruskin Museum
ruskinmuseum.com
Yewdale Road, LA21 8DU
015394 41164 | Open mid-Mar–mid-Nov daily 10–5.30, mid-Nov–mid-Mar Wed–Sun, 10.30–3.30. Discount vouchers available for cruises on Steam Yacht Gondola, Coniston Launch and Brantwood (see Take a Boat Trip, overleaf) Make sure to visit the amazing Ruskin Museum. John Ruskin's life is fascinating. He was an incredibly versatile and important political thinker,

writer and artist. The museum contains many of his watercolours, drawings, letters, sketchbooks and other memorabilia representing his life's work.

Equally fascinating is the story of *Bluebird*, Donald Campbell's iconic hydroplane, which has been resurrected from the lake and is being rebuilt. Permission has been granted for future low-speed engineering proving trials on Coniston Water. A newly built extension with interpretation boards and displays is ready for the arrival of *Bluebird K7*, and a new online ticketing scheme will start at the same time, so do check the website for details.

The other boat on display is Arthur Ransome's *Mavis*, the *Amazon* described in his classic children's tale, *Swallows and Amazons*. Arthur Ransome based the book on both Lake Windermere and Coniston Water, and described many actual features from the landscape, but he invented his own geography. If you loved the book (or film) as a child, no doubt you'll enjoy mixing and matching the descriptions and names in the story to the actual locations.

Add to this the history of the geology, mines and quarries of the area, lace and linen, dry-stone walling, Herdwick sheep, John Usher's miniature village

built in stone with painstaking detail and more, and you will realize that you need plenty of time for this visit. In fact you'll want to go back.

There are various guided walks available from the museum, including 'In Ruskin's Footsteps', 'Coniston Village walk' and 'The *Bluebird* walk', See opposite page for more details.

TAKE A BOAT TRIP
Steam Yacht Gondola
nationaltrust.org.uk/gondola
Coniston Pier, Lake Road, LA21 8AN
01539 432733 | Apr–Oct daily.
Check website or call for the
current timetable

Enjoy Coniston as wealthy Victorians did, by travelling in style in *Gondola's* saloons or relaxing on the decks. The crew will give you a commentary on Coniston's history and themes, such as *Swallows and Amazons* or *Bluebird*, while you enjoy the spectacular scenery in old-fashioned comfort. You can find out all about *Gondola's* steam engine and watch the engineer feeding the firebox. Originally launched in 1859, *Gondola* sailed Coniston Water until 1936. Having been beautifully rebuilt, she returned in 1980. You can take a full-lake cruise, a half-lake cruise or combine a part cruise with walking. There's also an afternoon tea or a picnic cruise. Check the website for details and times.

▶ Coniston Launch

conistonlaunch.co.uk
Pier Cottage, Lake Road, LA21 8AJ | 017687 75753
Check website for the timetable

This is a great way to enjoy the lake and explore the area. Since 2005, the boats have used electric motors instead of diesel, with solar panels helping to charge the batteries so that they are now environmentally friendly and quieter. You can take one of the themed cruises such as *Swallows and Amazons* or *Bluebird*. Alternatively buy a hop-on, hop-off ticket for a day or a week to make the most of your Coniston experience.

GO WALKING

Guided walks from Ruskin Museum (see page 107)

Tarn Hows

You can drive to Tarn Hows from Coniston along the B5285 Hawkshead road. Better still, you could walk one of the loveliest parts of the long-distance Cumbria Way (see page 94) to reach it. Once there, you can picnic at the tarn, which is studded with islands, surrounded by gorgeous conifer woodland and with the most beautiful backdrop of rolling hills.

In Ruskin's Footsteps

One of the great attractions of this guided walk is that it takes you right off the beaten track with hardly a tourist in sight. The route winds up steeply from the base of Long Crag, with rewarding views at every stage. Soon the whole of Coniston is laid out behind you, and your guide – an enthusiastic Ruskin scholar – will point out places with Ruskin connections. Once above the impressive waterfall, White Ghyll, you follow a footpath along a marshy plateau, down to a stream and finally up to the viewpoint at the

▼ Tarn Hows

top of Yewdale Crag itself. On the way back, the route heads down the old peat road near Tilberthwaite, returning to Coniston via Whin Woods. The walk is approximately five miles and generally takes about four to five hours. You'll need a reasonable level of fitness and suitable boots and clothing.

Coniston Village Walk

This short, low-level walk is easy and you can take it at a leisurely pace. The guide explains all about Coniston's history and heritage, including its connections with Arthur Ransome and Donald Campbell – the route visits Campbell's memorial and grave, Ruskin's Cross in the churchyard (see also page 107) and the old school where he gave lessons.

You can really appreciate Coniston's past as you visit the old station, the former miners' houses up on the Banks, the 16th-century Black Bull, and the forge. There are local legends and the story of the landscape, the mountains and Mountain Rescue. The distance is just over a mile and takes approximately two hours.

EAT AND DRINK

The Black Bull Inn & Hotel
blackbullconiston.co.uk
1 Yewdale Road, LA21 8DU
015394 41335
Tarry a while at this 400-year-old inn with a pint of Bluebird or Blacksmiths bitter, brewed at the rear of the pub. You can drink in grand views outside tables or in the bar, and look over the photos and artefacts in the main bar, recalling

▼ The Coniston Launch *Campbell* on Coniston Water

the exploits of Donald Campbell seeking the world water-speed record on the lake. Campbell himself was a regular here. Early birds can tuck into a full breakfast before hitting the peaks. Daytime and evening diners can enjoy hearty snacks, home-cooked main dishes and at least two vegetarian options.

The Bluebird Café

thebluebirdcafe.co.uk
Lake Road, LA21 8AN
015394 41649

Set in a stunning location overlooking the lake, this cafe offers a varied menu – from cakes and snacks to full main courses – all freshly cooked and moderately priced. You can combine a visit here with a cruise on the lake and they provide the picnics for the *Gondola* Picnic Cruises (see page 108).

The Green Housekeeper Cafe

16 Yewdale Road, LA21 8DU
015394 41925

The food in this friendly cafe is great. They serve freshly made sandwiches using homemade bread and fillings, hearty non-greasy breakfasts, soup and snacks. If you order afternoon tea, you will be given an enormous pot of tea with scones or cakes. Vegetarians will find a number of tasty options on the menu and they do their best here to cater to special diets too.

▸ **PLACES NEARBY**

The hamlet of Torver, on the old packhorse trail to the Duddon Valley, is a couple of miles outside Coniston on the road to Broughton-in-Furness. It once had a railway line for transporting stone and slate from the nearby quarries. It's a day's walking from the start of the Cumbria Way at Ulverston, so it's an ideal place to stop if you are walking it.

The Wilsons Arms

www.thewilsonsarms.co.uk
Torver, LA21 8BB | 015394 41237

You'll find a friendly welcome, a real log fire and open beams at the family owned Wilsons Arms. Children are welcome and they have dining areas reserved for those staying with pets. They serve good pub grub in generous portions all day from breakfast until dinner.

▶ Dalemain

dalemain.com

Two miles north of Ullswater, CA11 0HB | 017684 86450 | House open 6
Apr–Oct, Sun–Thu 11.15–4 (closes at 3 in Oct); Gardens, tea room & shop,
Sun–Thu 10.30–5 (closes at 4 in Oct)

Dalemain is a country house and garden that's still home to the
Hazell-McCosh family. The estate has evolved over time – at its
core there's a 12th-century pele tower with a kitchen garden,
an Elizabethan knot garden, a Stuart terrace from 1680 and the
facade is Georgian. In the gardens, there's a sense of continuity
with the past, as well as personal touches added by the present
family, such as the Children's Garden developed by Mrs
Hasell-McCosh when her own children were small.

The Terrace Walk, with its buttressed retaining wall, is much
as it was when Sir Edward Hasell laid it out in the 17th century,
although there are now several rambling roses attempting to
invade the gravel path and a deep herbaceous border below the
walls of the house. At the end of the terrace is a handsome
Grecian fir next to the Knot Garden, with a marble fountain as
its central feature surrounded by low, symmetrical box hedges
filled to overflowing with herbs, campanulas and antirrhinums.

From here, the ground slopes upwards to the west, with a
lawn planted with old apples, plums and pears on one side of a
gravel path and a deep border with splendid shrub roses edged
with sedums, phloxes, rodgersias, meconopsis and irises at the
other. At the top of the garden, a classically proportioned
summerhouse is built into an alcove.

A door leads into Lob's Wood where a path winds between
beech and oak trees on the top of a steep bank above the Dacre

▼ Dalemain House

Beck. Further along the wall is a pavilion, with a pointed roof and mullioned windows, dating from 1550. A flight of steep steps leads down to the Wild Garden – bright with drifts of daffodils in spring and flowering trees and shrubs and the Himalayan blue poppy, *Meconopsis grandis*, in the early summer months. The latter was planted by Sylvia McCosh, the current owner's mother.

The Children's Garden features plants with 'animal' names, including bear's breeches (*acanthus*), snapdragon (*antirrhinum*) and foxglove (*digitalis*). Each plant is identified by locally handcrafted wooden animal signs; similar examples are for sale in the gift shop.

John de Morville owned the oldest surviving part of the house, the pele tower, at the time when his brother Hugh was involved in the murder of Thomas à Becket. The Layton family, who held Dalemain from the 13th to the 17th centuries, added the buildings around the courtyard. These include the medieval Great Hall, with its Tudor ceiling, and the Priest's Hiding Chamber, originally reached by climbing the kitchen chimney, but now accessed from the housekeeper's room. The haunted solar holds 'The Luck of Dalemain', a superb wine glass of about 1730, engraved with the Hasell coat of arms.

Lady Anne Clifford, a rich heiress, whose portrait hangs here, left a legacy to her 'secretarie' Sir Edward Hasell, and he used it to buy Dalemain in 1679. Another Edward added the classical Georgian front that transformed the jumble of old buildings. The star of the show, however, is the Chinese Drawing Room, with its hand-painted wallpaper featuring a riot of pheasants, peonies and butterflies, Chippendale chairs and an English fireplace carved with spirited dragons.

▶ **PLACES NEARBY**

Church of St Andrew

North of Dacre centre, CA11 0HL

Parts of the building date from the 10th to the 19th century. Built in the local red sandstone, it is on a monastic site referred to by the Venerable Bede in AD 731. The existing building is Norman, with additions of the 13th and 14th centuries and then extensive alterations in the 18th and 19th centuries, but look for the remnants of an earlier age. The stone on the floor belongs to the 10th-century Viking period, and two ancient stone cross-shafts, carved with people and fantastical creatures, date from the 9th century. Don't miss the famous stone-carved Dacre Bears in the four corners of the graveyard. The first shows the bear asleep. The bear then wakes to find a cat or a lynx on its back, which it tries to remove in the third carving. In the fourth the bear appears to have eaten the animal.

Dalton-In-Furness

The ancient town of Dalton-in-Furness was once the principal town of Furness. You can enjoy a walk round the historic buildings at the Market Place. Look out for the unique cast-iron shopfront at No. 51 Market Place, the elegant Victorian drinking fountain, the market cross and the slabs of stone used for fish drying in the 19th century.

MEET THE ANIMALS
South Lakes Wild Animal Park
see opposite

EAT AND DRINK
Clarence House Country
Hotel & Restaurant ◉◉
clarencehouse-hotel.co.uk
Skelgate, LA15 8BQ | 01229 462508
At this white-fronted hotel, located between the sandy beaches and the lush green acres of Lakeland, you can dine on modern British cooking with a twist or choose from a range of steaks and chops. On Friday nights there's a popular carvery. The dining room, designed to look like an orangery, has windows on three sides and looks over the St Thomas Valley.

Dent

If there were a vote for the most attractive village in the Dales, it would hardly be surprising if Dent won first prize. It is a beautiful cluster of pretty whitewashed cottages and cobbled streets in the lush green valley that is Dentdale. This does, of course, mean that it's extremely busy in the holiday season, and you would be best to visit at other times if possible.

Dent is on the Settle–Carlisle railway line, a scenic 72-mile railway route, and is the highest mainline station in Britain, at 1,150 feet. However, if you're planning to travel by train, be warned that the station is five miles from the village itself. The connecting bus service only runs on Saturdays so you'll need to arrange a lift or a taxi. Apparently, when one local was asked why they built the station so far from the village, he replied bluntly, "Appen they wanted t'put it near t'track.'

Dent has a flourishing artistic community with knitters, musicians, authors and photographers among its diverse population, and you can see many of the craft they produce for sale in the area. The local Dent Brewery ales are also very popular. The brewery began life at the Sun Inn (see Eat and Drink, page 117) at the centre of the village but grew so successfully that it had to seek new premises at Cowgill, further up the valley.

Adam Sedgwick was born in Dent in the Old Parsonage in 1785, attended the local grammar school and then went on to

▶ South Lakes Wild Animal Park

wildanimalpark.co.uk
Crossgates, LA15 8JR
01229 466086 | Open daily Mar–
Oct 10–5, Nov–Feb 10–4.30
Whether you want to hand feed
giraffes, penguins and
kangaroos or get up close to
rhinos, tigers, bears, hippos,
monkeys, vultures and lemurs, the whole family will love South
Lakes. There are new aerial walkways and viewpoints, the Wild
Things gift shop and Maki restaurant, all overlooking a recreated
African Savannah where rhinos, giraffes and baboons wander.

become Woodwardian Professor of Geology at Cambridge. The pink Shap granite memorial fountain in the main street marks his distinguished career as a geologist. In 1985, to commemorate the 200th anniversary of his birth, the National Park Authority created the Adam Sedgwick Geology Trail, near Sedbergh. Leaflets are available at National Park Centres and Tourist Information Centres.

Both black and grey marble was quarried near here in the past. The Stone House Marble Works flourished in the 18th and 19th centuries at Arten Gill, southeast of Dent Station, where you will also find Dent Head Viaduct, one of the most amazing constructions on the Settle–Carlisle line. Many of the stations contain marble quarried at Dent. In the days when the quarries were working, the knitters were busy knitting and the mills were humming with weaving, Dentdale's population reached almost 2,000 – about three times what it is today.

VISIT THE HERITAGE CENTRE

Dent Village Heritage Centre
dentvillageheritagecentre.com
LA10 5QJ | 01539 625800
Open daily 11–4
The best place to start exploring Dent is at this centre, on the western edge of the village. Here you will find out the story of the valley, its people, industry and wildlife. Many of the exhibits are of genuine Dales provenance, with a large number from the collection

of Jim and Margaret Taylor of High Laning Farm – the centre's founders, who have spent many years rescuing and refurbishing the artefacts. You can see a kitchen with range and many other implements of a bygone age – the pantry where the butter was churned and the pig salted, and the parlour dressed out in its best for entertaining visitors. There is also a wealth of information on the farm animals in the area and Adam Sedgwick, Dent's most famous son.

EAT AND DRINK

Stone Close Tea Room

dentdale.com
Main Street, LA10 5QL
01539 625231

It's hard not to enjoy the convivial atmosphere conjured up at this lovely whitewashed tea room, where you'll find locals, writers, artists, talkers and walkers. The 17th-century cottage, with its cast-iron range, flagstone floor, exposed beams and original fittings, has a well-earned reputation for serving wholesome food, including vegan and vegetarian dishes. Everything is freshly cooked on the premises, using local, seasonal, organic and Fair Trade produce as far as possible.

Sun Inn

dentdale.com
Main Street, Dent, Sedbergh,
LA10 5QL | 01539 625208

Dent may feel like a village where time has stood still, but the Sun Inn was a true pioneer in the home-brewing and fine-dining revolution that has revitalised many country pubs. The Dent brewery was established behind the pub in 1990 and, although it has since moved up the road to larger premises, you can still enjoy its excellent output here, particularly when suitably accompanied by no-nonsense pub grub – the tasty sausages and pies are truly excellent. Charming public rooms, original coin-studded beams, an open coal fire and a fascinating collection of local photos will all add to your enjoyment.

◀ Dent Head viaduct

▶ Derwent Water (south of Keswick)

At 1.25 miles, this is the Lakeland's widest lake and it's attractively dotted with islands. These include, in the very centre, St Herbert's Island, named after the saint who lived here as a hermit in the seventh century. Derwent Isle was once home to German miners who came to work around Keswick and the Newlands Valley in the 16th century. With Borrowdale closing in to the south, and crags on either side of the lake's southern half, Derwent Water is a popular favourite. You can explore the lake and its surroundings using the ferries. They run between the seven landing stages around

▼ Derwent Water

the lake, so passengers can get off and walk the many footpaths through the woods and climb up to the various viewpoints. There are also good views from the high narrow road on the lake's western edge.

The eastern side of Derwent Water is rich in waterfalls, such as the spectacular Lodore Falls in the southeastern corner, which is one of the stops for the ferries. The National Trust owns much of the land, mainly due to the efforts of Canon Hardwicke Rawnsley, vicar of Crosthwaite and Secretary of the National Trust from its formation in 1895 until his death in 1920. The beautiful Friar's Crag, on the northern shore of Derwent Water close to the Keswick boat landings, was given to the National Trust (along with Lords Island and Calf Close Bay) to be his memorial. Ruskin declared that this view was 'one of the finest in Europe'.

GET ON THE WATER
Derwent Water Marina
derwentwatermarina.co.uk
Portinscale, CA12 5RF
01768 772912 | Open daily 9–5.50
If you want to explore Derwent Water, you can hire canoes, kayaks, sailing dinghies, windsurfers and rowing boats here. It is also the place if you want to learn to sail or brush up your skills – they have a range of courses to suit all abilities. Check the website for details. There are 58 berths afloat and ashore, and storage for dinghies, kayaks and canoes, should you have your own boat. There's also a small chandlery shop and boat repair services.

Nichol End Marine
nicholend.co.uk
Portinscale, CA12 5TY
01768 773082 | Open daily from 9 (until 5–8 depending on season). Check website for details
You can hire motor cruisers here as well as canoes, kayaks, sailing dinghies, windsurfers and rowing boats. There's a range of courses on offer here too. Check the website to find one that matches your level of skill and proficiency. If you own a boat, they have moorings for cruisers at the jetty, as well as berths afloat and storage for dinghies, kayaks and canoes. There are boat repair services and a chandlery shop.

▼ Sunset across Derwent Water

Platty Plus
plattyplus.co.uk
Lodore Boat Landing, CA12 5UX
01768 776572
This small family-run business is about three miles from Keswick. If you are looking for a quieter experience on the lake, this could be the place to go. You can hire canoes, kayaks, sailing dinghies, windsurfers and rowing boats. They also run a range of courses to suit all abilities. Check the website for more details.

Keswick Launch
keswick-launch.co.uk
CA12 5DJ | 01768 772263
You can take a 50-minute cruise right around the lake.

Alternatively hop on and off all day until you return to where you started or just buy a ticket for any part of the journey. The launches start from Keswick boat landings and cruise around the lake stopping at seven lakeshore jetties. Check the website for the current timetable.

GO FISHING
Angling
Keswick Anglers Association
keswickanglers.co.uk
You can fish here for brown trout, sea trout, salmon, perch and pike and you can get a permit from Keswick TIC and number of other places. See the website for details.

Dunnerdale

Dunnerdale, or the Duddon Valley, is as delightful and unspoiled today as it was when William Wordsworth first explored the valley. The River Duddon rises in the hills by the Wrynose Pass, and reaches the sea at the estuary of Duddon Sands. In between lies 10 miles of the most delectable scenery – not the most dramatic, or the most spectacular, but those who prefer more intimate landscapes will love Dunnerdale.

The little town of Broughton-in-Furness (see page 80) stands back from the Duddon Estuary – from Duddon Bridge a minor road takes you up Dunnerdale – but you are seldom far away from the river. Rocky and fast flowing, the river is the natural habitat of dippers and wagtails. There are grassy riverbanks just perfect for spreading out a picnic blanket. Ulpha, a straggle of houses and farmsteads, is the only village of any size in the valley.

As you continue to climb, fields and woods give way to a more rugged landscape, as Harter Fell (2,139 feet) and the higher peaks of central Lakeland begin to dominate the view. When you reach a road junction at Cockley Beck, you can either travel west to Eskdale, via the tortuous Hardknott Pass, or east, along Wrynose Pass, and down into the beautiful Little Langdale Valley.

Egremont

With the River Ehen winding past it, and a wide main street lined with trees (and with a variety of stalls on its Friday market day), Egremont is pretty famous for ugly faces. The World Gurning Championships are held here each September at the ancient Egremont Crab Fair (egremontcrabfair.com). There are athletics competitions, animal shows, hound trails and a greasy pole competition.

The crabs at the Egremont Crab Fair are crab apples not crustaceans. The fair dates from 1267, and on the third Saturday in September the Apple Cart parade passes through the town, throwing apples to people lining the route. The highlight of the fair is the famous 'Gurning through a Braffin' competition, where whoever can make the ugliest grin (gurn) while peering through a horse collar (a braffin), is declared world champion.

As old as the fair is the castle, now in ruins, on a hilltop overlooking the main street. It was largely destroyed in the 16th century but the original gatehouse is still standing.

▶ River Duddon at Dunnerdale

VISIT THE GALLERIES
Lowes Court Gallery
lowescourt.co.uk
12 Main Street, CA22 2DW
01946 820693 | Open Mon–Fri,
10–5, Sat 10–4. Closed Sunday
This listed 18th-century
building was a derelict coal
merchant's cottage until
it was renovated in the early
1970s as an exhibition centre
for local and Cumbrian
artists and craftsmen. You'll
find a great variety of artwork
here including prints, sculpture,
jewellery and textiles. The
Tourist Information Centre
is also here.

Florence Arts Centre
florencemine.com
Florence Mine, CA22 2NR
01946 824946 | Open Mon–Fri,
10–5. Check by phone or web for Sat
and Sun openings
Florence Mine was the last
deep-working iron ore
mine to survive in Western
Europe. Now the former
shower block of the mine
has been transformed into
a new kind of centre for the
arts. It has a high-spec studio
room, gallery space, workshops
and artists' residencies.
Check the website for a
list of forthcoming exhibitions
and events.

EXPLORE BY BIKE
Ainfield Cycles
ainfieldcycles.co.uk
Jacktrees Road, Cleator Moor,
CA23 3DW | 01946 812427
This bike shop stocks a
range of quality bikes to
buy or hire. You can pick
up a bike here and drop it
off in the northeast if you
are cycling coast to coast.
They also stock cycling
accessories of all sorts and
carry out repairs.

▶ Ennerdale
wildennerdale.co.uk
If you want to walk away from the 'madding crowd' you will
appreciate Ennerdale Water in the secluded valley of
Ennerdale. Access by car is limited and the bulk of its shores
can only be explored on foot. From the car park, either at
Bowness Knott or Bleach Green, you can follow the path around
the lake. If you go all the way round, it is eight miles and the
going can be tough in places.

Behind the rows of spruce and larch, the land rises steeply,
to over 2,600 feet in places. Looking south, the hills are higher
still, with Pillar at 2,926 feet, in front of which stands Pillar
Rock – popular with climbers since its first ascent in 1826.
There are biking and bridle paths as well as a wealth of wildlife.
For details of all the many paths, climbs and activities visit
the website.

SADDLE UP
Bradley's Riding Centre
walk-rest-ride.co.uk
Low Cock How, Kinniside,
CA23 3AQ | 01946 861354
You can go riding at this family run riding centre for 30 minutes, half-a-day or all day. They have horses to suit all sizes and abilities, and the owners will find you a riding helmet and tailor your trek to suit you.

EAT AND DRINK
Ennderdale Brewery
ennerdalebrewery.co.uk
Corasdale Farm, Ennerdale,
CA23 3AT | 01946 861755
One of the most out of the way small brewers producing rather splendid ales using water from Croasdale Fell.

▶ PLACES NEARBY
Shepherd's Arms
shepherdsarmshotel.com
Ennerdale Bridge, CA23 8AR
01946 861249
Set right in the centre of Ennerdale Bridge village this relaxed and informal free house serves Jennings and Yates's beers. They do a good line in vegetarian dishes, as well as locally sourced game, while the two open fires in autumn and winter make it very cosy. Local musicians sometimes play in the bar and the pub is a popular stopping point for weary walkers on the Wainwright Coast-to-Coast footpath.

▶ Eskdale

While so many other places in Lakeland are busy with tourists, Eskdale is another beautiful valley that remains relatively quiet. The reason? Inaccessibility. To explore Eskdale you have to take the twists, turns and hairpin bends of the Hardknott and Wrynose passes, or else go the long way round, meandering through south Lakeland. All the better, then, for those who venture this far west, for Eskdale is well worth the effort.

This is excellent walking country, with plentiful rights of way and room to roam. Take the Ravenglass & Eskdale Railway into the heart of Eskdale without blocking up the narrow road with your car. This delightful narrow-gauge railway used to carry iron ore from the Eskdale mines to the coast; now the engines carry passengers up the valley. There are seven stations along the line, all offering opportunities for scenic walks with the option of taking a later train back down to Ravenglass.

The terminus, at Dalegarth, is just a short walk from Boot, a tiny village with a friendly pub. Just up the valley, the Woolpack recalls a time when this was a watering hole for the men who drove pack ponies heavily laden with fleeces down to the coast. Beyond a packhorse bridge spanning Whillan Beck is the

▲ View over Eskdale

delectable grouping of tiny buildings that comprise Eskdale Mill (see page 202). Cereals have been ground here since 1578. Milling ended during the 1920s, but it is now restored to working order. See Ravenglass (page 200) for various attractions.

Furness Peninsula

Furness lies between the mountainous heart of the Lake District and the great sandy estuaries of Morecambe Bay. For centuries it was owned by the monks of Furness Abbey who grazed sheep on the hills, controlled fishing rights, grew crops, planted orchards, made charcoal, smelted iron, dug peat for fuel and manufactured salt.

The young William Wordsworth made a number of trips on horseback to this area of low hills, old woodlands and lush meadows by rivers and reedy tarns, which extends from Ulverston (see page 225), Broughton-in-Furness (see page 80), Coniston (see page 105), Hawkshead (see page 147) and the fringes of Lake Windermere (see page 240) to Barrow-in-Furness (see page 64) and Isle of Walney (see page 229) on the coast. The red sandstone ruins of Furness Abbey (see page 64), inspired Wordsworth to feature them in *The Prelude*

and a couple of sonnets. He knew Barrow-in-Furness too, but only as a small village as yet untouched by the shipbuilding industry that transformed the town so rapidly.

It's a place to walk, hike or cycle along stretches of unspoiled coastline, quiet country lanes or classic routes over and around the Furness Fells. Wildlife flourishes in the nesting and wintering grounds of Walney Island's two nature reserves and along a coastline, where various species of birds, moths, butterflies, natterjack toads and grey seals thrive.

WALK THE FURNESS WAY

contours.co.uk/walking-holidays

The 71-mile Furness Way meanders across this tranquil corner of the Lake District – from Arnside on the eastern side of Morecambe Bay to Ravenglass on the Irish Sea. If you follow the whole route you pass through the beautiful Lyth, Winster, Duddon and Eskdale valleys; cross Whitbarrow, Hampsfell and Muncaster Fell, all with breathtaking views of the mountains of the Lake District and the Furness coastline. Along the way the route visits a succession of attractive villages, where you can find accommodation. It also takes in several magnificent stately homes including Levens Hall (see page 180), Sizergh Castle (see page 213) and Muncaster Castle (see page 190).

▶ Glenridding

This small village at the southern end of Ullswater, near the foot of Kirkstone Pass, is popular with walkers, and there are routes to suit all levels of fitness and experience. Experienced walkers come here to do the classic Helvellyn walk along Striding Edge.

GET YOUR BOOTS ON
Helvellyn (see page 150)

GET ON THE WATER
St Patrick's Boat Centre
stpatricksboatlandings.co.uk
CA11 0QQ | 01768 482393 | Open Etr–Oct/early Nov daily 9–5
Motorboats, rowing boats and mountain bikes can be hired here. Hires are from 30 minutes to several days.

Glenridding Sailing Centre
glenriddingsailingcentre.co.uk
The Spit, CA11 0PE | 01768 482541
Open mid-Mar to mid-Oct, daily 10–5
If you want to explore Ullswater, you can hire canoes, kayaks, sailing dinghies and rowing boats here. If you want to learn to sail or brush up your skills you can take a course, they have a range of courses to suit all abilities – including a special *Swallows and Amazons* adventure, which kids will love. Check the website for details. If you have your own boat, they have storage for dinghies, kayaks and canoes.

TAKE A BOAT TRIP
Ullswater Steamers
ullswater-steamers.co.uk
The Pier House, CA11 0US
01768 482669 | Open all year, daily
You can buy a ticket for part of the cruise or all the way round, which allows you to hop on and off all day. This is the perfect way to combine a lake cruise with a spectacular walk. Ullswater Steamers are varied from Victorian to mid-20th century types. The company's been operating lake cruises on Ullswater for over 150 years.

EAT AND DRINK
Fellbites Café
fellbitescafe.co.uk
CA11 0PD | 01768 482781
If you want a tasty snack, homemade cakes or scones by day or a simple meal in the evening, this little cafe at the centre of Glenridding is conveniently placed, with good food, friendly staff and great views.

The Inn on the Lake ❀❀
lakedistricthotels.net
CA11 0PE | 017684 82444
You can explore 15 acres of fabulous grounds here, so there is plenty of opportunity to connect with the landscape. The Lake View Restaurant lives up to its name with a glorious panorama across the lake. You'll find imaginative food well deserving of its two Rosettes, cooked from the excellent produce available in

the region. If you'd rather have good pub grub, try The Ramblers Bar, in the hotel's grounds, where you can enjoy a pint of real ale.

Traveller's Rest
Greenside Road, CA11 0QQ
01768 482298
There is no better place to unwind after climbing Helvellyn than in this cosy pub, halfway up the road to the Greenside Mine. Stay for a generous home-cooked meal, or sit outside with a pint and watch the walkers go by.

▶ **PLACES NEARBY**
Watermillock is a small hamlet on the western edge of Ullswater between Pooley Bridge and Glenridding.

Macdonald Leeming Hotel ◉
macdonald-hotels.co.uk
Watermillock, CA11 0JJ
0844 879 9142
You will find luxury and a splendid location on the edge of Ullswater at this 200-year-old Lakeland manor. If you fish, you will be pleased to know that they offer fishing rights from

the shore here, and if not you'll still enjoy the glorious views of the lake through the French windows of the Regency Restaurant. Leeming House takes a traditional approach to the grande-luxe country house dining experience: a polished front of house team deliver correctly formal service, while the kitchen delivers gently modern ideas.

Rampsbeck Country House Hotel ◉◉
rampsbeck.co.uk
Watermillock, CA11 0LP
017684 86442
Rampsbeck is a tranquil country hideaway, where you can wander through 18 acres of splendid grounds down to the hotel's lake shore and enjoy views over Ullswater and the distant fells. The traditional 18th-century house is full of antiques, grand marble fireplaces and ornate ceilings. The staff deliver polished service in a calm, professional way, while the food is classic French – made with fresh local ingredients.

▶ **Gosforth**
Gosforth is situated between Wasdale and Sellafield and the closest large village to the Eskdale and Wasdale valleys, so it makes for a good base if you're planning to explore these dales. There has been a church on this site for more than 1,000 years so it's worth having a look for the ancient stone cross and tombs. There's also a cork tree, planted in 1833.

Close to the village is Blengdale Forest, where you can walk along the River Bleng and to the ancient packhorse bridge known as 'Monks Bridge' on Cold Fell.

SEE A LOCAL CHURCH
Church of St Mary
Wasdale Road, northeast of village, CA20 1AU

St Mary's has been a religious site since the eighth century and there are many ancient remains to see here. The most striking is the Gosforth Cross in the churchyard. It is Norse, from around 940, and the slender red sandstone stands 14-feet-tall with detailed carvings on all four sides of Viking and Christian symbols – including the crucifixion and the pagan god, Loki. Another ancient cross in the churchyard was, for some strange reason, converted into a sundial 200 years ago. Two 10th century 'Hogback' tombstones carved with battle scenes can also be found inside the church.

GET CRAFTY
Gosforth Pottery
gosforth-pottery.co.uk
Near Seascale, CA20 1AH
019467 25296

Visit to see the range of pots for sale or go for one of their courses. They run fun pottery making days for kids or short residential courses.

EAT AND DRINK
The Wild Olive
thewildolive.co.uk
CA20 1AH | 019467 25999

This is a family-run, family-friendly restaurant. They serve authentic Italian food with pizzas cooked in an authentic wood-burning oven. There's a small, separate playroom for children so that parents can relax at the table while the children are happily occupied.

▶ PLACES NEARBY
Seascale is a small attractive seaside resort, best known for the nearby nuclear power station. There used to be a visitor centre attached to the power station but this has gone. Rich in history, the village can trace its origins back to an early Norse settlement and to Roman Britain.

Seascale Golf Club
seascalegolfclub.co.uk
The Banks, CA20 1QL
019467 28202 | Open daily ex Wed

A tough links course, skilled golfers will enjoy the natural terrain and undulating greens, which give a variety of holes and add considerable character to the challenge. There are fine views of the western fells, the Irish Sea and the Isle of Man.

Sella Park House Hotel ◉
penningtonhotels.com
Calderbridge, Seascale CA20 1DW
0845 450 6445

This historic 16th-century manor house sits in six acres of lovely gardens running down to the River Calder. There's no faulting the splendid seasonal Cumbrian produce it hauls in, as the basis of its up-to-date cooking. Vegetables, fruit and herbs are plucked fresh from the kitchen garden at nearby Muncaster Castle, and great care is taken in tracking down the best local meat and fish.

▶ Grange-over-Sands

Neat white limestone buildings, colourful gardens, a sunny aspect and disposition quickly made Grange a popular seaside resort for Victorian visitors. The 'grange' in the town's name belonged to the monks of medieval Cartmel Priory (see page 96), who had a vineyard here and a small harbour for bringing in sea coal. There was a fashionable health spa using the water from St Ann's Well at Humphrey Head, which was said to be good for gout and 'the stone'. The railway arrived in 1857 and the promenade along the front was built in 1904.

The town looks south over the alluring and treacherous sands of Morecambe Bay, once the main route to Lancashire. It's the place to bring your binoculars if you're interested in birds and wildlife, but the whole area around here is packed with fascinating places to explore.

WALK THE CISTERCIAN WAY

If you're looking for two or three days of moderate walking, try this 33-mile walk from Grange-over-Sands to Roa Island, near Barrow-in-Furness. It follows the low limestone fells that fringe the shores of Morecambe Bay and the sands of the Furness and Cartmel peninsulas. It is an ancient waymarked trail, but some waymarks are missing or not entirely obvious, so make sure that you have the relevant OS map before you set out. The route passes the historic Cartmel Priory (see page 96), the market town of Ulverston (see page 225), Dalton-in-Furness (see page 114), the ancient capital of Furness and Barrow-in-Furness, (see page 64), an attractive Victorian seaside town where you can visit Furness Abbey (see page 64), and finishes at Roe Island, just beyond Barrow.

▼ The notoriously dangerous Morecambe Bay

PLAY A ROUND
Grange-over-Sands Golf Club
grangegolfclub.co.uk
Meathop Road, LA11 6QX
015395 33180
A fairly flat parkland course
with well-sited tree plantations,
ditches and water features, and
excellent drainage. If you are an
older golfer or have some
mobility problems, the flatness
is a bonus, but there are still
some tricky holes. The excellent
drainage makes it playable
when other courses are closed.

EAT AND DRINK
Clare House ●
clarehousehotel.co.uk
Park Road, LA11 7HQ
015395 33026
The friendly staff make
everyone feel welcome from the
moment they step into this
elegant Victorian country
house. The view from the hotel
extends over the gardens and
down to the expansive waters of
Grange-over-Sands. The
restaurant is split into two
nicely decorated rooms with
artwork hung on the modern
wallpaper, and clothed and
unclothed tables are set with
fresh flowers. The food is a
happy blend of modern and
traditional dishes, based on
local ingredients, wherever
possible.

Hazelmere Café and Bakery
hazelmerecafe.co.uk
1–2 Yewbarrow Terrace, LA11 6ED
015395 32972
Taste more than 25 different
types of cuppa at this traditional
Victorian tea room. Local
specialities include
Cumberland Rum Nicky
and pheasant burgers.
You can also buy artisan breads,
cakes and pastries to take
home. It's a great place to
select a picnic – choose
from savoury pies, homemade
preserves and sandwiches.
They also do a range of
ready-to-cook meals to
take away, which are just
perfect if you are on a self-
catering holiday.

▶ Grasmere

The village of Grasmere is central – geographically and historically – to the Lake District. The village is in a valley surrounded by hills, just a short stroll from Grasmere Lake. If you prefer low walks on gentler ground you'll find some round the lake here. On the other hand, if you want a challenge Grasmere is an ideal base for tackling the Scafell Pike, Helvellyn, Skiddaw and the Langdale Pikes.

William Wordsworth was on a walking tour of the Lake District, with his friend Samuel Taylor Coleridge, when he spotted the little house that would become his home for eight years. You can visit two of Wordsworth's homes in Grasmere – Dove Cottage and Rydal Mount (see page 206).

▼ Grasmere

VISIT THE MUSEUM
Dove Cottage and The Wordsworth Museum
wordsworth.org.uk
LA22 9SH | 015394 35544
Open Mar–Oct daily 9.30–5.30,
Nov–Feb 9.30–4.30. Closed 24–26
Dec & 5 Jan–3 Feb

Dove Cottage was the home of William Wordsworth between 1799 and1808, and it was here that he wrote some of his best-known poetry. The cottage has been open to the public since 1891, and is kept in its original condition. The museum displays manuscripts, works of art and items that belonged to the poet. There is a changing programme of special events, check the website for details. Although Wordsworth's home was small, there was a constant stream of visitors, many of whom belonged to the great and good of the world of art and literature. Previously home to an inn called The Dove and Olive Branch, at that time the cottage was known as Town End.

An adjacent coach house has been converted into the Wordsworth Museum. The attached Jerwood Centre is for academic studies. It was opened in 2005 and has won awards for its architecture. By the time Wordsworth's wife, Mary, was expecting their fourth child, Dove Cottage was becoming too small. The family moved first to Allan Bank and the Rectory (both in Grasmere, and both now private homes), before making one last move to Rydal Mount (see page 206), which you can also visit.

SEE A LOCAL CHURCH
Church of St Oswald
Church Stile, LA22 9SN

If you're exploring Wordsworth country, you'll find the great man's grave here in the churchyard along with those of his wife and sister and some of his friends. The tower, porch and south wall are all that remain of the 14th-century church. In around 1500, the church was enlarged with a new arch through the north wall and an aisle. It was not until 1841 that the church floor was flagged – prior to that it was earthen and parishioners were simply buried beneath it. The baptistery window depicts St Oswald, and two of the south windows are by the famous Pre-Raphaelite artist Henry Holiday. Every year in July, Grasmere celebrates its Rushbearing Festival, a custom dating back to the days when the earthen floor was strewn with rushes, both for warmth and cleanliness.

EAT AND DRINK
The Gingerbread Shop
grasmeregingerbread.co.uk
Church House, LA22 9SW
015394 35428

Next to the churchyard is the gingerbread shop, where the famous Grasmere gingerbread is made and sold. It is made to the recipe of Sarah Nelson, who first made it in the mid-19th century. She kept the recipe in a bank vault and passed it on to her niece. It is no longer in the family but the secret recipe has been passed down through the generations and is still made and sold today. Celebrities travel here just to taste it, brides use it for wedding favours and Jamie Oliver, among many others, swears it is the best gingerbread he ever tasted. So make some time between William Wordsworth and the scenery to sample some gingerbread – you'll probably want to take some home too.

Jumble Room
thejumbleroom.co.uk
Langdale Road, LA22 9SU
015394 35188
The Jumble Room in Grasmere is a small, long-established and colourful little restaurant. It is undoubtedly different and if you like quirky, relaxing, bohemian places in bright colours, you will love it here. Their ethos is to take the best local ingredients, organic if possible, and cook them with love and care. You will certainly feel relaxed, cared for and well fed by the time you leave.

Macdonald Swan Hotel ⓐ
macdonaldhotels.co.uk
LA22 9RF | 0844 879 9120
The historic Swan Hotel first opened its doors as a coaching inn in the 1650s and is mentioned in Wordsworth's *The Waggoner*. So, if you want to sit where the great man sat, this is one of the places to do it.

5 places to eat

▶ **The Pheasant**, Bassenthwaite Lake (page 69)

▶ **Jumble Room**, Grasmere (this page)

▶ **L'Enclume, Cartmel** (page 98)

▶ **The Watermill Tearoom**, Little Salkeld (page 139)

▶ **Drunken Duck Inn**, near Hawkshead (page 58)

Although the hotel has been much updated, it still looks handsome on the inside, with plenty of period details and timeless warming log fires. There is a bar called Walkers and a restaurant named The Waggoners, which is a smart-looking space with a broad menu including retro classics such as prawn cocktail and potted shrimps, pasta dishes and steaks.

Oak Bank Hotel ⓐⓐ
lakedistricthotel.co.uk
Broadgate, LA22 9TA
015394 35217
Go for a stroll through the well-tended gardens running down to the River Rother at this Victorian hotel before relaxing with a drink in front of the log fire in the lounge. In the elegant conservatory restaurant you'll find elegant food to match the surroundings. The kitchen is painstaking about sourcing locally and has a good eye for presentation.

Rothay Garden Hotel ◎◎

rothaygarden.com
Broadgate, LA22 9RJ
015394 35334

On the edge of Grasmere, this refurbished luxury hotel sits in a couple of acres of riverside gardens, with the panoramic sweep of the Lakeland fells in the background. The restaurant is in a thoroughly modern conservatory-style room with a bare floor and smartly clothed tables, with restful views of the gardens all around. Chef Andrew Burton has been with the hotel for many years and he gets the balance between country hotel and modern edge just right, to maintain their well-deserved two AA Rosettes.

The Travellers Rest Inn

lakedistrictinns.co.uk
Keswick Road, LA22 9RR
015394 35604

The Travellers Rest has been a pub for more than 500 years. Inside, you'll find a roaring log fire to welcome you to the beamed and inglenook bar area. Along with ales such as Sneck Lifter, you can choose from an extensive menu of traditional home-cooked fare.

Wordsworth Hotel & Spa ◎◎

thewordsworthhotel.co.uk
LA22 9SW | 015394 35592

As so often in the Lake District, what a setting this hotel has. The two acres of riverside gardens have stunning views of Grasmere Vale and the mountains all around, so before you even sit down to eat, this classic Victorian country house feels like Lakeland on a plate. The Signature Restaurant – with its airy conservatory extension – is plush and rather romantic, with mood lighting and a piano. The food is imaginative and constructed from a solid bedrock of fine Cumbrian ingredients. For a less formal meal, you can have simple pub grub and good ales in the Dove Bistro. There's a children's menu and afternoon tea option as well.

▶ PLACES NEARBY

The village and lake of Elterwater lie in the lovely valley of Great Langdale. Nowadays most of the houses in Elterwater are holiday cottages.

Langdale Hotel & Spa ◎◎

langdale.co.uk
The Langdale Estate, Elterwater, LA22 9JD | 015394 37302

Housed in a former Victorian gunpowder factory in a 35-acre estate dotted with streams, ponds, an original waterwheel and millstones, this is a wonderful place to relax and dine. In the restaurants you'll find imaginative menus with exotic touches featuring local produce – they tell you exactly where the ingredients in your meal come from – and. You can eat in the cosy bar overlooking the waterwheel, on the terrace next to the spa or in the elegant Purdey's Restaurant with its exposed Lakeland stone walls climbing to the raftered roof.

▶ Great Gable

Great Gable, standing at an impressive 2,949 feet (899m), is a classic Lake District climb with rough paths and a few scrambles – so you need to be fit to attempt it. It gets its name from its appearance from Wastwater, through Wasdale Head; its bulk resembles the great gable end of a house. If you are very fit, you can take this route to the top. Alternatively, you can approach it from the northeast, from Seathwaite Farm climbing up past the waters of the Sourmilk Gill and passing Great Gable's little brother, Green Gable. This is still a strenuous climb, but the views from the top are a fitting reward for your efforts – south to Scafell Pike (3,210 feet, 978m) and straight down Wasdale towards the Irish Sea.

At the top, a plaque proudly records the occasion, when the Fell and Rock Climbing Club gave the surrounding area to the National Trust in memory of their colleagues lost in the World War I. A memorial service is held here each year in November on Remembrance Sunday.

It was also in these hills that modern climbing first started to develop, late in the 19th century. The names alone are inspiring – Needle Ridge, Eagle's Nest Ridge, Windy Gap.

▶ Great Salkeld & Little Salkeld

These two small villages on opposite banks of the Eden River were linked in the Middle Ages by a bridge over the river. St Cuthbert's Church in Great Salkeld is where the Saint's body rested in 880 when it was brought over from Holy Island. Although it contains the remains of a Roman altar the present building is Norman. Its defensive, Pele, tower was added in 1380.

▼ Great Gable mountain, Wastwater

TAKE IN SOME HISTORY
Little Salkeld Watermill
organicmill.co.uk
Little Salkeld, CA10 INN
01768 881523 | Open daily 10.30–5
Little Salkeld Watermill is a bit of a rarity. It is one of Britain's few working water-powered corn mills still producing stoneground flour the traditional way. Even better, perhaps, is that after finding out how it works, you can then buy some of the organic produce in the bakery and visit the organic vegetarian cafe. There's also a pleasant gallery, which has knitwear and a series of changing exhibitions.

GO BACK IN TIME
Long Meg & Her Daughters Stone Circle
Little Salkeld
You shouldn't miss this stone circle. Wordsworth said of it, 'Next to Stonehenge it is beyond dispute the most notable relic that this or probably any other country contains.' The circle has a diameter of about 350 feet, the second biggest in the country. The red sandstone Long Meg is the tallest of the 69 stones, at about 12 feet high, and stands around 60 feet outside the circle – its four corners facing the points of the compass and carved with three mysterious symbols. The Daughters, in the circle, are boulders of rhyolite, a form of granite. The circle dates from around 1500 BC, and was probably linked to some form of religious ritual.

SADDLE UP
Bank House Equestrian
bankhouseequestrian.co.uk
Little Salkeld, CA10 1NN
01768 881257
Whether you want a lesson or just a ride, you can get it here either as a one-to-one session or in a group, and there are horses to suit all ages and abilities. If you have children who are pony club members, they can take part in a whole range of activities here at moderate prices. You can also stay here in one of the large caravans or bring a tent and camp, both options are offered as either self-catering or B&B.

EAT AND DRINK
The Highland Drove Inn and Kyloes Restaurant
kyloes.co.uk
CA11 9NA | 01768 898349
If you want to eat and drink where the locals do, then seek out this 300-year-old pub by the village church, on an old drove road, and named after the original Highland cattle that were bred in the Western Isles and then driven over the short channels of water to the mainland. It is a great all-rounder with a reputation for high-quality food, a wide range of cask-conditioned real ales and a good selection of wines. Inside, there's an attractive brick and timber bar, old tables and settles in the main bar area, and a lounge with log fire and tartan fabrics. The upstairs restaurant has an interesting hunting lodge feel, with a

veranda and lovely country views. Menus reflect the availability of local game and fish, and meat from herds reared and matured in Cumbria.

The Watermill Tearoom
organicmill.co.uk
Little Salkeld, CA10 1NN
01768 881523
This little cafe is attached to the watermill itself. Try some of the brilliant bakes and lunches, with five varieties of bread, all made from scratch right here. The Mill sells its organic flour and other goodies, and has a classroom for various bread making courses. The gallery displays local crafts. After tasting the wholesome vegetarian fare, you can pop next door and watch the flour being milled.

▶ Grizedale Forest
forestry.gov.uk
LA22 0QJ | 01229 860010 | Visitor Centre open daily 10–5 (Nov–Feb 10–4)

Your first stop here should be the visitor centre, where you can get a guide to the many waymarked trails in the forest. This estate, between Coniston Water and Windermere, was the first forest, where the Forestry Commission actively encouraged outdoor activities. It was opened to the public in the 1960s and is now the largest forest in the Lake District. Look for the original sculptures among the trees or on hilltops. Sculptors have been sponsored over the years to create these artworks in the woods and there are now more than 80 of them.

EXPLORE BY BIKE
The North Face Trail
If you're an experienced mountain biker you will enjoy this red trail, with an optional black section. This 10-mile loop, starting and finishing at the visitor centre, takes you on a roller coaster ride of rough tracks and curves, uphill and downhill, through woodland and

10 great days out

▶ **Windermere Lake Cruises** (page 247)

▶ **Lake District Visitor Centre** at Brockhole (page 246)

▶ **Whinlatter Forest and Visitor Centre** (page 232)

▶ **Ullswater Steamers** (page 128)

▶ **Grizedale Forest and Visitor Centre** (this page)

▶ **The World of Beatrix Potter** (page 245)

▶ **Honister Slate Mine** (page 72)

▶ **Theatre by the Lake,** Keswick (page 164)

▶ **The Ravenglass and Eskdale Railway** (page 200)

▶ **Hill Top, Beatrix Potter's farm, Near Sawrey** (page 193)

▲ Sculpture, Grizedale Forest

meadows with outstanding views along the way.

Grizedale Mountain Bikes

grizedalemountainbikes.co.uk
LA22 0QJ | 01229 860369
You will find one of the biggest fleet of bikes in the north of England at this hire centre, including varied mountain bikes, children's bikes, tag-a-longs, trailers and even electric bikes, for the not-so-fit or anyone not feeling energetic. Although you can often just roll up and hire a bike on the spot, it is worth booking in advance to avoid disappointment particularly in summer. A shop sells bikes and related gear, and there's a workshop for repairs and custom builds.

▶ Hadrian's Wall

In about AD 121, the Roman soldiers stationed in the north were ordered to build a wall, from the Solway Firth to the River Tyne, to keep out the wild tribes of northern Britain. Meanwhile Rome tried to civilise those south of the wall by introducing such modern comforts as central heating, public baths and an efficient drainage system. Working under the instructions of the Emperor Hadrian (AD 76–138), and taking advantage of a prominent natural ridge, the soldiers built a massive fortification around 73 miles long from a million cubic yards

▼ Hadrian's Wall

of stone, and strengthened at key points by forts, mile castles and turrets. The project took about five years to complete, but succeeded in holding back the Picts for more than 200 years.

There are several examples of Roman remains of houses, forts and baths along the wall, although the finest examples – Chesters, Corbridge, Vindolanda and Housesteads – are to the east. In addition to the fort at Birdoswald (see page 70), there are the remains of turrets at Piper Sike, Leahill and Banks East, while at Hare Hill, near Lanercost, is a section of the wall that stands nine-feet high. The entire structure now forms the western part of a UNESCO World Heritage Site – 'The Frontiers of the Roman Empire' – that includes large sections of wall across Germany too.

From Harrow's Scar, near Birdoswald, to its end at the Solway Firth – a distance of 30 miles – the wall was originally made of turf – and some of the turrets were free standing to enable turf ramparts to be run up them. Although the wall was rebuilt in stone, a two-mile stretch, west of the River Irthing from Gilsland to Bowness, did not follow the line of the original wall, and so remains of the older turf wall can still be seen running nearby.

The Hadrian's Wall Path National Trail between Bowness-on-Solway and Tynemouth opened in 2004 and is now one of England's most popular National Trails.

▾ Birdoswald Roman Fort and visitor centre

EXPLORE BY BIKE
Hadrian's Cycleway

If you want to get a real overview of Roman Britain this long-distance route – National Cycle Route 72 – will take you along the Cumbrian coast and right across country, following the Roman frontier. Allow three or four days for this 160-mile trip, which passes through some glorious countryside, taking in a series of Roman sites on the way. It more or less follows the path of Hadrian's Wall, but starts on the Cumbrian coast at the ancient village of Ravenglass. Even in Roman times, Ravenglass was recognized as an important natural harbour and the Roman fort of *Glannoventa* guarded it from invaders. After following the coast to the Solway Firth, the route continues by quiet roads along the wall to Tynemouth. You will find a hybrid bike the most suitable for this route but you could manage with a road bike.

WALK THE WALL
Hadrian's Wall National Trail

As long as you are moderately fit, you should be able to complete this walk in just over a week. It covers 84 miles, from Bowness-on-Solway to Wallsend on Tyneside and the scenery is breathtaking – taking you through rugged moorland, rolling fields and the cities of Carlisle and Newcastle-on-Tyne, as well as following the route of Hadrian's Wall. No wonder it's one of the most popular long-distance trails in England.

▼ Hadrian's Wall, Birdoswald

▶ Hardknott Pass & Roman Fort

To get to the Roman Fort here you have to drive up Hardknott Pass, which rises 1,000 feet out of Eskdale in little more than a mile. It is one of the most spectacular roads in the country with hairpin bends as steep as 1-in-3. If the road is icy, or you are towing a caravan, don't even consider this road! For cars, it is a scary drive, if you are not used to narrow, winding, hill roads; but most problems arise at peak holiday times. So take it slowly, carefully and use your gears – the views and the experience are well worth the effort.

When you gaze down from the remains of the fort at the western end of the Hardknott Pass (1,291 feet) it's easy to see why the Romans chose this site. Hardknott Castle Roman Fort enjoys a commanding position down into the green valley of Eskdale. Attacks from three sides were impossible and a trench prevented attacks from the east.

Soldiers were garrisoned here to safeguard the road they had constructed to link the fort at Ambleside and the port of Ravenglass. Preferring to take the most direct route, they drove

▲ Hardknott Pass and the Roman Fort

their road over the most difficult terrain in the Lake District, through the Hardknott and Wrynose passes. Despite the wonderful views, the Roman soldiers must have regarded isolated, windswept *Mediobogdum* as an unglamorous posting. The ruins, however, are still impressive. The soldiers drilled on a flat parade ground near by. The bath house would have been one of their few home comforts.

....

▶ Haverthwaite

Haverthwaite, beyond the southern tip of Windermere, is the southern terminus of the Lakeside and Haverthwaite Railway. As in the railway's heyday, you can combine the scenic journey with a leisurely cruise on Windermere. Newby Bridge (see page 177) marks the southern limit of the lake, where it drains into the River Leven. Some two miles from Newby Bridge is Stott Park Bobbin Mill (see page 177).

TAKE A TRAIN RIDE
Lakeside and
Haverthwaite Railway
lakesiderailway.co.uk
Haverthwaite Station, Nr Ulverston,
LA12 8AL | 01539 531594 | Call or
check the website for the timetable
This is one of the best days out
in Windermere, particularly if
you combine the scenic train
journey with a cruise on the
lake. Originally a branch of the
Furness Railway, the line used
to carry goods and passengers
from Ulverston to connect with
the Windermere steamers at
Lakeside. Four passenger
steamers began service in
1850; trains began running 20
years later. Passenger numbers
peaked just before World War I,
but sadly declined from then
onwards and finally, in 1967,
the railway closed.

A group of rail enthusiasts
fought to buy the branch line
and re-open it as a recreational
line, using steam-hauled trains.
Despite many setbacks they
succeeded in taking over the
3.5-mile stretch of line between
Haverthwaite and Lakeside and
have maintained the service
ever since.

▶ Haweswater

Haweswater lies east of Ullswater and Windermere and is the
most easterly of the lakes. But while it may sound like just
another lovely natural lake, modern Haweswater is, in fact, a
reservoir, created in the 1930s. The haunting secret beneath its
surface is the village of Mardale Green and the dairy farms of
the Haweswater Valley. Most of the houses were blown up, but
when the water levels are low the remains of roads and houses

▼ Haweswater, with Carling Knott

can still be glimpsed and you can even walk across a long submerged bridge. You can't help but feel an eerie shiver to see this long forgotten place emerge from the water.

You will also see an abundance of wildlife here, with peregrine falcons, buzzards, sparrow hawks and even golden eagles now breeding in the valley. Otters have also colonised the area, no doubt feeding on the rare char and freshwater herring that are also found here. Other mammals include both roe and red deer, and red squirrels

On the western shores of the reservoir steep crags rise to the ridge of High Street (see page 150) – the high fells taking their name from a Roman road across the summit. In the east is the ancient Naddle Forest, where you can find wood warblers, tree pipits, redstarts and several species of woodpecker.

▶ Hawkshead

When you visit Hawkshead you'll understand why the young William Wordsworth loved it. He was a pupil at the Grammar School between 1779 and 1787 and lodged with Ann Tyson, whose cottage still stands. The school also survives and you can see the desk on which he carved his name.

Wordsworth would easily recognise this intriguing maze of tiny thoroughfares, alleyways and courtyards. The whitewashed houses – many of them 17th century – possess an architectural anarchy that adds a great deal to the charm of the village. The monks of Furness Abbey once owned much of it, in the days when it was an important market town. Only one building now remains from monastic times: the sturdy little courthouse, just north of the village.

There is a large car park, leaving the narrow streets peacefully car-free and you will enjoy just wandering around this picturesque village. However, Hawkshead is extremely popular so if you don't like crowds, avoid visiting on a busy Bank Holiday.

VISIT THE MUSEUM AND GALLERY
Beatrix Potter Gallery
nationaltrust.org.uk
Main Street, LA22 0NS
015394 36269
Open 15 Feb–27 Mar, Sat–Thu
10.30–3.30, 29 Mar–22 May & 30
Aug–2 Nov Sat–Thu 10.30–5, 24

May–28 Aug, daily 10.30–5. Check website for Fri opening times. Admission by timed ticket including NT members
Revisit your childhood at this exhibition of Beatrix Potter's original illustrations from her storybooks. The gallery is housed in the former office of

her husband, William Heelis, and the exhibits change annually. There was much more to Beatrix Potter than her role as a children's author and artist, and here you'll also find a wealth of fascinating information about her life as a farmer and a pioneer of the conservation movement.

The Old Grammar School Museum

hawksheadgrammar.org.uk
Main Street, LA22 0NT
015394 36735 | Open Apr–Sep
Mon–Sat 10–1, 2–5, Sun 1–5, Oct
Mon–Sat 10–1, 2–3.30, Sun 1–3.30.
Closed Nov–Mar

Find out why boys were allowed to drink beer, smoke and carve their names on the desks at this fascinating museum. William Wordsworth's time at the school is well documented and you can see his name carved into his wooden desk. The museum has a fascinating collection of artefacts relating to the ancient school, some of which date back to the 16th century.

WALK THE HIGH ROPES
Go Ape! Grizedale

goape.co.uk
LA22 0QJ | 0845 643 9215
See website for details
(pre-booking advised)

The Grizedale course is the jewel in the crown of Go Ape! Built on a side of a hill, it's seriously high. If you're brave enough, you'll fly 656 feet across the top of the Grizedale Beck and view the forest canopy from a platform 60 feet up a magnificent Douglas Fir.

SEE SOME LOCAL CHURCHES
Hawkshead Methodist Chapel

The Square, LA22 0PG

Standing at the corner of The Square, this simple whitewashed building was converted in 1862 into a nonconformist chapel from two cottages – both possibly dating from the 17th century. The first floor juts out over Flag Street and is likely to be a remnant from these early buildings. Inside, the chapel is small and seats around 40 people. From the outside, you can see a graceful round-headed window and a handsome porch.

The Methodist founder John Wesley visited Cumbria 26 times. His last visit to Kendal was in 1788, when he was 85.

St Michael and All Angels Church

hawksheadbenefice.co.uk
LA22 0NT | 015394 36301

Take a stroll up to the parish church overlooking the village and have a look at its wall frescoes. It was built in around 1300 on the site of an older church and, as it exists today, mainly dates from the 16th and 17th centuries. Wordsworth referred to it in *The Prelude*. The church was painted white at the time:

> *I saw the snow-white church upon her hill*
> *Sit like a throned lady*

sending out
A gracious look all over
her domain

EAT AND DRINK
Hawkshead Relish Company
hawksheadrelish.com
The Square, LA22 0NZ
015394 36614
Pop in to sample the award winning relishes, which include some very unusual food combinations. But be warned you are unlikely to leave without buying something even if you have a sweet tooth because they also do scrumptious puddings.

Kings Arms
kingsarmshawkshead.co.uk
The Square, LA22 0NZ
015394 36372
Set in the square, this 16th-century inn is always packed in summer. In colder weather, bag a table by the fire in the traditional carpeted bar, quaff a pint of Hawkshead Bitter and tuck into lunchtime light bites or hearty evening meals. Look out for the carved figure of a king in the bar.

Old Hall Brewery
cumbrianlegendaryales.com
LA22 0QF
015394 36436
Established in 2003 using a small three-barrel kit, you'll find this successful brewery just south of Hawksead village on the shores of Esthwaite Water. Their Loweswater Gold was The Champion Ale of Britain in 2011.

The Queen's Head Inn and Restaurant
queensheadhawkshead.co.uk
Main Street, LA22 0NS
015394 36271
On the village's main street, the 17th-century Queen's Head is a stone's throw from Esthwaite Water. Behind the pub's flower-bedecked exterior, the low oak-beamed ceilings, wood-panelled walls, slate floors and welcoming fires combine to create a relaxed, traditional setting. You can sample real ales, an extensive wine list and a menu full of fresh, quality local produce.

The Sun Inn
suninn.co.uk
Main Street, LA22 0NT
015394 36236
This listed 17th-century coaching inn, supposedly, has two resident ghosts – a giggling girl and a drunken landlord. The wood-panelled bar has low, oak-beamed ceilings. If you are hill walking you will particularly appreciate being able to warm yourself next to the log fires, while the real ales and locally sourced food can't help but appeal to all.

▸ PLACES NEARBY
Outgate is a pretty but tiny settlement north of Hawkshead and west of Windermere.

Outgate Inn
outgateinn.co.uk
LA22 0NQ | 015394 36413
Once owned by a mineral water manufacturer and now part of

Robinsons and Hartleys Brewery, this 17th-century Lakeland inn is full of traditional features, including oak beams and a real fire in winter. The secluded beer garden at the rear is a tranquil place to enjoy the summer warmth. Food options include salads and light bites, as well as hearty options if you're coming in ravenous from the hills. There's a gluten-free menu and vegetarian choices.

▶ Helvellyn

This was Wordsworth's favourite mountain and you will join thousands more, if you trek to its summit at 3,116 feet (950m). It is a grand climb, but it has arduous stretches, especially on its jagged eastern edges. If you're thinking of venturing onto the hill, make sure you're prepared for sudden changes in weather. Snowfall is not unknown on the tops, even as late as June, and dense mist can envelop them at any time. If you're a novice, join one of the many organised groups.

Warnings aside, the peak is accessible by reasonably fit walkers as long as you make sure you have extra clothes for the top, sturdy boots and a map. A popular approach is from Wythburn on the southeastern shores of Thirlmere Reservoir (see page 219). This route heads up Helvellyn's steep southwestern slopes, with splendid views across Thirlmere to the west. The eastern approaches are longer but scenically more dramatic, from Glenridding (see page 128), for example.

The arduous climb may take your breath away, but the views from the top of Helvellyn will do so again – north along the valley towards Keswick, and east beyond the mountain lake, Red Tarn, to the distant high peaks of the Pennines. Just south of the summit is a memorial by Wordsworth and Sir Walter Scott. The words are a sign that you have reached the highest point in the area. Only Scafell Pike, at 3,210 feet (978m), and Scafell, at 3,162 feet (964m), are higher than Helvellyn.

▶ High Street Roman Road

The Troutbeck Valley was designated by the Romans to be the starting point for a remarkable road, High Street, which took an uncompromising route straight across the mountain ridges between the lakes of Ullswater and Haweswater. The road probably linked the Roman forts at Ambleside and Brougham with their port at Ravenglass on the west coast.

▶ Descending Helvellyn towards Thirlmere

▶ Holker Hall

holker.co.uk

Cark in Cartmel, Grange over Sands, LA11 7PL | 015395 58328 | Hall &
Gardens open late Mar–early Nov, Sun–Fri, Hall 11–4, Gardens 10.30–4.30,
(10.30–5.30 Jul & Aug). Café, food hall & gift shop: Mar–Dec daily 10.30–
4.30 (10.30–5.30 Jul & Aug)

Remarkably, despite the obvious grandeur of Holker Hall, it
still has the atmosphere of a family home – not least because
visitors are free to explore the rooms unhindered by ropes
and barriers.

Still home to Lord and Lady Cavendish, it is the sort of house
where, at every turn, you expect to see the hearty clergymen,
eager young noblemen, elderly housemaids and animated
younger daughters of the aristocracy straight from the pages of
an Anthony Trollope novel.

Holker is largely a creation of the third quarter of the 19th
century. A disastrous fire in 1871 destroyed the whole of the
west wing, including paintings and furniture. The seventh
Duke of Devonshire commissioned local architects Paley and
Austin – then among the best country-house designers in
Britain – to rebuild the wing in pale red sandstone in a grand
yet relaxed Elizabethan style, complete with large bay windows
and a copper dome.

The library has deep armchairs, French furniture and
family portraits. His microscope and copies of his learned
works remember Henry Cavendish, the scientist, who
discovered nitric acid. There is a portrait by Richmond of Lord
Frederick, who was assassinated in Phoenix Park, Dublin, in
1882. The drawing room still has its original red silk walls,
while the spectacular chimneypiece in the dining room is
constructed of local marble and finely carved wood – one of

▼ Holker Hall

several throughout the house – and incorporates a Van Dyck self-portrait.

Fine craftsmanship is everywhere. On the main staircase look at the balusters, every one of them is different. Each room retains some of that joyous sense of jewelled clutter so loved by the Victorians. One of the bedrooms has Wedgwood plaques and blue Jasper Ware on the fire surround while another has furnishings from 1937, when Queen Mary stayed at Holker. The family used to play carpet bowls down the gallery, a spacious and sunny contrast to the hall, which recalls winter evenings around a roaring fire.

The extensive gardens and woodland, some 25 acres in total, are formal and informal by turns. Here, you'll find the only surviving monkey puzzle tree planted from seeds that were brought to England in 1837, as well as a superb display of magnolias and rhododendrons and, of course, the Great Holker Lime. One of the largest trees of its kind in Britain, this one was planted in the 17th century and is 26 feet in circumference.

▶ Hutton-in-the-Forest

hutton-in-the-forest.co.uk

CA11 9TH | 017684 84449 | Gardens open Apr–Oct, Sun–Fri 11–5.
House open mid-Apr–mid-Oct, Wed–Thu, Sun & BHs

You really can walk back through history in this house. The oldest part is the fortified pele tower, built in the 1350s by the de Hoton family as protection against the Scots and the border reivers. The house reflects centuries of history and change, and is an incredibly rich illustration of the development of the country house in northern Britain.

The legendary Sir Gawain is said to have stayed with the Green Knight at Hutton, which was then surrounded by dense woodland. In 1292, Edward I was a visitor during the heyday of the royal hunting forest of Inglewood. The Fletchers, ancestors of the family who still live here, bought the property in 1605. The Long Gallery was built in 1630, and the light classical east front in the 1680s. The Renaissance facade, with its light-coloured stonework and delicate classical features, contrasts dramatically with the rest of the building.

The final additions were made in the 1820s, when Salvin designed the dominant southeast tower, and added battlements to the pele. The impressive Stone Hall with its barrel vaulted ceiling is the oldest room, contrasting with the later rooms, which are warm with wood panelling, good furniture and family pictures. The charming Cupid Staircase, with its carved cherubs, and the Cupid Room, with its delicate plaster ceiling of 1744, testify to the romantic associations of the house. There is a more formal air about Salvin's dining room and the Long Gallery retains its distinctly Jacobean flavour.

Look out for the portrait of John Peel who was employed here as a huntsman in the 18th century. Also 18th century is the engraving of the house, made by Kip. It is astonishing how little the house has changed since he put pen to paper.

Before you go, take a stroll around the beautiful gardens, which include a delightful walled garden, a woodland walk, terraces, topiary and three ponds with cascades.

▶ Kendal

As you drive from the M6, the first sight of Kendal in the valley below, means that the Lakes are 'only just round the corner'. The one-way traffic system can be frustrating, so it's better to go on foot if you want to investigate Kendal's numerous 'yards' or alleyways. The castle is in ruins but the splendid view from the top is worth the climb. It is best known for being the home of the Parr family and you may hear that King Henry VIII's sixth wife Catherine Parr was born at Kendal Castle. This is very unlikely, since by the time Catherine was born, the castle was beyond repair and her father based in London.

Near the parish church is Abbot Hall. This elegant Georgian house is now an equally elegant art gallery, showing works by the many artists – including Ruskin and Constable – who were inspired by the Lakeland landscape. Also at Abbot Hall is the Museum of Lakeland Life and Industry, which aims to bring recent history to life. At the opposite end of town, close to the railway station, the Kendal Museum has fascinating displays of geology, archaeology and natural and social history.

▶ Kendal

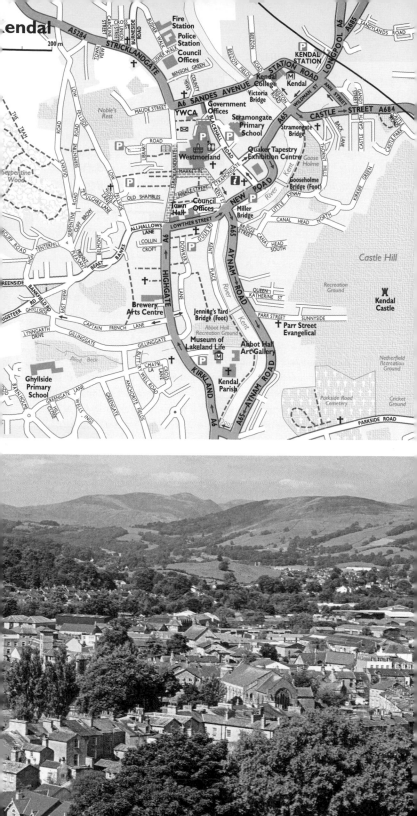

VISIT THE MUSEUMS AND GALLERIES

The Quaker Tapestry

quaker-tapestry.co.uk
Quaker Tapestry Exhibition Centre,
New Road, LA9 4BH
01539 722975 | Open Mon–Sat
10–5. Closed mid Dec–Feb
Look for this exhibition in the Friend's Meeting House. The tapestry is made up of 77 beautifully embroidered panels, the work of 4,000 men, women and children from 15 countries. Anne Wynn-Wilson, author of *Quakers In Stitches* had the vision of a number of tapestry panels telling something of the Quaker story and beliefs. Here, you can also learn about Quaker events and insights, and of the considerable contribution that these quiet non-conformists have made to the modern world. Finally completed in 1996, the 77 panels, each measuring 25 by 21 inches, show stories from the forefront of the industrial revolution, developments in science and medicine, astronomy, the abolition of slavery and stages of social reform.

There is also a collection of documents, photographs and samplers associated with the making of the embroidered panels. As well as the tapestry, there are articles of clothing, embroidery and other domestic items relating to Quaker history, and interactive displays and activities for children.

The building itself is one of the finest Georgian buildings in Cumbria with a beautiful, peaceful walled garden. It is a Grade II listed building that was designed by local architect Francis Webster in 1816. The tea room serves a range of healthy lunches and snacks, and caters for vegetarians and vegans.

▼ Abbot Hall Art Gallery

Museum of Lakeland Life

lakelandmuseum.org.uk
Abbot Hall, LA9 5AL
01539 722464 | Open mid-Jan–
mid-Dec Mon–Sat 10.30–5 (10.30–4
Nov–Feb), Sun 5 Jul–28 Sep. Closed
mid Dec–mid Jan

Find out how people lived and
worked in bygone days as you
explore the reconstructed
shops, room settings and a
farming display. You can see the
toys that children played with,
and how different Georgian and
Victorian life was from today.
There's a farmhouse kitchen
with traditional recipes and
utensils, a bedroom full of
period furniture, including a
magnificent 16th-century
four-poster bed, and a parlour
with rare 17th-century oak
panelling. You can go into the
study of Arthur Ransome and
immerse yourself in the world
of *Swallows and Amazons* with
the author's typewriter, desk,
personal mementos and
original illustrations. Other
displays include a traditional
chemist's shop, Lakeland
industries, and the local Arts
and Crafts Movement.

Kendal Museum

kendalmuseum.org.uk
Station Road, LA9 6BT
01539 815597 | Open Tue–Sat
10.30–5. Closed Xmas & New Year

This quirky museum is based
on the collection of 'curiosities'
first exhibited by William
Todhunter in 1796. He charged
admission at the rate of 'one
shilling per person; children
and servants 6d each'. There
are displays of wildlife, both
local and global including a
case full of iridescent humming
birds which seems unpleasant
by today's standards. You can
find out about the archaeology
and natural history of the Lakes
and there's also a display

▼ Kendal Castle

devoted to author Alfred Wainwright, one of Kendal's best-known adopted sons. His seven handwritten guides to the Lakeland hills became classics in his own lifetime. You can see Wainwright's little office in Kendal Museum, where he held the post of honorary curator for many years. A hand-drawn map reveals his interests were already in place at the tender age of ten. However, it wasn't until he was 45 that he began the mammoth task of writing his *Pictorial Guides*. Other books about his beloved 'North Country' followed, until his death in 1991.

Abbot Hall Art Gallery

abbothall.org.uk
LA9 5AL | 01539 722464 | Open mid-Jan–mid-Dec Mon–Sat 10.30–5 (closes at 4 Nov–Feb). Closed mid Dec–mid Jan. (Also open Sun Jul–mid-Sep)

This Grade I listed Georgian villa on the banks of the River Kent is one of Kendal's most important buildings. There are two floors of light-filled spaces, where you can see a permanent collection of works by George Romney spanning his entire career; 18th- and 19th-century paintings and watercolours; a large number of drawings and watercolours by Ruskin; and an exhibition of contemporary art. The upstairs galleries have commanding views of the River Kent and Kendal Castle and show works by major British artists, including Sean Scully, Frank Auerbach, and Ben and Winifred Nicholson. Check the website for temporary exhibitions planned throughout the year.

GET INDUSTRIAL

Greenside Lime Kiln

This scheduled Ancient Monument is all that remains of a much larger lime burning operation. The interpretation boards provide an invaluable introduction to this once prolific industry.

SADDLE UP

Holmescales Riding Centre

holmescalesridingcentre.co.uk
Holmescales Farm, Old Hutton, LA8 0NB | 01539 729388

Whether you're a novice or an experienced rider, this centre has horses and courses to suit all ages and abilities. You can go hacking or take lessons with one of their horses or your own.

CATCH A PERFORMANCE

The Brewery Arts Centre

breweryarts.co.uk
122a Highgate, LA9 4HE
01539 725133

If you fancy an injection of culture, popular or high-brow, you'll find it here. Housed in an old Victorian brewery, the centre has theatre productions from Shakespeare to edgy drama. Live music ranges across contemporary, folk, rock, jazz, blues and classical. The arts centre also commissions and presents dance, from hip hop to ballet to contemporary dance. You'll find comedy performances as well,

from solo stand-ups to sketch shows and musical comedy. Alternatively, you might decide to take in a movie, maybe the latest big-screen blockbuster releases or specialised and classic films from around the world.

PLAY A ROUND

Carus Green Golf Course & Driving Range

carusgreen.co.uk
Burneside Road, LA9 6EB
01539 721097 | Open all wk & BHs
Surrounded by the rivers Kent and Mint, this picturesque flat course has views of the Kentmere and Howgill fells. The course is a mixture of relatively easy and difficult holes. The rivers come into play on five holes and there are also a number of ponds and bunkers.

Kendal Golf Club

kendalgolfclub.co.uk
The Heights, LA9 4PQ
01539 723499 | Open Mon–Fri, Sun and BHs
More than 100 years old, this is an elevated parkland and fell course with breathtaking views of Lakeland fells and the surrounding district. You can see as far as the Yorkshire Dales to the east and the Lake District to the north.

EAT AND DRINK

The 2 Sisters Cafe

plumgarths.co.uk
Crook Road, Lakeland Food Park, LA8 8LX | 01539 729551
This little cafe, next to Plumgarth's Farm Shop, serves delicious breakfasts, lunches and snacks. Monika and Magda love cooking and they produce everything fresh on the premises, using ingredients from the farm shop. If you go here once, you will definitely return for a warm welcome and great food in comfortable relaxed surroundings.

Best Western Castle Green Hotel ◉◉

castlegreen.co.uk
Castle Green Lane, LA9 6RG
01539 734000
The Greenhouse Restaurant here is light and airy while the sweeping picture windows open onto views of Kendal. You can also watch the chefs in action through a large glass window without the inconvenience of noise and smells. The kitchen uses locally produced ingredients and the Cumbrian tasting menu comprises ingredients supplied from within a 55-mile radius.

Burgundy's Wine Bar

burgundyswinebar.co.uk
19 Lowther Street, LA9 4DH
01539 733803
This wine bar has a real village 'local' atmosphere where young, old and inbetweeners get together in friendly, convivial surroundings. You will often find live music on here – Thursday night is live jazz night. Four real ales are always on, as well as speciality Belgian and German beers and a phenomenal choice of wines.

Castle Dairy

castledairy.co.uk
26 Wildman Street, LA9 6EN
01539 733946

Housed in Kendal's oldest, this restaurant and art gallery welcomes customers with its log fires, antique furniture and historic ambience, and which all add to the unique feel of the place. It is a stunning piece of medieval architecture in excellent condition, and probably Kendal's only surviving 'true' medieval house. The name 'Dairy' is most likely the result of a historical misspelling, as its true name relates to 'Dowry', meaning a house where a Dower or a widow would have lived. There are many other stories to this ancient building, just ask one of the staff and they will tell you. Kendal College apprentices staff the place under the careful eye of the chef. The restaurant menu is short but high in quality and imagination. There's also an interesting bar menu at very reasonable prices. The art gallery allows Kendal College's art students to display and sell their pieces, which makes for very interesting exhibitions.

Deja Vu

dejavukendal.com
124 Stricklandgate, LA9 4QG
01539 724843

A perfect little restaurant, serving authentic French food with a Cumbrian twist. It's always busy here – a reliable recommendation in itself. If you want to be guaranteed a table, you should book.

▶ **PLACES NEARBY**

The Sun Inn

Crook, LA8 8LA | 01539 821351
Warm yourself next to a roaring open fire in this gorgeous, oak-beamed country pub, which evolved over time from a row of early 18th-century cottages. Hand pumps in the bar dispense Coniston Bluebird and Hawkshead, and the seasonal menus feature a fine range of starters and light snacks, as well as locally sourced dishes.

▶ Kentmere

The valley of Kentmere begins at Staveley, just off the A591 between Kendal and Windermere. From Staveley the road meanders prettily along the valley bottom heading northwards, clinging to the River Kent before coming to a halt at the charming little village of Kentmere. The village church, St Cuthbert's, has a bronze memorial to Bernard Gilpin, who was born at Kentmere Hall in 1517 and eventually became Archdeacon of Durham Cathedral. From Kentmere, you can continue to explore the head of the valley on foot, or take footpaths 'over the top' into either the Troutbeck Valley or the remote upper reaches of Longsleddale. Be warned, parking is limited in the village.

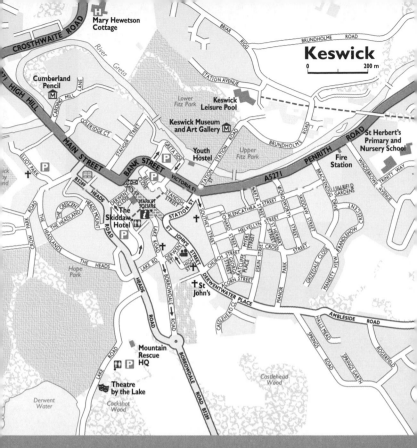

▶ Keswick

Keswick is a natural centre for mountain climbers, country walkers and more leisurely tourists alike. It is small, with a population of less than 5,000, but is said, for its size, to have more beds for guests than anywhere else in the country. This gives an idea of what it can be like on a sunny bank holiday weekend, when its reliance on tourism is most obvious.

In the past, however, it was mining that kept it alive. The industry flourished in the 16th century with the formation, at the behest of Elizabeth I, of the Company of Mines Royal. Expert miners came from Germany and settled on Derwent Isle. The mining industry declined by the second half of the 19th century, but a new source of prosperity came in 1865 when the Cockermouth–Penrith railway line was built.

Graphite is the reason that the Cumberland Pencil Museum exists here today. A delightfully quirky specialist collection, it shows that even the humble pencil has a fascinating history.

Keswick also has one of the oldest museums in the county, the Keswick Museum and Art Gallery, which has a good display on Lakeland's literary connections, while the Keswick Mining Museum covers the area's geology and industrial history.

On the northern edge of Keswick at Crosthwaite is the Church of St Kentigern (see page 250), whose best-known incumbent, Canon Rawnsley, was the first Secretary of the National Trust. A friend of Beatrix Potter, he was also an author, journalist, educationalist and orator. His influence pervades almost every corner of Keswick and Cumbria.

▼ Keswick and north end of Derwent Water

▶ Cumberland Pencil Museum

pencilmuseum.co.uk
Southey Works, Greta Bridge,
CA12 5NG | 017687 73626
Open daily 9.30–4

This interesting and forward-thinking museum investigates the history and technology of an object most of us take utterly for granted – the humble pencil. Did you know that the first pencil was made locally in the 1550s? Well, it was, and you do now! You will find lots more well-presented information about pencils here, including details of modern production methods, and the whole thing is very much geared to keeping children interested, with an on-site giant and other exciting innovations, such as a replica of the Borrowdale mine, where graphite was first discovered. You can see the world's longest coloured pencil, manufactured in 2001, and there's a children's activity area, a shop selling artists' materials, and Sketchers Coffee Shop, where all the food they serve is locally sourced. The coffee shop has an enviable riverside location with views of Catbells.

Throughout the year, there are artist demonstrations and tuition workshops showing various techniques using pencils. Family fun days are just what the doctor ordered on rainy days, with quiz trails all around the museum, drawing competitions and a host of fun and creative things to make and do in the Kid's Art Studio. Check the website for details.

▲ Vintage pencil making machine tool

▶ Theatre by the Lake

theatrebythelake.com

Lakeside, Lake Road, CA12 5DJ | 01768 774411 | Open all year

This theatre has been described as 'the most beautifully located and friendly theatre in Britain'. It is a short stroll from Derwent Water on the edge of Keswick and sits amid the magnificent western fells of the Lake District. You will find a huge range of presentations here and it is well worth checking their website to see what is showing while you are visiting the Lakes.

The theatre has two stages, a 400-seat main house and 100-seat studio, putting on up to nine productions of classic, modern and new plays throughout the year. The resident company of around 14 actors performs six plays in repertory from May to November, and produce a new play every year. If you are in the area at Christmas, particularly with children, go to their Christmas play if you can get a ticket.

The theatre also hosts a variety of festivals, visiting companies and musicians.

▼ Peter Macqueen and Richard Earl in *She Stoops to Conquer*

▲ Derwent Water

VISIT THE MUSEUM AND GALLERY
Keswick Museum and Art Gallery
keswickmuseum.webs.com
Fitz Park, Station Road, CA12 4NF
01768 773263 | Open Mon–Sat 9–5, Sun 10–4
In this museum, you'll find displays of letters and manuscripts, as well as information about the local geology and natural history of the area. It covers in particular, the poet Robert Southey – who moved to Greta Hall in Keswick (now part of a school) to join his brother-in-law, Samuel Coleridge – and remained there for over 40 years until his death in 1843. He became Poet Laureate in 1813. There is also a fine period scale model of the Lake District as it was in the early 19th century and, even older, a 500-year-old mummified cat. The geology collection is of national importance and contains mineral examples from the Caldbeck Fells.

TAKE A BOAT TRIP
Keswick Launch
see page 121

EXPLORE BY BIKE
Keswick Mountain Bike Centre
keswickbikes.co.uk
133 Main Street, CA12 5NJ
017687 75202
You can hire mountain bikes suitable for all sizes here, as well as helmets, spare parts and bike locks.

Whinlatter Bikes
whinlatterbikes.com
82 Main Street, CA12 5DX
017687 73940
Mountain bikes for men, women and children, plus tagalongs and buggies can be hired here. There's a workshop for repairs to your own bike as well.

PLAY A ROUND
Keswick Golf Club
keswickgolfclub.com
Threlkeld Hall, Threlkeld, CA12 4SX
017687 79324 | Open all year, daily
This parkland course is not very long, at just over 6,200 yards, but the par of 71 shows that it is a good test for golfers of all abilities – its numerous hazards, tree-lined fairways and well-protected greens will testify to that, as will its 500 members.

The natural landscape with outstanding, panoramic views of Blencathra, Skiddaw and Clough Head among others makes this an especially impressive and beautiful course to play.

EAT AND DRINK
The George
georgehotelkeswick.co.uk
3 St John's Street, CA12 5AZ
017687 72076
This is Keswick's oldest coaching inn and it's a handsome 17th-century building in the heart of the town. Restored to its former glory, The George still has its traditional black panelling, Elizabethan beams, ancient settles and log fires. You can get local Jennings ales on tap and classic pub food prepared from local ingredients.

The Horse & Farrier Inn
horseandfarrier.com
Threlkeld Village, CA12 4SQ
017687 79688
Built in 1688, this lovely Lakeland inn is on the ancient route between Keswick and Penrith, at the foot of Blencathra. Walkers are welcome and there are splendid views across Skiddaw and Helvellyn. Within the thick, whitewashed walls of this long, low building are slate-flagged floors, beamed ceilings and crackling log fires, with hunting prints decorating the traditional bars and panelled snug. Good pub grub made from seasonal produce is served here.

▼ Keswick and Skiddaw

The Inn at Keswick

theinnkeswick.co.uk
Main Street, CA12 5HZ
017687 74584

On the corner of Keswick's vibrant market square, you'll find contemporary comfort with charming reminders of its place in local history in this friendly 18th-century coaching inn. Lancaster Bomber is one of the award-winning Thwaites ales on tap, and Kingstone Press cider is deservedly popular too. The wine selection is small but thoughtfully chosen. The kitchen endeavours to source ingredients from ethical suppliers, ensuring sustainability as well as freshness and local artisan suppliers are named on the menu. The slight price premium for these policies is all but unnoticeable, as the menu represents excellent value for money. The food is served in hearty Cumbrian portions and the inn welcomes walkers and their dogs.

Keswick Brewery

keswickbrewery.co.uk
The Old Brewery, Brewery Lane,
CA12 5BY | 017687 80700

This small craft brewery was established in 2006 on the site of a much older brewery that closed way back in 1897.

Morrels ⊛

morrels.co.uk
34 Lake Road, CA12 5DQ
017687 72666

Located bang in the centre of Keswick, between the market and the Theatre by the Lake, the outside of this restaurant is a classic Lakeland stone-built townhouse. Inside, however, you'll find a stripped-out contemporary style, with pine floors, bare wooden tables, chocolate and cream high-backed chairs and etched-glass screens. The eclectic modern menu is simple, international and imaginative. Friendly staff and a laidback soundtrack make for an easy-going ambience.

Pheasant Inn

pheasantinnkeswick.co.uk
Crosthwaite Road, CA12 5PP
017687 72219

This is an open-fired, traditional Lakeland inn owned by Jennings Brewery, so you will find their regular range on tap, and a monthly guest beer. The seasonal menus, using home-cooked, locally sourced food, range from Cumbrian traditional to international favourites.

Swinside Lodge Country House Hotel ◉◉

swinsidelodge-hotel.co.uk
Grange Road, Newlands, CA12 5UE
017687 72948

You'll enjoy a dinner at this trim, whitewashed Georgian house at the foot of Catbells, just a five-minute stroll from the shore of Derwent Water (see page 118). The fells –

Skiddaw, Blencathra, and Causey Pike – crowd all around, making you want to pull on your boots to get the view from the top. The food is traditional Lakeland, while menus change daily and with the seasons.

▶ PLACES NEARBY

Church of St Kentigern

see page 250

Threlkeld Quarry and Mining Museum

threlkeldquarryandminingmuseum.co.uk | Threlkeld, CA12 4TT
017687 79747

You can take a trip through a reconstructed mine and wander around the vintage excavators and machinery in the quarry. There are also rooms explaining the story of mining and quarrying. You will find out about all aspects of Cumbrian mining, quarrying and geology.

▼ Catbells and Derwent Water

▶ Kirkby Lonsdale

This tiny market town in Cumbria marks the far western limit of the Yorkshire Dales. It is a delightfully unspoiled place, and its charms have been recognised by artists and authors, from Constable and Turner to Ruskin and Wordsworth, all of whom have sung its praises over the years. Even the street names such as Jingling Lane and Salt Pie Lane are quaint.

A Roman fort has been excavated at Burrow, just two miles south of the town, and in 1227 King Henry III granted a market charter, which allowed for a weekly market and an annual fair to be held in the town. The fair died out in the 19th century, but the market still thrives every Thursday in Market Place – the lovely butter cross here dates from the early 20th century.

Make sure you walk to the edge of town to see the medieval Devil's Bridge spanning the River Lune. It is one of the town's most notable features, with its three graceful arches striding over the water, and a very popular meeting place for bikers. Its date is not known for sure, though records from the late 14th century tell of repairs to a bridge in the town. No one knows when it first acquired its cheerful name, although a poem of 1821 tells the tale. A Yorkshire woman, known for being a cheat, one night heard her cow and pony calling from the far side of the swollen river. The devil appeared and offered to build a bridge, and his payment would be to keep the first thing that crossed over the bridge. He knew that her husband was coming home and thought he would capture him, but the canny

▼ Ruskin's View, Kirkby Lonsdale

woman tricked him by throwing a bun across the bridge, which her dog chased after. The devil grinned at the woman's trickery, and disappeared in flames. The bridge is now open for pedestrians only, to help preserve it.

A short way downriver you can see a piece of limestone, known as the Devil's Neck Collar, which has a hole worn through it by the action of the water.

SEE A LOCAL CHURCH
The Church of St Mary the Virgin
Queens Square, LA6 2AU

This impressive building probably dates from the late 11th and early 12th centuries. Look for the lovely Norman archway beneath the solid square tower. It has some fine stained glass and a delicately carved pulpit. Outside, near the north entrance, is a tower, which can be seen in J M W Turner's famous painting of 1822, *Kirkby Lonsdale Churchyard*, which serves as another reminder of the timeless and inspirational nature of this attractive little town.

PLAY A ROUND
Kirkby Lonsdale Golf Club
kirkbylonsdalegolfclub.com
Scaleber Lane, Barbon, LA6 2LJ
015242 76365

A parkland course on the east bank of the River Lune and crossed by Barbon Beck, Kirkby Lonsdale Golf Club is surrounded by the beautiful scenery of the Lune Valley and mainly follows the lie of the land. The course is gently undulating and the beck creates a number of water hazards.

EAT AND DRINK
Hipping Hall ⊛⊛⊛
hippinghall.com
Cowan Bridge, LA6 2JJ
015242 71187

In this rugged lunar landscape, you'll find a warm refuge, away from the wilds of the northern weather. The hotel is named after the hipping-stones, which once allowed travellers on foot to cross the stream that runs past the old wash house. You can eat, either in the fine medieval dining room – complete with minstrels' gallery, stately fireplace and raftered ceiling – or in the old conservatory, now upgraded to a smart new orangery. There is a choice of menus each evening, either a straightforward three-course menu with a choice of four dishes at each stage, or a seven-course tasting extravaganza, including pre-dessert, with cheeses as an optional extra. The combination of ingredients is fairly classic, but there are some novel additions. You can order an imaginative vegetarian seven-course menu, for example, which is very unusual. All the food choices live up to the hotel's three AA Rosettes.

The Sun Inn ◉

sun-inn.info

Market Street, LA6 2AU

015242 71965

This 17th-century free house, situated next to the church, is a short stroll from the famous Ruskin's View. Inside, there are natural stone walls, oak floors, log fires and furniture hand-made by the landlady's father, a cabinet maker. Some of the chairs were previously used on the RMS *Mauretania*. You'll find a selection of cask ales and an extensive wine choice. The all-day lunch or snack menu is called 'Meats, fishes, loaves and dishes', which allows you to choose starter-size meals for nibbling and/or sharing. The restaurant menu changes seasonally. In the evening, three-course meals come with a complimentary taster of soup. There is a good range of choices on the three-course vegetarian menu too.

The Pheasant Inn

pheasantinn.co.uk

Casterton, LA6 2RX | 015242 71230

Below the fell on the edge of the beautiful Lune Valley is this sleepy hamlet with its whitewashed 18th-century coaching inn. You'll get a warm welcome from the staff and the owners, the Wilson family. You can choose from guest ales and beers from Tirril and a broad wine list. The menu is interesting with quality seasonal produce sourced from the valley farms.

▶ PLACES NEARBY

A quiet and pretty village off the main tourist routes, Barbon makes the perfect base to explore the South Lakes. Lupton has a good pub.

The Barbon Inn

barbon-inn.co.uk

LA6 2LJ | 015242 76233

Sitting happily in the Lune Valley, between the River Lune and with the looming fells rising to Whernside, this whitewashed small village inn oozes the character only centuries of heritage can generate. The cosy Coach Lamp bar is particularly welcoming, with its vast fireplace and old furnishings. The Oak Room restaurant is equally enticing with polished old settles, grand beers and good food.

The Plough at Lupton ◉

theploughatlupton.co.uk

Cow Brow, Lupton, LA6 1PJ

015395 67700

The Plough had fallen on hard times before being given a shot in the arm by the good people behind the Punchbowl Inn in Crosthwaite (see page 250). It's surely never looked better. You'll find that it has kept the best of the traditional elements – wooden floors, beams and real fires – but added a contemporary finish with leather sofas and a Brathay slate-topped bar. You can sample real ales and a decent slate of wines by the glass alongside a broad menu of hearty British food.

▶ Kirkby Stephen

kirkby-stephen.com

This is a traditional market town of historic buildings, cobbled yards, quaint corners and interesting shops in the beautiful Upper Eden Valley. Although it is in Cumbria, it stands at the foot of Mallerstang, a dale that stretches south, half-in and half-out of the Yorkshire Dales National Park. You will find this area much quieter than the better-known parts of Cumbria, but equally appealing. You can walk through this landscape of pastoral rural scenery and wild uplands and find breathtaking views in every direction. It is remote from large towns and population centres and has a strong, self-sufficient identity and community spirit.

TAKE IN SOME HISTORY
Pendragon Castle

If you are passing, it is worth having a quick look at these atmospheric remains about four miles south of Kirkby Stephen, by the side of the B6259. Although, it's worth noting, there is more myth than historical fact here. The castle was named after King Uther Pendragon, the legendary father of King Arthur, although the building only dates from the 12th century. The crumbling castle is not very big but you can wander at will, despite it being on private land.

SEE A LOCAL CHURCH
Church of St Stephen

Vicarage Lane, CA17 4QT

Go into the church from the Market Square through the handsome cloisters built in 1810, where the butter market was held. The oldest part of the present church dates from 1220. Prior to that, this was the site of a Norman church, which only survived for 50 years, and before that a Saxon church stood on this spot. You can see many ancient relics here. There are some well-preserved bread shelves, a fine Shap granite and Italian marble pulpit, and a 17th-century font. Look for the beautiful engraved panel over the entrance to the Hartley Chapel showing the Stoning of St Stephen, crafted by John Hutton. He was also responsible for the memorable glass screen in Coventry Cathedral. Inside the chapel is a tub, which was used to measure a bushel of wheat.

The best feature is at the west end. It is the 10th-century Viking Loki Stone, decorated with a carved horned figure of the Norse god Loki. It is the only example in Britain, and one of only two in of Europe. There is also a hogback stone, a Viking grave marker with a curved ridge, which is thought to represent the shingled roofs of these 'houses of the dead'. The tower was built in the early 16th century and in the nave you can still see fragments of a painted weave pattern.

In the churchyard look for a flat stone table, the Trupp Stone. This is where the tenants of church properties traditionally paid their tithes. It was in use until 1836.

HIT THE SHOPS
Rocke That Frock
rockethatfrock.co.uk

acoustictearoom.com

39 Market Street, CA17 4QN

017683 72123

Don't miss the chance to browse through this fascinating treasure trove. It is a chic 1960s inspired boutique upstairs and an Aladdin's cave of antique treasures in the cellar downstairs – a unique vintage shopping experience indeed. The store has a vast collection of women's classic vintage clothing dating from the 1920s to 1980s and a wide variety of period furniture and collectables. With help on hand to help you find that perfect look or item, Rocke That Frock is the place for complete vintage indulgence. In the evening, they also run excellent monthly folk music gigs in the nearby Masonic Hall under the name 'acoustic tea room'. Check the website for details.

EAT AND DRINK
Mango Tree
Market Square, CA17 4QT

017683 74960

If you fancy a change from all the hearty Cumbrian food in the Lake District, you might want to try this excellent Bangladeshi restaurant. However, it gets very busy, so it's a good idea to book. They do great takeaways too, if your accommodation is self-catering.

▶ PLACES NEARBY
Ravenstonedale is an unspoiled picturesque village lying at the foot of the Howgills.

The Black Swan
blackswanhotel.com

Ravenstonedale, CA17 4NG

015396 23204

A previous winner of the AA Pub of the Year for England, The Black Swan sits below Wild Boar Fell beside the headwaters of the River Eden. You can see red squirrels in the tranquil riverside garden. The ever-changing selection of northern beers includes the likes of Dent, Hawkshead and Tirril. Reliance on local produce is also evident in the choice of dishes, with all meat traceable. This is a handy stop if you are walking the Howgill Fells or touring the Yorkshire Dales.

The Fat Lamb Country Inn
fatlamb.co.uk

Crossbank, CA17 4LL

015396 23242

High above the green meadows of Ravenstonedale, this 350-year-old stone coaching inn has its own nature reserve, some seven acres of open water and wetlands, surrounded by flower-rich meadows. From The Fat Lamb's gardens, you can see some of England's most precious and remote countryside. An open fire in a traditional Yorkshire range warms the bar in winter, where you'll find plenty of friendly locals mingling and nattering with visitors. Snacks and meals are served here and in the traditional, relaxed restaurant, which is decorated with old prints and plates. Check out the day's specials board or order from the five-course set menu. Whatever you choose, it will have been prepared on site using the best available local ingredients.

The King's Head
kings-head.com
CA17 4NH | 015396 23050
It's hard to believe that this old whitewashed pub was closed for three years, re-opening in 2011 after major refurbishment. Three regularly changing real ales and eight wines by the glass are served in the open-plan bar. There are real fires in the restaurant, where a three-course lunch or evening meal will be homemade and Cumbrian. Cyclists will love the bike lock-up facility.

▶ Kirkstone Pass

Kirkstone Pass is, at a maximum of 1,489 feet, the highest road in the Lake District, as well as one of the most spectacular. You can imagine the effort it took in days of yore for charabancs to labour up the long haul, from either Ambleside or Troutbeck. The Kirkstone Inn, where these roads converge, would have been a welcome sight for passengers. It takes its name from the nearby Kirk Stone, which resembles a church steeple.

The Kirkstone Pass continues through some magnificent mountain scenery, before dropping down, past Brothers Water, into Patterdale.

▼ Kirkstone Pass

EAT AND DRINK

Kirkstone Pass Inn

kirkstonepassinn.com

LA22 9LQ | 015394 33888

It is worth stopping here just for the view, but it is also 500 years old and the highest pub in Cumbria. It will not disappoint you with its oak beams, open fire, home-cooked meals and friendly welcome.

▾ Kirkstone Pass

5 hauntings

▶ **The Kirkstone Pass Inn** (see page 175) is crawling with ghosts, including a boy who was killed by a coach and a ghostly coachman who pops in for a pint.

▶ The spectre of Lord Lonsdale apparently drives a ghostly coach and horses round **St Peter's Church in Askham**

▶ **Broughton Moor** is supposed to be haunted by a character known as Bible John who carries a Bible with a pistol inside it.

▶ **Cartmel Priory** (see page 96) is the scene of ghostly apparitions of monks.

▶ **Muncaster Castle** (see page 190) is one of the most haunted buildings in England and you can register to take part in one of their ghost sits or overnight ghost vigils – that's if you dare.

▶ **Lake District National Park**

lakedistrict.gov.uk

The Lake District National Park includes the central and most visited part of Cumbria, but stops short of the towns of Carlisle (see page 88), Kendal (see page 154) and Penrith (see page 195). The Furness Peninsula, Morecambe Bay, the northern coast and the Solway are not included.

The National Park Authority's main aims are to promote conservation, public enjoyment and the well-being of the local community, and to protect the landscape by restricting change, which would be detrimental to it. The biggest landowner within the Lake District National Park is the National Trust, which looks after large tracts of some of the finest Lakeland landscapes for the enjoyment of future generations. The Forestry Commission is another major landowner. United Utilities, too, owns three large areas within the National Park, including Haweswater (see page 146), Thirlmere (see page 219) and Ennerdale (see page 124). Most of the land is, however, in the hands of individual farmers and estates.

The area was the second national park in Britain, designated in 1951, just after the Peak District and it is the most visited national park with more than 20 million tourists visiting every year. Based in Kendal, the national has a visitor centre on Windermere at Brockhole (see page 246).

▶ Lakeside

Lakeside started life as a steamer pier. Then it became the terminus of the Lakeside branch of the Furness Railway. A hotel was built to cater for the passengers. It's still possible to travel here by steamer from Bowness on Windermere and then travel on the short distance to Haverthwaite and back via the heritage railway.

MEET THE WILDLIFE
Lakes Aquarium
lakesaquarium.co.uk
LA12 8AS | 015395 30153
Open daily 9–4
Here you can see creatures that live in and around freshwater lakes across the globe making it an ideal place to come if you have children. They will love discovering things that swim, fly and bite in beautifully themed displays. Find out about otters in Asia, piranhas in the Americas and marmosets in the rainforest, not forgetting all your favourite creatures that live a bit closer to home. This includes diving ducks and otters in spectacular underwater tunnels, and freshwater rays and seahorses in the Seashore Discover Zone. Don't miss the world's first virtual dive bell. Experience a spectacular interactive adventure and come face to face with awesome virtual creatures – including a terrifying shark, charging hippo and fierce crocodile – without getting wet. Special themed events take place throughout the year.

TAKE A TRAIN RIDE
Lakeside And Haverthwaite Railway
lakesiderailway.co.uk
Haverthwaite Station, Nr Ulverston, LA12 8AL | 015395 31594
This is one of the best days out in Windermere, particularly if you combine the scenic train journey with a cruise on the lake. Originally a branch of the Furness Railway, the line used to carry goods and passengers from Ulverston to connect with the Windermere steamers at Lakeside. Four passenger steamers began service in 1850; trains began running 20 years later. Passenger

numbers peaked before the World War I, but sadly declined from then and finally, in 1967, the line was closed.

A group of rail enthusiasts fought to buy the branch line and re-open it as a recreational line, using steam-hauled trains. Despite many setbacks they succeeded in taking over the 3.5-mile stretch of line between Haverthwaite and Lakeside and have maintained the service ever since.

TAKE A BOAT TRIP
Windermere Lake Cruises
see page 247

EAT AND DRINK
Lakeside Hotel 🏵🏵
lakesidehotel.co.uk
LA12 8AT | 015395 30001
Originally a simple 17th-century coaching inn, the Lakeside Hotel has spread its wings to cater to the influx of visitors who want to enjoy its splendid setting and linger in the spa. Embraced by thickly wooded hills and overlooking nothing but the boats nodding at anchor on Lake Windermere, an atmosphere of rest and relaxation pervades the luxurious Lakeside Hotel. Luckily, the building's expansion has not been at the expense of its period charm – there are cosy lounges and snug traditional bars for an aperitif, before you head to the more formal oak-panelled Lakeview restaurant. Local produce forms the backbone of the modern British menu.

Whitewater Hotel 🏵
whitewater-hotel.co.uk
The Lakeland Village, LA12 8PX
015395 31133
The Whitewater is a resort hotel in Lakeland Village, constructed around a converted stone-built mill, offering the latest pampering spa treatments in an area that's all about tranquil relaxation. The thoroughly hospitable dining room has rough stone walls, hung with Lakeland scenes, smart table linen, high-backed chairs and views through expansive windows of the cascading River Leven. The modern British food on offer is full of punchy, vivid flavours and subtle additions.

▶ **PLACES NEARBY**
Newby Bridge
Newby Bridge marks the southern limit of Lake Windermere, where it drains into the River Leven. There is a convenient stop here on the Lakeside–Haverthwaite Railway (see opposite page), so you can combine a train journey and a lake cruise with a visit here.

Stott Park Bobbin Mill
www.english-heritage.org.uk
015395 31087 | LA12 8AX | Open Apr–Oct, 10–4.30
Here, you can see the journey from tree to bobbin on the original belt driven machinery. The 1835 building is an evocative reminder of a local industry that produced bobbins for the clattering textile mills of Lancashire. Now preserved

by English Heritage, at one time, this extensive working mill produced millions of wooden bobbins for the Lancashire spinning and weaving industries. There's a family trail to give you an idea of what it was like to work at the mill. Although it is small compared to others, some 250 men and boys worked here to produce 250,000 bobbins a week.

Fell Foot Park

nationaltrust.org.uk
Newby Bridge, LA12 8NN | 015395 31273 | Open daily dawn til dusk
Fell Foot Park is one of the few sites on Lake Windermere's eastern shore where you can get access to the water. At this 18-acre park you'll find safe bathing, boats for hire, an adventure playground and space to spread a picnic blanket. A ferry runs between Fell Foot Park and Lakeside, where you can see the terminus of the restored railway and steamer berth, as well as the Aquarium of the Lakes with its imaginative naturalistic displays of water and bird life in rivers, lakes and nearby Morecambe Bay.

▶ The Langdales

The Langdales must be two of the most beautiful valleys in the Lake District. They are no secret, as you will discover if you try to make the circular drive around Great Langdale and Little Langdale on a weekend in summer. The road is very narrow, so it's best to park at Skelwith Bridge or Elterwater, and tackle the area on foot. There are climbs and scrambles here to challenge the sure-footed, as well as lowland rambles if you just want to enjoy the view.

At Skelwith Bridge, where the B5343 Langdale road branches off from the A593, is Skelwith Force. The path to the waterfall continues to Elterwater, where you can enjoy the view of the distinctive silhouette of the Langdale Pikes.

You can see the twin humps of Harrison Stickle at

2,415 feet and Pike of Stickle at 2,323 feet from many different points.

Beyond the village of Chapel Stile, the Great Langdale Valley opens up spectacularly. The valley floor is divided up by stone walls, dotted with farmsteads and surrounded by mountain peaks. The valley road meanders past the Old Dungeon Ghyll Hotel, and after a steep climb the road drops, with views of Blea Tarn, into Little Langdale Valley. Though not as stunning as the main valley, it is delightful and has good footpaths. It is from Little Langdale that a minor road branches west, to become first Wrynose Pass and then Hardknott Pass (see page 144) – exciting driving if your brakes are good.

One of the best walks in the Great Langdale Valley begins at the New Dungeon Ghyll Hotel. The route passes the foaming white water of Dungeon Ghyll Force before climbing steeply uphill by Stickle Ghyll waterfalls. A surprise awaits you at the top – the still waters of the beautiful Stickle Tarn, with the vertiginous cliff-face of Pavey Ark behind.

EAT AND DRINK

The New Dungeon Ghyll Hotel
dungeon-ghyll.co.uk
Great Langdale, LA22 9JX
Sitting in a spectacular spot at the foot of the Langdale Pikes and Pavey Ark, this traditional stone building is full of character and charm. It was once a farmhouse, before being transformed into a hotel in 1832. If you are returning from a walk on the fells, you will

▼ Little Langdale

enjoy relaxing in the rustic bar and if you're hungry, local specialities are served in the bar and smart dining room.

Old Dungeon Ghyll Hotel

odg.co.uk

Great Langdale, LA22 9JY

015394 37272

You'll find a warm welcome, excellent beer and good value food in this family-run hotel. The ODG has been catering to weary travellers here for 300 years and is usually full to overflowing with walkers, climbers and campers. The Hiker's Bar is deservedly popular. As well as real ales there is a large selection of the finest Scottish whisky's and a large wine cellar. The setting, below the towering Langdale Pikes, probably helps too.

Three Shires Inn

threeshiresinn.co.uk

Little Langdale, LA22 9NZ

015394 37215

This classic Lake District hotel is on the winding lane that squeezes from Little Langdale towards the daunting Wrynose and Hard Knott passes, England's steepest roads. You'll find superb Lakeland beers, tasty Cumbrian fare and a blazing fire in the traditional beamed bar during the winter months. In summer, the landscaped garden with its magnificent fell views is the place to savour a pint of local real ale. Personally run by the Stephenson family since 1983, everyone – including families with children and dogs – is welcomed in the bar. The food is freshly prepared using local Lakeland ingredients.

▶ Levens Hall

levenshall.co.uk

LA8 0PD | 015395 60321 | Open Apr–mid-Oct Sun–Thu; Gardens 10–5, Hall 12–4.30

Levens Hall, just south of Kendal, is well worth a visit. The beginnings of the hall can be traced back to a 14th-century pele tower. Typically square, with thick walls and narrow windows, the towers allowed the wealthier landowners to protect their families, livestock and servants in times of danger. The grim medieval tower at Levens was later incorporated into a more elaborate Elizabethan building to create a comfortable family home. Levens Hall has passed through many hands, but in 1688 it came into the possession of Colonel James Grahme, supposedly as a result of a card game, and was passed on to Grahme's descendants, the Bagots, who still live at Levens.

As a result of this long family connection, you'll find an atmosphere of care and comfort here. Levens is still full of furniture and possessions, brought to the house by Colonel Grahme at the end of the 17th century. One of the Bagot ancestors married the Duke of Wellington's niece, bringing into the family a number of Napoleonic relics, including his cloak clasp of two bees, taken after Waterloo, and a superb Sèvres chocolate service made for the Emperor's mother. You can also see the earliest English patchwork quilt, made by Colonel Grahme's daughters from rare Indian cottons in about 1708. The family even owns one of the bowls Sir Francis Drake was using on Plymouth Hoe when the Armada was sighted.

As fine as the house is, its most famous feature is the topiary gardens. Colonel Grahme had a passion for gardening and engaged Monsieur Beaumont to create a topiary garden, in which yew trees were clipped into a variety of shapes – resembling nothing so much as a surreal set of chess pieces. Beaumont laid out the Hampton Court Palace gardens and spent the last 40 years of his life working at Levens Hall. You can see a portrait of him in the hall with the inscription: 'Gardener to King James II and Colonel James Grahme.' The designs seen today, probably the finest examples in the country, are much as they were designed three centuries ago. It is the finest, oldest and most extensive topiary garden in the world. There are over 100 pieces here, each clipped to an unusual and individual design. Beaumont's imagination knew no limits and he created designs representing graceful birds, elegant beasts, chess pieces and even teacups and saucers.

Levens Hall has more than its share of ghosts too. One is the Grey Lady, able to walk straight through walls, and supposed to be the ghost of a gypsy woman who was refused refreshment at the hall. It is reported that she put a curse on the house, saying that no male would inherit Levens Hall until the River Kent ceased to flow and a white deer was seen in the park.

▼ Levens Hall

The hall did indeed pass through the female line until the birth of Alan Desmond Bagot in 1896 – an event that coincided with the river freezing over and the appearance of a white fawn.

▶ Little Salkeld
see **Great Salkeld & Little Salkeld**, page 137

▶ Lorton

Lorton Vale is the valley that sweeps south from Cockermouth – passing the village of Loweswater, Crummock Water and finally Buttermere – before ending in the lofty Honister Pass. Five miles southeast of Cockermouth is the village of Lorton, which is divided in two. High Lorton clings to the side of Kirk Fell at the start of the Whinlatter Pass, and is famous for its yew tree. Wordsworth described this magnificent tree, which stands behind the village hall, in his poem *Yew Trees*. It was beneath its boughs that the founder of the Quaker movement, George Fox, preached to a large crowd under the watchful eyes of Cromwell's soldiers.

At Whinlatter (see page 232), there is a Forestry Commission Visitor Centre, where you can watch the local ospreys on CCTV and discover more about this vast forest.

EAT AND DRINK
The Wheatsheaf Inn
wheatsheafinnlorton.co.uk
CA13 9UW | 01900 85199/85268
At this white-painted, 17th-century pub you'll find an open fire in the bar and panoramic views of the lush Vale of Lorton from the child-friendly beer garden. They serve real ales from Jennings Brewery and hearty pub grub.

▶ Loweswater

One of the smaller lakes, Loweswater is no less delightful for it and has the added bonus of often being less crowded than those lakes that are easier to access. To reach it, drive on the B5289 down Lorton Vale from Cockermouth but instead of continuing down the main road that leads to Crummock Water and Buttermere – as many motorists do – take a turning through Brackenthwaite. This road will take you along the north shore of the lake with parking at either end.

Loweswater village is little more than a church, a village hall and a pub, with a scattering of whitewashed farm buildings surrounded by woodland and meadows. Explore one of the leafy footpaths through the woods, cared for by the National Trust.

GO FISHING

Water End Farm

CA13 0SU | 01946 861465

The fishing here is controlled by the National Trust and you can get a permit from Waterend Farm. You might find the odd trout but it is mainly pike fishing here. You can also hire a rowing boat at the farm, whether for fishing or just to mess about on the lake.

▶ Maryport

A comparatively new Cumbrian town, Maryport was founded in 1749 to serve as a port for the coal trade, and named after Mary, the wife of the Lord of the Manor, Humphrey Senhouse II. The port quickly grew and, for a short while, was the biggest in Cumberland, with trade from the coal and iron-ore mines and also a healthy shipbuilding industry.

You can find the story of its rise and subsequent decline in the Maryport Maritime Museum. Also by the quayside is the Lake District Coast Aquarium, where you can see a surprising range of native marine and freshwater fish. On the hill above the town, the Senhouse Roman Museum, begun in 1570 by the Senhouse family, has an important collection of Roman artefacts, many found locally.

VISIT THE MUSEUMS

Maryport Maritime Museum

maryportmaritimemuseum.btck. co.uk | 1 Senhouse Street, CA15 6AB 01900 813738 | Open Apr–Oct, Tue, Thu–Sun and BHs 10–5. Winter Fri–Sun, 10.30–4

Maryport Maritime Museum is on the quayside in the building formally known as The Queen's Head public house. This is one of the oldest buildings in the town and, in its day, entertained and boarded a great many sailors between voyages. You can see exhibits ranging from a whale's tooth to luxury china designed for the *Titanic*. The sperm whale tooth is etched with a picture of the whaler 'Eagle'. The sailors of the 19th-century whaling ships made these intricate carvings of bone and ivory, known as 'scrimshaw' work.

Senhouse Roman Museum

senhousemuseum.co.uk

The Battery, Sea Brows, CA15 6JD 01900 816168 | Open Fri–Sun, 10.30–4

This small but fascinating museum is in the Battery, an old naval building, overlooking the Solway Firth. Most of the objects in the museum come from the fort at Maryport and the Roman settlement attached to it. John Senhouse rescued some pieces from Maryport's Roman fort in the 1570s and the family continued to add to it over the centuries. You can see the largest group of Roman military altar stones and inscriptions from any site in

Britain. In the grounds, you can climb the observation tower for a clear view of the full extent of the settlement, which is one of the largest and best preserved in the north.

MEET THE SEALIFE
Lake District Coast Aquarium
coastaquarium.co.uk
South Quay, CA15 8AB
01900 817760 | Open daily 10–5
You can see aquatic life, both native and exotic, seawater and freshwater in the myriad tanks and pools in this award-winning attraction. There is a rock pool to investigate, rays that can be stroked, cascading pools of trout and even a shipwreck. If the kids have had enough of sea life, they can let off some steam in the nautical themed adventure play park.

TIE UP
Maryport Marina
maryportharbour.com
Marine Road, CA15 8AY
01900 814431
If you're cruising the west coast, this is a good place for boats of up to 60 feet to stay for a short stopover. There are 190 pontoon berthings sheltered at all points from the weather. There is range of services and amenities, including electricity and water on pontoons, showers and toilets and boat repairs.

PLAY A ROUND
Maryport Golf Course
maryportgolfclub.co.uk
Bankend, CA15 6PA
01900 812605 | Open all year daily
This is a tight seaside links course exposed to Solway breezes, with fine views across Solway Firth. The course has nine links holes and nine parkland holes, and the small streams can be hazardous on several holes. The first three holes have the seashore on their left and you can easily land in the water with a badly judged tee shot. Holes 6–14 are gently undulating open parkland, with holes 15–18 reverting to links.

▶ PLACES NEARBY
Allonby beach
This is a superb long sand and shingle beach with views across the Solway to the hills of southern Scotland and, on a clear day, as far as the Isle of Man. It has been popular for sea bathing since the 18th century.

▶ Millom
Sitting on its own peninsula, overlooking the estuary of the River Duddon, Millom is well off the beaten track. The town grew with the iron and steel industries in the latter years of the 19th century. The Millom Folk Museum and Tourist Information Centre are both in the imaginatively redeveloped railway station, now called the Millom Discovery Centre.

The Hodbarrow Iron Works, which closed in the 1960s, have been encouraged to go back to nature. The result is a brackish lagoon, adjacent to the Duddon Estuary, which is now an RSPB reserve. This stretch of water acts as a magnet for breeding wildfowl, waders and the rare natterjack toad.

VISIT THE MUSEUM

Millom Discovery Centre
millomdiscoverycentre.co.uk
Station Buildings, LA18 5AA
01229 772555 | Open all year
Mon–Sat 10.30–3.30, Sun 10.30–1.30

Completely refurbished, this museum features vivid reminders of the town's iron-mining days, including a mining cage from the Hodbarrow Mine. There's a reconstructed miner's cottage and displays of clothing in the dressmaker's shop. You can also find out about Millom in the war years and its ship-building past; Norman Nicholson – Millom's own poet – and, of course, in the station building, the story of the extensive rail network of yesteryear.

SEE A LOCAL CHURCH

Holy Trinity Church
Salthouse Road, LA18 5EY
Surrounded by farmland, Holy Trinity is close to the ruined 12th-century Millom Castle. The church was built in the 12th century, extended in the 13th century with a south

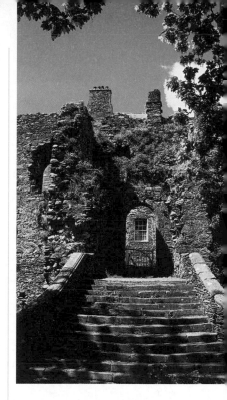

▲ Millom Castle

aisle and enlarged again in the 14th century. Inside you'll find monuments to the Huddleston family of Millom Castle – the highlight is a fine 15th-century carved alabaster tomb of rare beauty and workmanship. It consists of the reclining effigies of a man and a woman, with the representation of six angels on either side, each bearing a scroll. Although the communion rail contains work from the 1630s and the box pews remain, many of its interior features are Victorian. There are several interesting stained-glass windows, one called the 'fish' window due to its shape. In the churchyard are further monuments to the Huddlestons, including a sundial.

▶ **PLACES NEARBY**
Hodbarrow Nature Reserve
rspb.org.uk
01697 351330 | Open all year daily
This is a small RSPB Nature Reserve on the site of the Hodbarrow Mine, which ceased production in the late 1960s. It's part of the Duddon Estuary Site of Special Scientific Interest, and you'll stand a good chance of hearing natterjack toads even if you don't see them.

(Cumbria is home to about 50 per cent of the country's population.) You'll also find pleasant walks in flower-rich grasslands, with marsh orchids, bee orchids and rare flora and fauna. Look out for butterflies, skylarks, peregrine falcons, terns and occasionally the sight of dancing crested grebes.

Swinside Stone Circle
see page 215

▶ Milnthorpe

Seven miles south of Kendal, Milnthorpe is an ancient market town of beautiful, old, limestone buildings and narrow lanes. The Market Square is bordered on three sides by pretty cottages and shops. The fourth side opens out on to green lawns and trees leading up to the 19th-century Church of St Thomas.

WALK THE CUMBRIA COASTAL WAY
see page 94

EAT AND DRINK
The Cross Keys
thecrosskeyshotel.co.uk
1 Park Road, LA7 7AB
015395 62115
In the heart of the village, this pub makes a good pit stop for cask-conditioned ales and hearty pub food. Levens Hall (see page 180), Leighton Moss Nature Reserve and Morecambe Bay (see page 187) are all within reach.

▶ **PLACES NEARBY**
Lakeland Wildlife Oasis
wildlifeoasis.co.uk
Hale, LA7 7FE | 015395 63027
Open daily

This is a great all-weather activity for children of all ages. There are free-flying butterflies, exotic vegetation, fish, reptiles, birds and mammals. There are working models, hands-on exhibits, computer programmes and a range of live animals to demonstrate life on Earth, through 3,000 million years of evolution. The meerkats are a particular favourite with children, especially when there are babies to coo over. Check the website for special events.

Heron Corn Mill
heronmill.org
Mill Lane, Beetham, LA7 7PQ
01539 564271 | Open al year
Wed–Sun 11–4; closed Mon–Tue
Here you can see a working watermill grinding corn.

It is a Grade II listed 18th-century mill on the banks of the River Bela. A mill existed on this site before 1096 and then in 1220 the Lord of the Manor gave the monks of St Marie's York the right to grind their grain at his mill.

The Wheatsheaf at Beetham
wheatsheafbeetham.com
LA7 7AL | 015395 62123
Once a coaching stop on the road from Lancaster to Carlisle, it's worth a visit to the Wheatsheaf just for the opportunity to sample the penny menu, a starter and dessert for 1p each, when you order a main course. Jean and Richard Skelton, the owners, think that's probably much the same as would have been paid by a farm labourer to the farmer's wife for a meal here back in the early 1600s. For a pre-meal pint, the Old Tap Bar offers Thwaites Wainwright, Tirril Queen Jean and Cross Bay Nightfall, as well as an impressive range of malt whiskies.

▶ Morecambe Bay

With the mountains of the Lake District to the north, and changing patterns of water and light on the largest area of inter-tidal sands and mudflats in Britain, Morecambe Bay is an impressive sight on a vast scale. Water levels can vary by up to 34 feet at spring tides – be aware, the incoming waters advance faster than anyone can run.

At low tide, in favourable weather conditions and only with an expert guide (ask at the tourist information centre if you would like to book one), it is possible to walk across the sands from Morecambe, on the south side, to Grange-over-Sands. You should never attempt this on your own, however – the shifting sands, quicksands and currents make it extremely dangerous.

Morecambe's rail link to West Yorkshire made it a popular holiday resort for people from the Bradford area, but it saw a serious decline in the 1980s and 1990s. More recently, it has turned itself around. The town's revival has included the conversion of the former promenade railway station into the Platform Arts Centre, a stylish restoration of the gracefully curved art deco Midland Hotel, and transformation of the remains of the 1850s harbour into the Stone Jetty walkway. You can walk along here and enjoy the sculptures, games and poems carved in the stone and then watch a breathtaking Morecambe Bay sunset. There's also a campaign to re-open the Winter Gardens, a gorgeously Victorian theatre.

On the four-mile long promenade you can see a slightly
larger-than-life statue of the town's favourite son, Eric
Morecambe (born Eric Bartholomew), who took his stage
name from his boyhood home and became as popular as
the resort in its heyday. All this is a long way from Morecambe's
humble origins as the little fishing village of Poulton-le-Sands,
though the boats still fish locally for whitebait, cockles and,
perhaps most famously, shrimps.

5 top beaches

▶ **St Bees beach** at St Bees Head (page 205) – a mile-long sandy beach with rockpools and a RSPB reserve for top-notch birdwatching.

▶ **Grange-over-Sands** (page 131) on the edge of Morecambe Bay – don't attempt to cross the bay unless accompanied by the Queen's Guide to the Sands, the excellent Cedric Robinson MBE.

▶ **Whitehaven beach** (page 235), located just north of the docks, is small but rather splendid.

▶ **Allonby beach** (page 184), between Maryport and Siloth, is a sand and shingle beach. There's an enormous expanse of sand at low tide.

▶ **Silecroft beach,** south of Ravenglass, has a Marine Conservation Society award (page 212).

◀ Morecambe Bay

INDULGE YOURSELF
Morecambe Bay
Brown Shrimps
Available from local fishmongers, Morecambe Bay Brown Shrimps are renowned for their delicate taste and texture; they have been caught locally for hundreds of years. Fishing methods may have changed but you can still find the shrimps made to the same traditional recipe. Locally caught shrimps are cooked in butter and then sealed with butter and packed into pots.

▶ Muncaster Castle

muncaster.co.uk

CA18 1RQ | 01229 717614 | Castle open Sun–Fri, 12–4 (closed most Sats for weddings); Gardens and owl centre open daily 10.30–4.30

Few stately homes have a view to match the panorama from the grand terrace of Muncaster Castle. Directly below are the gardens, with one of the largest collections of rhododendrons in the country. In the middle distance, the River Esk meanders prettily through the lowlands, while the horizon is a series of stark Lakeland peaks, of which Scafell Pike (3,210 feet, 978m) is the most prominent.

In 1208, the land at Muncaster was granted to the Pennington family, who still own it today. The pele tower still survives beneath later stonework, but virtually everything here today dates from the 1860s. Lord Muncaster commissioned Anthony Salvin to remodel both the medieval remains and the modest 18th-century house. You can tour the house accompanied by a taped audio guided tour, recorded by the present owner, detailing the many treasures and artworks on view.

Two massive towers on the garden front add weight and grandeur to the outside of this solid Victorian building, while inside there are plenty of individual touches – for example, the hall with

▼ View from Muncaster Castle

its enclosed staircase, and the octagonal library, with a brass-railed gallery and fine vaulted ceiling. The rooms have splendid woodwork and panelling from Britain and the Continent, and carved chimneypieces – including one by Adam – brought from other houses. The furniture includes an Elizabethan four-poster and a superb set of Charles II walnut settees and chairs. The house contains a collection of glittering silverware by Paul Storr and a series of family portraits from the 17th century to the present.

Muncaster Castle is also the headquarters of the World Owl Trust, which is dedicated to worldwide owl conservation. You can see a variety of owls, from the pygmy owl to the gigantic eagle owl, and from native species to some of the rarest owls in the world. On fine summer afternoons you get a chance to meet the birds and watch them in flight.

As Lords of the Manor, the Pennington family owned Muncaster Mill from the 15th century right up to 1961, when the mill closed. You can easily reach the present buildings, dating from about 1700, by car on the A595 or by taking a ride on the Ravenglass & Eskdale Railway (see page 200), known affectionately as La'al Ratty. Note: Muncaster Mill is a request halt on the line. The tiny mill, with its overshot wheel turned by water from the River Mite, is a reminder of a time when every village had its own corn mill. Though now restored to full working order, it is currently closed and its future is again uncertain.

SEE A LOCAL CHURCH
Church of St Michael
CA18 1RJ
In the wooded grounds of Muncaster Castle, this church dates from the 15th century or earlier: there is evidence of a 12th-century stone in the nave. It has stained-glass windows by Henry Holiday, a Pre-Raphaelite artist, who had a home in Ambleside. The west window shows the Day of Judgement: Christ in Glory with Archangel Michael, and the 'saved' and the 'damned'. In the churchyard is a cross-shaft and wheel-head believed to date from the 10th century, a reminder of the Norse Vikings who settled here.

▶ Near Sawrey

A picturesque village, two miles from Hawkshead on the eastern side of Esthwaite Water, this tiny place is world famous for the work of one rather extraordinary woman. Beatrix Potter first came here on holiday in 1896, fell in love with the place and used the royalties from her first book, *The Tale of Peter Rabbit* (1901), to buy Hill Top. It was in this unpretentious little 17th-century farmhouse that she wrote many more of the books that have delighted children throughout the world.

The success of her books allowed Beatrix Potter to focus on her other interest – conservation – and in particular, the indigenous fell Herdwick sheep. In 1923 she bought a former deer park and farm in the Troutbeck Valley – restoring its land and thousand-strong flock of Herdwick sheep. On her death in 1943, all her properties were bequeathed to the National Trust.

TAKE IN SOME HISTORY
Hill Top
see page 193

EAT AND DRINK
Ees Wyke Country House ◉
eeswyke.co.uk
LA22 0JZ | 015394 36393
This Georgian house above Esthwaite Water, with glorious fell views, was at one time Beatrix Potter's holiday home before she bought Hill Top and moved to the village. It's now a comfortable, country house hotel, where dinner is served in the dining room overlooking the lake. The daily changing five-course menu has only a couple of choices per course, but the quality is always excellent. Vegetarians or those on special diets will be catered for too, but you do need to let the proprietors know in advance. Good local ingredient sourcing is clear, and the kitchen combines solid classical ideas with gently modern notions.

Tower Bank Arms
towerbankarms.co.uk
LA22 0LF | 015394 36334
The National Trust owns this 17th-century village pub on the west side of Lake Windermere although it is independently run. Situated just in front of Hill Top, Beatrix Potter's old home, it was once known as 'The Blue Pig' and later 'The Albion'. It has been the Tower Bank Arms for over a century and Beatrix Potter illustrated it perfectly in her *Tale of Jemima Puddleduck*. In the low-beamed, slate-floored main bar there's an open log fire, fresh flowers and a grandfather clock, and local brews on hand pump from the Hawkshead and Barngates breweries. The full lunch and dinner menus are available daily, and the hearty country food makes good use of local produce, whether you come in search of a snack or a filling main dish. From the garden you have a panorama of farms, fells and fields.

▶ Hill Top

nationaltrust.org.uk
LA22 0LF | 015394 36269 | Open
mid-Feb–Oct, Sat–Thu. Opening
hours vary; check website for details
This small 17th-century house
is where Beatrix Potter wrote
many of her famous children's
stories. It remains as she left it,
and In each room you can find
something that appears in one
of her books. Her will decreed
that Hill Top should remain
exactly as she had known it.

You will easily recognise
details from the pictures in her
books and, disregarding its
rather unprepossessing
exterior, Hill Top is chock full of
Beatrix Potter memorabilia, including her original drawings.
However, the place is so popular that it's best to avoid visiting at
peak holiday times.

If you love Beatrix Potter, you'll also find lots to interest you at
the Beatrix Potter Gallery (see page 147) at Hawkshead and the
World of Beatrix Potter (see page 245) at Bowness.

▼ Hill Top

▶ Newlands

Although it's close to Keswick and the busy A66, the delightful Newlands Valley is a quiet backwater. With its rolling green fields, there is little evidence left today that this was once a busy industrial mining community. In fact, you'd have to search hard to find any communities at all, as there are only a handful of farms and the two tiny hamlets of Little Town and Stair. A farmhouse at Stair has the inscription 'TF 1647'. The initials are believed to be those of Thomas Fairfax, commander of the Parliamentary forces, who stayed here after the Civil War in 1646.

Little Town's fame could hardly be more different, as its name features in Beatrix Potter's *The Tale of Mrs Tiggywinkle* – in fact Catbells, Skelgill and Little Town can all be recognised from her sketches for this book.

Copper and lead were mined on the valley's eastern slopes, and small deposits of silver and gold were also found there. Today the landscape has returned to nature, a beautiful, gentle and green landscape down in the valley, but rising up through a steep and rugged pass in the southwest before descending to Buttermere.

▶ The Pennine Way

The country's premier National Trail, which follows the high Pennine ridge, has something to offer every long-distance walker. If you want to test your stamina and endurance, you could walk the whole 270 miles from the Peak District National Park along the Pennine ridge through the Yorkshire Dales, up into Northumberland and across the Cheviots. Twenty miles of the route heads through East Cumbria from Alston through Garrigill and over Cross Fell – which at 2,930 feet is the highest point on the Pennine Way – then through Great Dun Fell towards Dufton and on to High Cup Nick and Cow Green Reservoir, which are on the border between Cumbria and County Durham.

▲ Penrith Castle

▸ **Penrith**

Another border market town that was vulnerable to Scottish raiders is Penrith and in fact it was sacked in the 14th century. Penrith Beacon on Beacon Hill at the town's northern edge was lit to warn the inhabitants of impending raids, and today it is a good viewpoint. The ruined red sandstone castle, which stands in Castle Park, dates from the early 15th century.

There are many more buildings of architectural and historical interest, including Penrith Museum and the Church of St Andrew. the graveyard here contains the reputed grave of Caesarius, the giant 10th-century Cumbrian king.

Just one mile south of Penrith at Eamont Bridge stands Mayburgh Henge. Dating from prehistoric times, its 15-foot banks surround an area of 1.5 acres, inside which is a huge and solitary stone. Close by, King Arthur's Round Table is another ancient henge monument.

Wetheriggs Pottery, four miles south of Penrith, has been here since 1855 and you can still see the steam-powered pottery site. When the pottery closed, its buildings were converted into an animal sanctuary.

Rheged Discovery Centre on the A66, interprets the history of the area through film and a range of innovative techniques. It has some useful shops, play areas and a cafe.

TAKE IN SOME HISTORY
Penrith Castle
Opposite Penrith railway station

The castle was built in the 14th century to protect the town against border raids, and it then became a residence of Richard III in the 15th century. Although the castle is now in ruins, some of the walls stand to their full height. If you are looking for somewhere to picnic in Penrith, the park where this castle stands is an ideal spot.

VISIT THE MUSEUM
Penrith and Eden Museum
eden.gov.uk
Robinson's School, CA11 7PT
01768 865105

You will find Penrith Museum and Tourist Information Centre in the former Robinson's School, an Elizabethan building altered in 1670 and used as a school until the early 1970s. The building is an ideal starting point if you want to explore Penrith. The museum covers the history, geology and archaeology of the area. Exhibits include some Roman pottery from the Roman Fort near Plumpton, and 'cup and ring' stones from Maughanby. There are also displays and information relating to Lady Anne Clifford, who was powerhouse of energy in 17th-century Cumbria. There's also a temporary gallery with changing exhibitions of local interest.

MEET THE ANIMALS
Wetheriggs Animal Rescue and Conservation Centre
wetheriggszoo.co.uk
Clifton Dykes, CA10 2DH
01768 866657 | Open daily Apr–Oct 10–5. Closes at 4 in winter

Wetheriggs is an animal rescue centre with a mixture of farm and exotic animals. Children will love it here as they can get very close to the animals. It operates as a registered charity and all the proceeds go towards rescuing and looking after the animals. You can also learn about the heritage of the steam-powered pottery and engine room, and paint your own pot. There is a pond, play area, petting farm and reptile house, cafe and gift shop, all

▼ Mayburgh Henge

set in 7.5 acres of the beautiful Eden Valley.

ENTERTAIN THE FAMILY
The Rheged Centre
see page 204

SEE A LOCAL CHURCH
Church of St Andrew
Kings Street, CA11 7XX
Rebuilt in 1720 on an ancient site, St Andrew's is said to have been modelled on Wren's St Andrew's Church in Holborn, London. The original 13th-century tower here still stands, while the nave and chancel is built of regular sandstone blocks. The splendid and spacious Georgian internal layout is intact, with its galleries on three sides supported by two tiers of columns, and a richly decorated box-panelled ceiling. Colourful Victorian murals surround the large, vibrant stained-glass east window. In the graveyard is the Giant's Grave, a grave consisting of two tall Norse crosses between which lie four hogback stones, or grave markers. Legend has it that this is either the grave of Owen Caesarius, King of Cumbria 920–37, or his son.

GO FISHING
Blencarn Lake Stillwater Trout Fly Fishing
tuftonarmshotel.co.uk
Near Penrith | 01768 88284
First impressions of this rainbow trout fishing lake simply take your breath away. Cross Fell and the North Pennines form a majestic backdrop to this attractive spring-fed, 15-acre lake with excellent stillwater fly fishing for rainbow trout. Kenny Stamper, the owner, rears the rainbow trout on site and optimum numbers are maintained. There's a little bothy with toilets and an area to eat and to boil a kettle. Recommended flies when fly fishing this rainbow trout lake are Lake Olives, Buzzers, Daddies, Pheasant Tail Nymphs, Hoppers and White Lures.

PLAY A ROUND
Penrith Golf Club
penrithgolfclub.co.uk
Salkeld Road, CA11 8SG
01768 891919
This beautiful, well-balanced course is always changing direction and demanding good length from the tee. It is set on rolling moorland with occasional pine trees and splendid views of the mountains of the northern Lake District.

EAT AND DRINK
Cross Keys Inn
kyloes.co.uk
Carleton Village, CA11 8TP
01768 865588
Located on the edge of Penrith, with sweeping views to the nearby North Pennines from the upstairs restaurant, this is a much-refurbished old drovers' and coaching inn. Traditional pub meals are the order of the day with only Cumbrian meats used. You'll find appreciative

locals warming their toes by the ferocious log-burner or laying a few tiles on the domino tables, while drinking beer crafted in nearby Broughton Hall by Tirril Brewery.

Greystone House Farm Shop and Tearoom

Stainton, CA11 0EF | 01768 866952

The oak-beamed loft house tea room is a great place to sample some of the locally sourced ingredients sold in the shop. Lunches, snacks, home-baked scones and cakes are all freshly prepared and a speciality is the farm's own beef and lamb.

North Lakes Hotel & Spa ◉

shirehotels.com

Ullswater Road, CA11 8QT

01768 868111

The North Lakes is just the spot if you want to explore the great outdoors, but if hill-walking isn't your bag, you can come here to indulge in spa treatments or swim in the pool. In the restaurant and bar, oak beams and six real fires help create the feel of a hunting lodge. The menus specialise in comfort food and they've got a children's menu and early bird option, as well as locally brewed Daniel Thwaites ales.

▸ **PLACES NEARBY**

Lakeland Bird of Prey Centre

visitcumbria.com

Old Walled Garden, Lowther

CA10 2HH | 01931 712746

Open daily 11–5

There are flying demonstrations with 150 falcons, hawks, eagles, buzzards and owls from this country and abroad. The birds fly every day at 2pm and you can actually have them come to you. Children particularly like this. The bird handler is very knowledgeable and will tell you all about the birds and answer any questions. There is a small tea room serving snacks and cakes.

Church of St Andrew

Church Road, Greystoke, CA11 0TL

This church is famous for its ancient choir stalls in the chancel with carved misericords featuring Christian symbols such as a pelican and a dragon, and a fine collection of medieval glass. According to village lore, the glass was removed in haste and buried as Cromwell and his army approached, and then finally restored in 1848. But the restorers had difficulty in re-assembling the pieces in the original order and substituted fragments from other, destroyed, windows. In the East window look at the extreme left, middle height, and you will see a curious sight – a red devil beneath the feet of a bishop – but the devil was originally in another window, whispering to Eve in the Garden of Eden.

The bestiary window on the north side of the chancel is the oldest glass; other ancient glass is behind the organ and in the clear window above the Lady Chapel altar. Because of the value of this clear glass, fragments have been joined with lead.

Modern times have left their mark on St Andrew's too. A sculpture of the Madonna and Child was carved by two German prisoners of war who were stationed at Carlisle at the end of World War II. Another, of the crucified Christ on the west wall, is by the sculptor Josefina de Vasconcellos, who lived in Cumbria.

Look for the stone by the path leading from the church to Thorpe. Known as the Plague Stone, its hollowed top, which fills with rainwater, may have once held vinegar in which coins were purified when plague victims paid their dues.

Yanwath

A small village between the North Pennines and the hills bounding Ullswater. Yanwath Hall, on the southern side of the River Eamont, is a splendidly preserved low 14th-century pele tower and a 15th-century hall, reputed to be the finest manorial hall in England.

The Yanwath Gate Inn

yanwathgate.com
Yanwath, CA10 2LF | 01768 862386
This is the former 17th-century toll gate, or 'yat', on the long road from Kendal to Scotland. Today's incarnation is a place where 'free range' and 'organic' are the watchwords. Menus vary according to what is seasonally and locally available, with the Eden Valley providing much of the produce. With your meal, you can sample authentic Trappist beer, wine from an excellent list or a beer from one of the local breweries.

Queen's Head Inn

queensheadinn.co.uk
Tirril, CA10 2JF | 01768 863219
Dating from 1719, this traditional English inn is chock-full of beams, flagstones and memorabilia. As well as enjoying a pint of Unicorn, Cumbria Way or Dizzy Blonde, you'll find they serve decent pub grub. Notice the original hooks used for smoking meats that are still in the fireplace.

Church of St Michael

Finkle Street, Pooley Bridge, off the B5320, CA10 2LR
In open countryside with views to the Lakeland fells, the church is on a mound in the centre of a circular graveyard, perhaps a pre-Christian site. The church has a squat 12th-century central tower, with narrow windows, which may have been used for defence during the border raids. Although the church has been extended, you can still clearly see the original Norman structure in the recently exposed stonework. All four corners of the Norman nave survive, and the north and south aisles were added in the 13th and early 14th centuries. Have a look at the attractive, stained-glass west window, designed by Charles Kempe in 1912.

▶ Ravenglass

Up to 1,000 Romans were garrisoned in Ravenglass, and the fort and harbour at Ravenglass were known to them as *Glannoventa*. Little remains of this settlement, just a short stroll to the south of the village, except for the ruins of the bath house. Ravenglass today comprises a short street of houses that ends abruptly at a slipway down to the beach and the estuaries of the rivers Mite and Esk. The town is now best known for the Ravenglass and Eskdale Railway, affectionately known as 'La'al Ratty'.

TAKE A TRAIN RIDE

Ravenglass & Eskdale Railway
ravenglass-railway.co.uk
CA18 1SW | 01229 717171 | Open mid-Mar–early Nov daily, most winter weekends, daily between Xmas & New Year & Feb half term. Call or check website for timetable. Discounts for online booking
The Lake District's oldest, longest and most scenic steam railway, stretching from the coast at Ravenglass, through two of Lakeland's loveliest valleys for seven miles to Dalegarth Visitor Centre and the foot of England's highest mountains. There are at least seven trains daily from March to November, plus winter weekends and holiday periods. If you have children, this is a perfect day out for them. Check the website for all sorts of children's activities with Ratty the Water-vole Stationmaster and special event days. Though it is now one of the most popular visitor attractions in western Lakeland, the line has had a distinctly chequered career. The railway – with a

▼ Ravenglass and Eskdale Railway

three-foot gauge track – was built in 1875, to carry iron ore and a few passengers from the Eskdale mines down to the coast and the main Furness line. When the mines became unprofitable, the railway closed. Then on a narrower 15-inch gauge track, it reopened in 1913 to serve Eskdale's granite quarries and to carry a few tourists until it came to a halt once again in 1953. Fortunately, a group of enthusiasts bought up the line in 1960 to run it as a tourist attraction.

Ravenglass Roman Bath House
english-heritage.org.uk
CA18 1RW | 0870 333 1181
Opening times vary. Call or check website for details
The remains of the bath house are among the tallest Roman structures in northern Britain: the walls still stand almost 13 feet high. You can also see the earthworks of the fort near the bath house.

WALK THE CUMBERLAND WAY
This is an old path and no longer completely signposted. It is tough and you have to be fit but it takes you through the heart of the Lake District. It is about 80 miles from Ravenglass to Appleby and takes about a week to 10 days to complete. It takes you to remote Wastwater, the most atmospheric of all the lakes, through spectacular scenery over Black Sail Pass and then below the high peaks – Great Gable, Scafell Pike, Pillar and Haystacks. There's another high-level route to the gentler Newlands Valley, the shores of Derwent Water and Keswick. From here you climb again to the Castlerigg Stone Circle (see page 101), with views back to Derwent Water and Bassenthwaite Lake. You continue through high moorland and farmland and come in sight of the Pennines before finally reaching Appleby.

Top 5 fells

▶ **Scafell Pike**, 3,210 feet/978m

▶ **Scafell**, 3,162 feet/963m

▶ **Helvellyn**, 3116 feet/949m, page 150

▶ **Skiddaw**, 3,054 feet/931m, page 215)

▶ **Great Gable**, 2,949 feet/899m, page 137)

EXPLORE BY BIKE
The Eskdale Trail

Have a cycling day out with a difference. Take your bike on a converted carriage on the Ravenglass & Eskdale Railway then ride from the foot of the Scafell range via riverside pastures, meadows and historic oak woods of the Eskdale Valley back down to Ravenglass. The train ride from Ravenglass to Dalegarth takes 40 minutes, biking down around two hours, depending on how often you stop. It's easy biking most of the way on country lanes, rough tracks and fields, though it can be muddy at times. On the way look out for red squirrels, roe deer and buzzards or you could visit Muncaster Castle (see page 190) or St Bega's Church (see page 205).

EAT AND DRINK
The Pennington Hotel ❀

penningtonhotels.com
CA18 1SQ | 0845 4506445
This refurbished 16th-century coaching inn, overlooking the estuary, is an appealing blend of period character and smart contemporary style. It is just a stone's throw from the sea and Muncaster Castle, whose historic kitchen gardens provide freshly picked seasonal fruit and herbs. The kitchen focuses on care, skill and simple good food.

▶ PLACES NEARBY

Tiny Boot, with a population of less than 100, can be found along the Ravenglass and Eskdale Railway. Picturesque Eskdale is another popular stop and a good base for walking. The hamlet of Santon Bridge in the Wasdale Valley is laid out around the bridge over the River Irt. It's famous for its World's Biggest Liar contest, held each November at the Bridge Inn.

Eskdale Mill

eskdalemill.co.uk
CA191TG | 01946 723335
Open Apr–Sep 11.30–5.30 (occasionally closed Mon & Sat, check website for details), Oct–Mar by arrangement, call for details
Eskdale Mill promises a fascinating day out, as here you can take a tour of the historic machinery of one of the oldest water-powered corn mills in England. The setting on the leafy banks of Whillan Beck, cascading down from the flanks of Scafell is truly stunning. The miller's tour is a mixture of tales of historic characters, demonstration of the workings of the mill and answering any questions you care to fire at him.

Boot Inn

bootinneskdale.co.uk
Boot, CA19 1TG | 01946 723224
The Boot Inn dates back to the 17th century. Although renovated, it retains much of its historic character. This is a friendly pub, good for families. There are glorious views of the surrounding fells from the conservatory. They serve simple freshly cooked food all day.

Brook House Inn

brookhouseinn.co.uk

Boot, CA19 1TG | 019467 23288

Lakeland fells rise behind the inn to England's highest peak, while footpaths wind to nearby Stanley Ghyll's wooded gorge with its falls, red squirrels and the charming La'al Ratty narrow-gauge railway steams to and from the coast. There's a small drying room for walkers' or cyclists' wet gear. Up to nine real ales are kept, an amazing selection of 175 malt whiskies and there are 10 excellent wines available by the glass. They serve lunch and dinner and the food is homemade, simply prepared from Cumbria's finest produce with a decent vegetarian selection. This is a great community pub and it participates in the Boot Beer Festival each June.

Fellbites

ravenglass-railway.co.uk

Dalegarth Station, CA19 1TF

01229 717171

At the valley terminus of 'La'al Ratty' the Fellbites cafeserves a trainload of passengers at a time with freshly cooked, locally sourced food. Not to mention that it's handily placed for the train back to Ravenglass.

Bower House Inn

bowerhouseinn.co.uk

Eskdale Green, CA19 1TD

019467 23244

Walkers, families and dogs are welcome and you'll find good pub grub at this traditional Lake District hotel, which has been serving locals and walkers since the 17th century. Inside, oak beams, ticking clocks and crackling log fires create a comfortable atmosphere to enjoy a pint of Bower House bitter in the bar, which opens out on to the garden. The restaurant has candlelit tables, exposed stone and log fires.

King George IV Inn

kinggeorge-eskdale.co.uk

Holmrook, Eskdale, CA19 1TS

019467 23470

Another traditional coaching inn is the King George IV, which provides a warm welcome for walkers, families and dogs. Inside you'll find open fires and flagged floors. They serve a range of food from plain and wholesome to more sophisticated dishes and there's a good range of beers.

Bridge Inn

santonbridgeinn.com

CA19 1UX | 019467 26221

The Lake District was formed, not by ice or volcanic action, but by large moles and eels. Actually, that's a lie, one of the many told in this comfortable old inn at the annual World's Biggest Liar competition, held every November. No doubt pints of local real ales help to inspire such outrageous fibbing. Main courses here are traditional and hearty, pub grub. The inn is licensed for civil marriages, when, hopefully, 'I do' is not a lie.

Woodlands
santonbridge.co.uk
Santon Bridge, Near Holmrook
CA19 1UY | 019467 26281
With a great view of the local red squirrels, Woodlands tea room is attached to the Santon Bridge Craft Shop and concentrates on providing wholesome homemade food. It's handy for visiting Muncaster Castle and Eskdale, as well as Wasdale. Browse through the pretty craft shop while you are here. You will find a range of china, ceramics, leather goods, sheepskins and much more to take home with you.

▷ Rheged

rheged.com
Redhills, CA11 0DQ | 01768 868000 | Open all year daily 10–5.30
Rheged was the name of an ancient Celtic kingdom that dominated northwest England and southern Scotland in the sixth century AD. Today it is Cumbria's largest visitor complex, and Europe's largest grass-covered building. You could happily spend a rainy day or two rattling around in here. As well as the theatre, cafes, specialist food shops and shops selling outdoor gear, books and toys, there is a large exhibition space, which hosts touring exhibitions from time to time. You can watch a changing selection of movies suitable for all the family on a giant screen and there are both indoor and outdoor play areas for children.

▷ Rydal Mount & Gardens

see page 206

▷ St Bees

St Bees is the start of Lake District walking writer Alfred Wainwright's most celebrated route, the 192-mile Coast-to-Coast walk to Robin Hood's Bay in North Yorkshire. The impressive sandstone cliffs of St Bees Head rise to 300 feet.

Out to sea are views across the Irish Sea to the Isle of Man and over the Solway Firth to the hills of Galloway in Scotland. This part of the coast is Cumbria's only Heritage Coast, with land on the cliffs forming the St Bees Head RSPB Reserve. From the viewing areas, maintained by a seasonal warden, you can watch the noisy birdlife nesting on the cliffs below. Many thousands of birds return here each spring to lay their eggs and hatch their chicks before returning to the sea, where they spend three-quarters of their lives. Most prolific are the guillemots, which resemble dumpy little penguins; some 5,000 squeeze precariously onto the narrow open ledges. Razorbills, not so common, can also be seen here along with fulmars, gulls and some 1,600 pairs of kittiwakes.

The first St Bees Lighthouse consisted of a round tower of some 30 feet in height, supporting a large metal coal grate. It was the last coal-fired lighthouse in use in Great Britain when it burned down in 1822. The present lighthouse, which replaced it the same year, was automated in 1987 and is now monitored by Trinity House Operations Control Centre at Harwich in Essex.

In the village is the Church of St Mary and St Bega, once the nave of a priory that was partly demolished after the Reformation: the massive west door has fine Norman stonework. St Bega is said to have been an Irish princess who fled across the sea in the ninth century to escape an enforced marriage.

SEE A LOCAL CHURCH
Priory Church of St Mary and St Bega
Abbey Road, off the B5345, CA27 0DR

The splendid 12th-century Priory Church of St Mary and St Bega has a magnificent tower, which is a significant landmark in the village. The south transept, the base of the tower and the west door remain from the original 12th-century building. Have a good look at the west door with its five semi-circular arches decorated with beaked heads of men and serpents. In the wall opposite the door is the Dragon Stone, which has a carving of St Michael killing a dragon.

The priory has had a number of restorations. In 1855–68, the outstanding decorative chancel screen was installed, along with bright tiles and patterns designed to take the place of an east window. Before the restoration, the priory had a flat ceiling with box pews in the nave; in the 1960s, a central aisle was created. Within the church there are a number of carved stones, medieval slabs and effigies dating from the 10th century onwards, as well as part of the shroud of St Bees Man, one of England's best-preserved medieval bodies, which was found in the priory during an archaeological dig in 1981. A ninth-century carved Celtic cross stands in the graveyard, a reminder of the pre-Norman church that once stood on this site.

HIT THE BEACH
St Bees
St Bees Bay extends in a long sweep from the promenade to Seamill Lane about a mile away. At low tide it is a vast expanse of red sand and rock pools. At the foot of the cliffs there is a shingle bank composed of dozens of types of rock sloping down to the sand. For two to

▶ Rydal Mount & Gardens

rydalmount.co.uk

LA22 9LU | 015394 33002 | Open Mar–Oct daily 9.30–5, Nov–Dec & Feb Wed–Sun 11–4. Closed Jan

Rydal Mount was William Wordsworth's home from 1813 until his death in 1850. He came to this lime-washed yeoman's house on May Day. 'The weather is delightful and the place a Paradise,' wrote his sister Dorothy. His was a large household – it included not only the poet and his wife Mary, but his three surviving children and Mary's sister Sarah Hutchinson, as well as Dorothy. The move was partly financed by Wordsworth's appointment as Distributor of Stamps for Westmorland, which brought him his first and only steady income, and earned Browning's scorn: 'Just for a handful of silver he left us,' he wrote in *The Lost Leader*, 'Just for a riband to stick in his coat.'

More than half of Wordsworth's published poetry was written at Rydal Mount. The house was originally a farm built in 1550; the dining room still has its early timbers and slate floor and was enlarged about the middle of the 18th century. Wordsworth was particularly attracted to the traditional style of the house and its spectacular views over Rydal Water and Windermere.

He never owned the house but leased it from the le Flemings of nearby Rydal Hall.

Wordsworth believed that a house and its garden should harmonise with each other and with its locality, and the garden here is still much as he left it, with terraces stretching across the hillside. The highest was already there when he took over the house, but he added two others – one so that Dorothy could be pushed in her invalid chair to enjoy the view. Wordsworth would pace along behind, booming new poems to himself. If you visit on a spring day you will find nearby Dora's Field – bought for, and named after, the poet's daughter – crowded with wild daffodils. Even those who cannot recall another line of his poetry will know about the 'host of golden daffodils', a walk that his sister Dorothy took along the shores of Ullswater, recorded in her diary, inspired the poem.

While living in Rydal Mount, William Wordsworth accepted the post of Poet Laureate at the age of 73, but on the strict condition that he would not be expected to compose verses on demand, the bane of most Poet Laureates.

The house was bought in 1969 by Mary Henderson, the poet's great great-granddaughter, and opened to the public the following year, displaying mementoes of a life devoted to literature and the Romantic movement.

three hours on either side of high tide only the shingle is clear of the water. The beach was awarded a 2013 Quality Coast Award in recognition of its cleanliness.

Fleswick Bay

This bay has one of the grandest situations of any beach in Britain between the North Head and the South Head of St Bees. You can only reach it on foot or by boat, as towering red sandstone cliffs enclose the shingle beach. If you want to walk here, you can cross the footbridge at the north end of the promenade and walk up the South Head and along the cliff path. There is a footpath down to Fleswick Bay. There is no sand, but a very fine shingle. At one time the shingle had many semi-precious stones, such as agates, but years of collection by visitors have made these rare; have a look though, you might find one along with the odd pretty pebble or two.

GO WALKING

Coast-to-Coast Walk

This 190-mile walk from St Bees Head to Robin Hood's Bay, North Yorkshire, was created by Alfred Wainwright (see page 36). It passes through some of the most beautiful and varied scenery in the country, the rugged mountains and beautiful lakes of the Lake District, the rolling hills and pretty valleys of the Yorkshire Dales and the expansive heather moorland of the North York Moors, with some dramatic coastal scenery at each end. Wainwright suggested a way of breaking the walk miles into stages, each of which to be completed in a day. With one or two rest days, this makes the route fit into a two-week holiday. However, Wainwright explicitly stated that he did not intend people to necessarily stick to these stages or even to his route: for example, by reducing day-lengths to

▼ The coastline of St Bees

10 or 12 miles, the walk becomes a much easier three-week trip with time to 'stand and stare'.

Although unofficial, the Coast-to-Coast Walk uses public rights of way, public footpaths, tracks and minor roads and is one of the most popular of all the long-distance footpaths in the UK. Much of it is now waymarked, but you still need your map and compass for this walk and a copy of Alfred Wainwright's book will add even more to your enjoyment. Wainwright recommended dipping your toes in the Irish Sea at St Bees at the start of the Coast-to-Coast Walk and dipping your toes in the North Sea at Robin Hood's Bay at the end. In between, as well as the scenery you will enjoy the camaraderie of fellow walkers, the welcoming inns with dark, time-worn beams, cosy nooks and open fires and the satisfaction of achievement at the end.

PLAY A ROUND
St Bees Golf Club
stbeesgolfclub.org.uk
Peckmill, Beach Rd, CA27 0EJ
01946 824300
Overlooking St Bees beach, this picturesque 10-hole layout on the cliffs was originally designed as a golf course for St Bees School. It has glorious views of the Solway Firth and the Isle of Man. Although it's not very long there are some testing hazards for golfers of all abilities.

▶ Sedbergh

Thanks to the quirks of local government boundary changes, the largest town in the Yorkshire Dales National Park is actually in Cumbria. Even so, Sedbergh's population is still under 3,000. To the north are the high Howgill Fells. To the south the green fields fall away, across the River Rawthey to the River Dee, which runs through Dentdale. Take some time to explore this delightful and historic little town.

The old buildings of Sedbergh are its main attraction. Much of the Main Street has been designated a Conservation Area. As well as narrow alleys and tucked-away yards, Main Street contains many fine dwellings. Webster's Chemist's Shop dates from the first half of the 17th century, and behind it is Weaver's Yard, where the first weaving looms in Sedbergh were set up. From here, just at the back of Webster's, a 17th-century chimney breast can be seen – one of the many places around Britain in which Bonnie Prince Charlie is said to have hidden at one time or another. You'll also find lots of book shops because Sedbergh is a 'Book Town' and holds a Book Festival each September and lots of other book events.

Little remains of the Norman castle save a few grassy mounds, but the Church of St Andrew is worth seeing, with its ancient pews and alms boxes. Close by is the minuscule Market Place, where a market has been held for almost 750 years. The Market Cross was removed in 1897 when Finkle Street was widened and other alterations made to the town as part of Queen Victoria's Diamond Jubilee celebrations. The top of the cross now stands in the garden of the Quaker Meeting House in Brigflatts, a tiny village, just over one mile away. The Meeting House, built in 1675, can still be visited. It is the oldest in the north of England and retains many of its original furnishings.

ENTERTAIN THE FAMILY
Holme Open Farm
holmeopenfarm.co.uk
Off A683, LA10 5ET | 015396 20654
Open Mar–Sep Wed–Mon 10–5.
Closed Tue
Holme Open Farm is a traditional dales working farm. You can take a tour of the farm, giving children chance to touch, hold and feed as many different types of animal as possible. Holding and bottle-feeding baby lambs is really exciting; stroking the goats and kids is fun; sometimes being nibbled by them produces shrieks of laughter. And even the most timid children love feeding the tiny chicks. There are also ducks, geese, pigs, ponies and kittens. You can take a wander with the kids on the nature trail through the 120-acre farm, where you'll see a variety of birds, plants and other wildlife. There's even a badger hide where you can sit in the evening and watch quietly for these nocturnal beasts.

GO FISHING
Rawthey, also Clough and Dee
Permits available from Three Peaks Ltd, 25 Main Street, LA10 5BN
015396 20446
The Rawthey, which flows south from the Howgill Fells behind Sedbergh, is open and easy to fish it but it doesn't hold quite as many trout as the Dee, which flows down Dentdale. The Rawthey has sea trout and salmon later in the season.

EAT AND DRINK
The Cross Keys Temperance Inn
cautleyspout.co.uk
Cautley, LA10 5NE | 015396 20284
The Cross Keys is a 400-year-old National Trust, located at the base of Cautley Spout. It has a small farmhouse-style restaurant, serving lunches, snacks and evening meals. All the food is home cooked and prepared using fresh local produce where possible. You should note that this really is a temperance inn and serves no alcohol, but they are quite happy to provide glasses and a corkscrew without a corkage charge for your own drink. The famous Cumbrian ham and eggs is always the menu. On Sundays, they always prepare

▲ The confluence of the rivers Rawthey and Dee near Sedbergh

a roast and it's best to book a table, as it's a very popular little place.

Dalesman Country Inn
thedalesman.co.uk
Main Street, LA10 5BN
015396 21183
This family business is a free house and serves an ever-changing range of cask ales, wines and spirits. They have five cask ale pumps, which they change as often as possible but they keep people's favourites such as Timothy Taylor, Old Speckled Hen, Black Sheep and Tunnel Vision while mixing other beers from time to time. The food menu changes with the seasons and where possible all ingredients are sourced locally such as their lamb from Hebblethwaite – less than two miles away.

Duo Café, Bar & Bistro
duo-sedbergh.co.uk
32 Main Street, LA10 5BL
015396 20552
At this friendly little cafe you will find a delicious selection of homemade light bites, main meals, snacks and cakes using fresh local produce and a wide variety of drinks. Pop in for and try a Yorkshire tea or latte with your full English in the morning or a glass of wine or beer with your Cumberland sausage and mash in the afternoon.

Ewe Tree Café
holmeopenfarm.co.uk
Off A683, LA10 5ET | 015396 20654
You can get a range of snacks and baking at this little tea room and, while you're waiting, browse the gift shop.

Settle–Carlisle Railway
settle-carlisle.co.uk
Appleby Station, CA16 6TT
see page 61

GO WALKING
Guided Walks
foscl.org.uk/guided-walks
Settle–Carlisle Railway
There are guided walks from several stations in the Eden Valley (see page 61). Check the website for the current programme.

▶ Silecroft

Silecroft is a relaxed coastal village and beach a few miles to the north of Millom on the A 5093. It is a small pleasant resort, overlooked by the 1800-foot-high Black Combe from where, on a clear day, you can see Scotland, Wales, the Isle of Man and 14 counties of England.

HIT THE BEACH

Silecroft and Haverigg are both award-winning, extensive sandy beaches. There's plenty of space for children to play as well as other activities such as angling, kiting, dog walking and horse-riding. Silecroft has a quality coast award for its clean waters and facilities, while Haverigg is a Blue Flag beach with a restored lighthouse.

PLAY A ROUND

Silecroft Golf Club
silecroftgolfclub.co.uk
LA18 4NX | 01229 770467
Parallel to the coast of the Irish Sea, this seaside links course has spectacular views inland of Lakeland hills. It looks deceptively easy but you will find that an ever-present sea breeze ensures a sporting challenge.

▶ Silloth

Silloth is a small town on the shores of the Solway Firth, facing the hills of Southern Galloway and backed by the Lake District Fells. Turner, the famous landscape artist painted some of Silloth's glorious sea views and sunsets. Economically it relies heavily on the number of caravan parks in the surrounding countryside. It is also the venue for Silloth Beer Festival every September (www.sillothbeerfestival.co.uk) and Solfest music festival (www.solfest.org.uk) which is held on the August bank holiday and attracts over 10,000 visitors. After ten years Solfest is having a year off in 2014 but will be back in 2015.

VISIT THE MUSEUM

Solway Coast Discovery Centre
solwaycoastonb.org.uk
Liddle Street, CA7 4DD
016973 31944 | Open Mon, Wed, Fri 10–5, Sat 10–4. Closed Tue, Thu, Sun
There's something to keep the whole family interested here, as this exhibition interprets 10,000 years of the Solway's history. It describes the wildlife, heritage, landscape and communities. It shows a historic timeline from the last ice age, through the spread of forests that were home to wolves and giant deer, the clearing of the forests for farming, the Romans and later the Vikings and then to the Norman Conquest. Place names, field sizes, drainage ditches and saltmarsh ponds are all explained. The Industrial Revolution exhibit describes ports, canals and railways until we reach the present day. The

new art exhibition includes the work of local artists and has a bi-monthly featured artist. The Tourist Information Centre is also here, with exhibitions about the history of Silloth Airfield and the Carlisle to Silloth railway.

HIT THE BEACH
Grune Point
North of Silloth, Grune Point is a sandy, raised shingle beach approximately one mile long. You'll find a variety of interesting plants here including sea sandwort, sea holly and sand couch-grass. Note that bathing is not safe when the tide is ebbing.

TAKE THE ALLERDALE RAMBLE
If you're feeling energetic, try this 55-mile walk from the Borrowdale Valley that ends at Silloth. It is an excellent route through a fascinating variety of land and seascapes, which most people complete in four to five days. From central Lakeland the route heads north along the western side of Borrowdale and Derwent Water to Keswick. Here you can either cross the foothills of Skiddaw or go over the summit, then head along the Derwent Valley to Cockermouth. From here onwards you are in a much flatter pastoral landscape to the coast at Maryport, where you turn along the coastline enjoying the amazing panorama that is visible across the Solway Firth.

PLAY A ROUND
Silloth on Solway Golf Club
sillothgolfclub.co.uk
The Clubhouse, CA7 4BL
016973 31304
A championship links course with stunning views to the Lake District and across the Solway to Scotland. You'll find that the dunes, narrow fairways and heather and gorse make these superb links on the Solway an exhilarating and searching test.

EAT AND DRINK
The Gincase Tearoom
gincase.co.uk
Mawbray Hayrigg, CA7 4LL
016973 32020
Located in a converted farm building, this tea room is housed where once horses would have powered a grinding stone. There is also a shop, art gallery and rare breed animal park, so you can browse away an hour or two over a leisurely lunch or home baking.

▶ PLACES NEARBY
Beckfoot Beach
A flat sandy beach, south of Silloth, popular for fishing, this area is designated as an area of Historic and Scientific Interest and an Area of Outstanding Natural Beauty. There are spectacular views, particularly at sunset, across the Solway Firth towards the coast of Scotland.

Sizergh Castle & Gardens
nationaltrust.org.uk
LA8 8AE | 015395 60951 | House open Mar–Nov, Mon, Thu & Sun 1–5.

Garden, cafe & shop open 4 Jan–9 Feb & 1–8 Mar, Sat–Sun 11–4, 10–23 Feb & 3 Nov–Dec, daily 10–5. Closed 25 Dec. Timed tickets apply Sun, BHs and school holidays

Just a mile north of Levens Hall (see page 180) is Sizergh Castle, now owned by the National Trust, although the Strickland family still live here. In 1239, the heiress of Sizergh Castle married into the Strickland family, and their occupancy of the castle has been unbroken except for a short time when the family accompanied King James II into exile.

The fact that it has been lived in by the same family since before 1239 makes the story of its history more immediate. You can see their ancestors in portraits on the walls along with the Stuarts that they supported. You can see the furniture that they acquired over the centuries and most of the house is their Tudor additions to the original pele tower. The pele tower dates from the Scottish border raids of the 14th century.

You can still see parts of the intricately inlaid panelling of the Inlaid Chamber, which was sold in 1891 to the V&A in London. The museum has loaned two panels back to Sizergh so that you can imagine how the room would have looked in its heyday. The museum also loaned the inlaid bed, which was made to match the room.

EAT AND DRINK

Low Sizergh Barn Farm Shop and Tearoom
lowsizerghbarn.co.uk
LA8 8AE | 015395 60426
Stop here for breakfast, cakes and pastries, soups, quiches and snacks, as well as a children's menu. All make use of fresh local ingredients from the farm shop, which also sells milk, fresh morning bread, and meat from locally reared animals, vegetables and the farm's free range eggs. Follow the farm trail through ancient woodlands, with an abundance of wildlife and plants.

The Strickland Arms
ainscoughs.co.uk/strickland-arms
LA8 8DZ | 015395 61010
You'll find this pub beside the lane leading to Sizergh Castle and just a stride from paths alongside the River Kent. The essentially open-plan interior is Edwardian, with high ceilings, flagstone floors and grand fires, creating an instantly welcoming atmosphere. You can enjoy classic pub grub, snacks and salads as well as a range of real ales.

▼ Sizergh Castle

▲ View of Skiddaw across Bassenthwaite Lake

▶ Skiddaw

When the Lakes first began to attract tourists in numbers in the 19th century, it was to Keswick that many of them came, and the one peak they would all walk to was Skiddaw. It is not the most attractive ascent lower down, but even though it rises to 3,054 feet (931m) it is a safe climb that most can manage in little more than two hours. You can even avoid the first 1,000 feet by parking above the village of Applethwaite, north of Keswick off the A591, and starting the climb from there. Wherever you start from, the path to Skiddaw is clearly signed. At peak times walkers will be going up in droves, so don't attempt it then if you want solitude.

However, even if you do have to share them, the views are spectacular. To the north are the Scottish mountains, and in the far west is the Isle of Man. The Pennine peaks rise to the east, while all around you can identify Lakeland's other hills and dales. If you want to escape the crowds, take the Cumbria Way (see page 94), which circles behind the main peak into the area known as 'Back o' Skiddaw'.

▶ Swinside Stone Circle

Millom

The Swinside Stone Circle is on a spur of Black Combe, a little-explored fell, off the A596 between Millom and Broughton-in-Furness. Though it is on private land, you can see the circle of 57 standing stones from the adjacent right of way. The circle is similar in size to Castlerigg stone circle, near Keswick, though the setting is somewhat bleaker.

Talkin Tarn
carlisle.gov.uk
CA8 1HN | 01697 73129
Ideal for boating, fishing and swimming, this 65-acre lake lays just north of Talkin at the heart of Talkin Tarn Country Park. There are sandy bays around the tarn and you can follow a sign-posted nature trail through attractive woodland. From the top of the wooded rise behind the Victorian boathouse there are some lovely views over the surrounding countryside.

GO FISHING
Talkin Tarn Country Park
carlisle.gov.uk
CA8 1HN | 01697 73129
You can fish here for pike and perch but all fish must be returned to the tarn. You need to buy a day permit on arrival and you will need an Environment Agency rod licence, unless you are under 12 years old.

EAT AND DRINK
The Boathouse Café
CA8 1HN | 01697 741050
Upstairs from one of the tarn's boathouses, this welcoming cafe is the perfect place to reflect on the view and tuck into homemade cakes and hot chocolate. There's also a little gift shop.

Blacksmiths Arms
blacksmithstalkin.co.uk
Talkin, CA8 1LE | 01697 73452
Facing the green in this picturesque Pennine fell-side village of Talkin, the Blacksmiths serves à la carte meals in a small restaurant or simpler fare in the lounge bars. You can always choose from a range of cask ales.

▲ Swinside Stone Circle, near Duddon Bridge

▷ Temple Sowerby

The houses in this pretty village, between Penrith and Appleby, cluster around the village green. The village gets its name from the Knights Templar, who as long ago as 1228 had a religious house here. The oldest parts of the present buildings date back to the 16th century and the remainder are mainly 18th and 19th century. This is the place to go to see and be inspired by a true host of golden daffodils. In spring you can see whole swathes of yellow bobbing in the wind beneath the grand oak trees in the gardens at Acorn Bank on the edge of the village.

Near Acorn Bank you can follow the Crowdundle beck to the River Eden and one of the largest bridges in the Eden Valley, spanning the river on four arches of red sandstone.

TAKE IN SOME HISTORY

**Acorn Bank Garden
and Watermill**
nationaltrust.org.uk
CA10 1SP | 017683 61893
Open 9 Feb–10 Mar weekends 10–5,
16 Mar–3 Nov, Wed–Mon 10–5
Particularly noted for its walled herb garden, this is a delightful garden, of some 2.5 acres. It contains the largest collection of medicinal, culinary and even narcotic herbs in northern Britain which includes some 250 species. Some are poisonous, so you are warned not to try nibbling them. There are traditional orchards, too, and fine collections of roses, shrubs and herbaceous borders. If you are a gardener,

you can stock up with plants from the small shop. The garden is not just of interest to gardeners, though. You can follow the circular woodland walk through the woods alongside Crowdundle Beck to the restored watermill.

EAT AND DRINK
Acorn Bank
nationaltrust.org
CA10 1SP | 017683 61893
A visit to Acorn Bank's tea room is the only chance you'll get to see inside this 17th-century mansion. You can get excellent homemade cakes, lunches and a children's menu along with Fair Trade teas and coffees.

The Kings Arms
kingsarmstemplesowerby.co.uk
CA10 1SB | 017683 62944
In 1799, William Wordsworth and Samuel Coleridge set off from this 400-year-old coaching inn for their exploration of the Lake District. Today the kitchen serves a mix of old pub grub and modern dishes. There is a good vegetarian choice and a children's menu

Temple Sowerby House Hotel & Restaurant ◉◉
templesowerby.com
CA10 1RZ | 017683 61578
This small-scale 18th-century country house hotel overlooks the village green and makes a great base for exploring the area. When you come in from the hills, warm up by a real fire in the winter, or on balmy days, sip an aperitif in the pretty walled garden before moving indoors to the smart dining room. The kitchen, which has retained its two AA Rosettes for 10 years, turns out an inventive bang-up-to-date British menu crammed with fine Cumbrian produce and local game.

▶ PLACES NEARBY
Church of St Lawrence
Church Lane, Morland, CA10 3AX
You'll find a wonderful mix of styles here, spanning 1,000 years. The tower is 11th century but its height was raised in 1588, and the small spire was added later. The nave and aisles are 12th century and include some Norman features. The chancel and transepts were added in the next century. The chancel was rebuilt in 1600, the north aisle in the 18th century and the church was restored in both the 19th and 20th centuries.

◀ Walled Herb Garden, Acorn Bank

▶ Thirlmere

The A591, from Grasmere to Keswick, runs along the eastern side of the long thin lake of Thirlmere. There's a car park at the southern end, near the 17th-century Wythburn chapel. From here a track leads up to Helvellyn (see page 150), and before 1879 many paths would have led downwards, too. For the chapel is all that remains of Wythburn village, flooded in the 1890s when Thirlmere was dammed at the northern end and turned into Manchester's first Lakeland reservoir. Armboth in the northwest is also now beneath the waters, along with several farms on the shores of the original lake.

Thirlmere, an attractive, tree-fringed expanse, is one of the few lakes that you can drive round, as well as walk around. There's a lovely drive down the western edge through the lakeside woods with several car parks, each with forest trails leading off from them. You can walk up one of the trails to the summit of Raven Crag, but you also get good views halfway down the western edge at Hause Point, where the lake was once narrow enough to have had a bridge running across to the other side.

▶ Townend

nationaltrust.org.uk

Troubeck, Windermere, LA23 1LB | 01539 432628 | Open mid-Mar–Nov Wed–Sun & BHs 1–5

Come here to see how Lakeland farmhouses used to look. This mainly 17th-century house has no electricity, and epitomizes the remoteness of the Lake District in centuries past. This fascinating house belonged to the farming Browne family for more than 300 years until it was taken over by the National Trust in 1943. You can see domestic implements, the down house for washing, cooking, pickling and brewing, and a firehouse with living quarters. You can also see the Brownes' hand-carved furniture. George Browne added his own designs to older pieces of furniture, copying older patterns – so that you sometimes can't tell which decorations were done by George, and which by his ancestors. He even added older dates and initials to his designs to make them look more antiquated. He carved the date 1687, together with the initials of his ancestors, into a bookcase he made in 1887.

George had a quirky sense of humour too. Look for the row of tiny, smiling faces in the fireplace in the main bedroom or the feet sticking out of a long case clock. His sense of humour and indeed his work was not appreciated by Beatrix Potter, who described him as 'the tiresome Mr Browne', who added 'copied patterns to a splendid old bedstead'. Don't miss the library with its unique collection of books, complete with turned-down corners and finger-marks. These amusing and often slightly bawdy storybooks were meant for the lower orders of society and beneath the attention of serious libraries, so they haven't survived elsewhere. You'll get a real sense of the ordinary people of the past, laughing and passing round passages from their favourite books.

▶ Troutbeck

Troutbeck is a Conservation Area. The houses here are spread out along narrow country lanes, around a number of wells and springs, without a recognisable centre. However, you will find a superb collection of buildings, dating from the 16th to the 19th centuries, with original features such as mullioned windows, heavy cylindrical chimneys and a rare example of an exposed spinning gallery. The best-preserved building in the Troutbeck Valley is Townend (see page 219) – a fine example of a yeoman farmer's house. Townend offers a fascinating glimpse into what domestic life was like for Lakeland's wealthier farmers, with its low ceilings, original home-carved oak panelling and furniture, and stone-flagged floors.

SEE A LOCAL CHURCH
Jesus Church
A592, LA23 1PE

A church has stood here since the 16th century. In 1736, however, the entire church was dismantled and rebuilt. The only remnants of this structure are the massive beams, the tiny three-light window in the tower and the coat of arms of George II, painted on wood in the gallery. Dating from the time of its 1861 restoration, the light and colourful east window was designed by Sir Edward Burne-Jones in collaboration with William Morris and Ford Madox Brown. According to local tradition, Morris and Madox Brown came to Troutbeck on a fishing holiday at the time when Burne-Jones was working on the window, and they stayed on in the Lake District to assist him.

SADDLE UP
Rookin House Equestrian and Activity Centre
rookinhouse.co.uk
CA11 0SS | 01768 483561

The centre caters to all levels of ability – from total beginners to experienced riders – and there's a choice of over 35 well-mannered horses and ponies of all shapes, sizes and temperaments. The rides, led by experienced instructors, go along bridleways and quiet country lanes, across open fells and through shady forests, offering glorious views of the Ullswater and Matterdale Valleys along the way.

Lakeland Pony Trekking
lakelandponytreks.co.uk
Limefitt Park, LA23 1PA
015394 31999

You can take rides or treks here combining some of the finest views and stunning scenery that the Lake District has to offer. With direct access on to the tracks and bridleways of the fells, the majority of rides have no road work. You can choose from a variety of fully supervised treks from half an hour to full-day rides, catering to all ages and levels of experience.

◀ Troutbeck

EAT AND DRINK
Queen's Head
queensheadtroutbeck.co.uk
Townhead, LA23 1PW
015394 32174

This 17th-century inn has cosy nooks and crannies, and a log fire burns all year. In ages past, farmers on their way home stuffed the low beams here with old pennies from market. Look below bar counter level at the carved panelling while ordering a pint of Dizzy Blonde. Well-behaved dogs on leads are allowed on the slated area in the bar, and there are toys and games for children.

International dishes are served here, ranging from French to South African, as well as hearty traditional British pub grub.

▶ Ullswater

This is the second largest lake in the Lake District, at around 9 miles long, 0.75 miles wide and just less than 200 feet deep at its deepest – and for many, it is the most beautiful of the lakes. On the western shores, some splendid waterfalls tumble down through the wooded gorge of Aira Beck into the lake. The largest is the 70-foot drop of Aira Force.

Near the falls you can find an arboretum, a cafe and a landscaped Victorian park. Back in 1802, William and Dorothy Wordsworth were walking near here, when Dorothy observed the 'daffodils so beautiful... they tossed and reeled and danced.' Her brother transformed her words into one of the best-known and best-loved of English poems, *Daffodils*. Aira Force itself inspired another of Wordsworth's poems, *The Somnambulist*.

The southern tip of the lake, below the shoulders of Helvellyn, is reached via the dramatic and high Kirkstone Pass, which rises to 1,489 feet. On the lake's northern tip, at Pooley Bridge, there used to be a fish market in the main square, and this area is still rich in trout and salmon.

If you take a short walk up to Dunmallard Hill you can see Iron Age remains. Below here from the pier near the 16th-century bridge, two 19th-century steamers, *Lady of the Lake* and *Raven*, take visitors down the lake. Combine a cruise with a walk to enjoy the lake and the land at their best. Near Howtown the lake narrows to about 400 yards at the strangely named Skelly Nab. The name comes from the freshwater herring, the schelly, found only here, in Haweswater and high up in the Red Tarn on Helvellyn. The silvery foot-long fish were once caught in nets strung between Skelly Nab and the opposite shore.

▶ Ullswater, seen from Hallin Fell

10 top walks

TAKE A BOAT TRIP
Ullswater Steamers
see page 42
The 'steamers', which have been diesel-powered since the 1930s, call at Pooley Bridge at the north end of the lake, then Howtown, roughly halfway along the eastern shore, then travel on to Glenridding (see page 128), at the southern end. So take a cruise from Pooley Bridge to Howtown, walk from here to Glenridding and hop back on the boat to Pooley Bridge and you'll not find a finer walk in the Lakes. There is no road through the steep cliffs of the lake's southeastern shore, so walking the 7.5-mile rough

footpath is the only way to see it. It really makes you appreciate the magnificent views across the waters, with Helvellyn rising beyond.

GO FISHING
Fishing here is free; a rod licence is all that you need. There are perch, perhaps an odd pike and schelly – an endangered and protected whitefish relic from the last ice age. However the only serious fishing is of wild brown trout. Boats are available for hire from St Patricks Boat Landings at Glenridding (see page 128). There are only a couple, so book well in advance.

EXPLORE BY BIKE
Park Foot Caravan Site
parkfootullswater.co.uk
Pooley Bridge, CA10 2NA
017684 86309 | Open mid-Mar–Oct. Opening varies with weather. Call for details
You can hire mountain bikes here with helmets and accessories for a day or a half-day. There is a range of sizes to suit all. You can't book in advance, except for large groups or a bike with a child seat, so turn up early if it is a fine day.

▶ **PLACES NEARBY**
Howtown is a hamlet and small harbour on the east shore of Ullswater. It is about 3.5 miles from Pooley Bridge and the Ullswater steamers regularly stop here.

Sharrow Bay Country House Hotel ◉◉

sharrowbay.co.uk

Sharrow Bay, CA10 2LZ

017684 86301

If any view is guaranteed to bring out the landscape artist or poet in you, it is the majestic, tranquil panorama over Ullswater enjoyed by the delightful Sharrow Bay Country House Hotel. The establishment recalls a venerable country house with cultivated, flawlessly courteous service. At its heart is the unreconstructed dining room, all pink flounce and heavily draped comfort. The food is classically based using quality Cumbrian produce, with a wide range of choice, including some new-fangled food combinations among the more traditional.

▶ Ulverston

If you want to get off the beaten track then Ulverston, on the fringe of Morecambe Bay, generally has a tranquil, unhurried air, although on Thursdays and Saturdays, you'll find the market square thronged with stalls. On top of Hoad Hill, overlooking the town, is a 90-foot copy of the Eddystone Lighthouse, which is a monument to Sir John Barrow, born in Ulverston in 1764.

He was a founder member of the Royal Geographical Society and his story is told in the town's heritage centre. Another famous son of Ulverston, Stan Laurel of the world-famous duo Laurel and Hardy, was born in Ulverston in 1890. Not surprisingly, therefore, one of the main attractions of the town is the tiny, quirky Laurel and Hardy Museum.

Ulverston has the shortest canal in Britain. At just one mile long it links the town to the sea. Built by the engineer John Rennie in 1794, it represents the high point of Ulverston's iron ore industrial history; nearby were the town's foundry and blast furnace. Ships could navigate along the canal into the town where they would be loaded with cargoes of iron and slate. The canal had a short working life of just 50 years, before the railway took over. Ulverston also went into decline as the iron ore industry gradually moved to Barrow. Today, the canal towpath provides a pleasant walk down to the sea.

TAKE IN SOME HISTORY

Swarthmoor Hall

swarthmoorhall.co.uk

LA12 0JQ | 01229 583204

See website for opening times

A 16th-century country house set in beautiful gardens and grounds amid 130 acres of farmland, Swarthmoor Hall has a real sense of place and of the people who have lived here. A new courtyard garden features a Living Quilt, a copy of a quilt in one of the bedrooms. The history of the hall is fascinating too. In the 17th century, it was the home of Judge Thomas Fell and his wife Margaret. They provided protection and hospitality for early Quakers and allowed the hall to be used as the headquarters for the movement. Fell was able to serve the Quaker Movement too, when he had charges of blasphemy against its founder, George Fox, dismissed. Years later, after the death of Thomas Fell, Margaret married George Fox. In the six historic rooms here, you can see a fine selection of 17th-century furniture as well finding out more about early Quaker history. You can get a cup of tea or coffee and a biscuit; self-catering accommodation is available.

VISIT THE MUSEUMS
Ulverston Heritage Centre
visitoruk.com/Ulverston
Lower Brook Street, LA12 7EE
01229 580820 | Open Mon–Sat
9.30–4.30
Located in one of Ulverston's fascinating ginnels, the Heritage Centre is staffed by highly knowledgeable volunteers and is bursting at the seams with useful information about the local

▼ Swarthmoor Hall, near Ulverston

area. The centre also contains a set of records, dating from the 18th century, a museum, book shop and gift shop.

Laurel and Hardy Museum

laurel-and-hardy.co.uk
On Stage at the Roxy, Brogden Street, LA12 7AH | 01229 582292 | Open daily 10–5

Bill Cubin started the museum with his collection of memorabilia, gathered from his lifelong love of 'the boys'. Starting out as a few scrapbooks of photos, the collection grew over time until it filled one small room, with pictures covering all the walls and even the ceiling. There was also a tiny viewing room for the movies. With encouragement from friends, he opened the museum. After many years at this cramped site, however, the museum had become overcrowded and, due to the hobbyist way the collection had been started, some of the pictures were beginning to look past their best. Bill's daughter and grandson, who still run it, decided to move everything to the Roxy cinema complex. In this light and spacious area, you can see the collection much more easily but it has lost that quirky feeling created by the muddle of memorabilia.

WALK THE CUMBRIA WAY

This 70-mile route will take you from Carlisle to Ulverston through the heart of the Lakes (see page 94).

CATCH A PERFORMANCE

Coronation Hall

corohall.co.uk
LA12 7LZ | 01229 588994

Coronation Hall has the largest capacity of any hall in south Cumbria. You can see a whole range of events here, including performances by touring companies in the fields of music, theatre, ballet and opera, as well as lively local presentations. It was built on the site of the famous County Hotel, which burned down in 1911. The building was completed during World War I and named to commemorate the coronation of King George V.

PLAY A ROUND

Ulverston Golf Club

ulverstongolf.co.uk
Bardsea Park, LA12 9QJ
01229 582824

Between 1923 and 1924, H S Colt, the highly respected golf course architect designed this course – and today it still looks almost as it did then. You'll find this undulating parkland course overlooking Morecambe Bay testing but fair and at the same time you can enjoy the glorious panoramic views of the Lakeland fells and mountains.

EAT AND DRINK

Farmers Arms Hotel

thefarmers-ulverston.co.uk
Market Place, LA12 7BA
01229 584469

This is one of the oldest inns in the Lake District. Here, you'll find a hospitable welcome, whether in the traditionally decorated restaurant, with its oak beams and impressive views of the Crake Valley, or in the 14th-century stable bar complete with a log fire and original slate floors. You can drink local ales, including Hawkshead Bitter, and enjoy a wide range of hearty pub grub.

Old Farmhouse
old-farmhouse.com
Priory Road, LA12 9HR
01229 480324

Just south of the town, and a short distance from Morecambe Bay, this is a busy community pub in a beautifully converted barn. You can enjoy local Cumbrian ales, choose from an extensive traditional menu and, in summer, sit in the suntrap courtyard garden. If you're a sports fan, this is the place for you. It has a separate snooker room and a lively bar with a big screen for live sports.

The Stan Laurel Inn
thestanlaurel.co.uk
31 The Ellers, LA12 0AB
01229 582814

When the old market town of Ulverston's most famous son – the comic actor Stan Laurel – was born in 1890, this town-centre pub was still a farmhouse with two cottages surrounded by fields and orchards. Today it serves a selection of locally brewed real ales and a full menu of traditional pub food plus a specials board.

▶ **PLACES NEARBY**

Great Urswick is in the Furness Peninsula, southwest of Ulverston, on the banks of Urswick Tarn.

St Mary the Virgin and St Michael
Church Road, Great Urswick, LA12 0TA

St Mary the Virgin and St Michael's church is said to have very early origins, perhaps ninth- and tenth-century. Richly carved crosses were found on the site and are now on display in the church. You can see clues to its history in changes in the stonework, including evidence of a Georgian ceiling, which was removed in the early 1900s to reveal the roof structure. The tower has very thick walls and was possibly used as a place of refuge. Have a look inside for the rare 18th-century three-decker pulpit and the 16th-century roof timbers – look for the date 1598. You can also see some interesting stained-glass windows, including fragments of medieval armorial stained glass in the chancel and a gallery at the west end dating from 1828.

General Burgoyne
generalburgoyne.com
Church Road, Great Urswick, LA12 0SZ | 01229 586394

Walkers, cyclists, bikers, families and dogs are always welcome here – they even provide crayons and paper for the children. Known as Gentleman Johnny, General

Burgoyne was a British army officer, politician and dramatist, infamous for surrendering his men to the enemy during the American War of Independence. A skull – not Burgoyne's – was found during renovations in 1995 is displayed in the fire-warmed bar, where you can enjoy Robinsons beers and decent pub grub.

▶ Isle Of Walney

Walney Island is connected to Barrow-in-Furness by Jubilee Bridge. Originally opened in 1908, it operated as a toll bridge but was renamed Jubilee Bridge in 1935. The ends of the island are designated Sites of Special Scientific Interest, and contain an abundance of nesting sea birds as well as amphibians and rare geological features.

GET OUTDOORS
North and South Walney Nature Reserves
Barrow-in-Furness, LA14 3YQ
A road bridge links Barrow with the Isle of Walney, which shields the tip of the Furness Peninsula, and Barrow itself, from the ravages of the sea. The southern tip of the Isle of Walney is a haven for a huge variety of birds; 250 different species have been recorded here, including migrants passing through. In the northern part of the reserve, you can walk by the saltmarshes, sand dunes and mudflats and where you might hear the loud and raucous call of the rare natterjack toad.

EXPLORE BY BIKE
W2W Cycle Route
This superb 151-mile trans-Pennine route (Sustrans Regional Route 20) begins on Walney Island and passes through a variety of wonderful countryside from Walney Island to Wearmouth in Sunderland. This is a classic 'coast to coast' cycling adventure, challenging in both distance and terrain, but if you are reasonably fit you should be able to do it. Thanks to the distinctive blue National Cycle Network signs and the official maps it's easy to follow in either direction. The route is mostly on country lanes, back roads and cycle paths, and you should easily manage the few off-road bits with a touring, trekking or hybrid bike.

PLAY A ROUND
Furness Golf Club
furnessgolfclub.co.uk
Central Drive, LA14 3LN
01229 471232 | Open all year, daily
This is one of the oldest golf courses in England, with beautiful views of the Lakeland hills and the Irish Sea. Enjoy the views with six outward holes, six inward holes along the beach and six alternating in each direction.

▶ Wasdale & Wastwater

You need to approach this bleakly beautiful valley from the west, which means a long drive for most people. The reward is that Wasdale will be spectacularly empty at times when the more accessible Lakeland places are crowded with visitors. If the view up to the head of the valley seems oddly familiar, that's because the National Park Authority created their logo from this view of Wastwater and the three peaks – Yewbarrow, Great Gable and Lingmell. Scafell Pike, near the head of the valley is the highest peak in England at 3,210 feet (978m) and although it is just three miles long, Wastwater is the deepest lake. The huge screes that dominate the southern shore continue their descent fully 250 feet into the cool clear waters. If you're tired of the busy Windermere waters, you will relish the tranquillity and awesome landscape at Wasdale.

The road hugs the water's edge until you reach Wasdale Head; communities don't come much smaller than this. St Olaf's, at Wasdale Head (CA20 1AZ) is at least as old as 16th century and is one of the smallest churches in England. Some of the roof beams are believed to have been made from Viking longships. It is open during daylight hours.

▲ Wastwater

EAT AND DRINK
Wasdale Head Inn
wasdale.com
CA20 1EX | 019467 26229
Walkers and climbers congregate here to drink local ales, take in some hearty pub grub and swap tales of the mountains. Dramatically situated at the foot of England's highest mountain, this Victorian inn is reputedly the birthplace of British climbing – photographs decorating the oak-panelled walls reflect this. Will Ritson, who was born in 1808, was the first and is still the most famous landlord of the hotel, renowned as 'The World's Biggest Liar'.

Top 5 views

▶ Ashness Bridge looking over Derwent Water

▶ Tarn Hows

▶ Rydal Water from any angle

▶ Wastwater looking towards Wasdale Head

▶ King's How on Grange Fell looking over Borrowdale and across Derwent Water

A beer festival on the first Sunday in October is a great reason to hang up the climbing boots for a day and maybe stay over in one of the comfortable bedrooms.

▶ Wetheral

Nestling on the banks of the River Eden, conveniently located close to Carlisle (see page 88), is this attractive village of Wetheral. Centred around a large triangular green and edged with gracious houses, built from the distinctive local red sandstone, this is a lovely place to stop and explore. Two buildings stand out from the rest:– Eden Bank, a grandiose mock château of the 19th century, which has mill stones set in its garden wall; and the elegant Crown Hotel, with a columned porch. Look for the early five-arched railway bridge spanning the wide River Eden, and if you take one of the footpaths into Wetheral Woods to the south of the village, you will find charming views of the picturesque ruins of Corby Castle on the opposite bank. Nearby, a 15th-century gatehouse is all that survives of the local Benedictine priory. Also overlooking the river is Holy Trinity Church, with an unusual octagonal tower and some splendid effigies. The quiet village of Faugh is also nearby.

▶ Whinlatter Forest

Whinlatter Forest is a mixed plantation of trees ranging from Sitka and Norway spruce to Scots pine, Douglas fir and Lawson cypress. Look out also for native broadleaves such as birch and oak, and the more exotic western hemlock and Japanese larch. The forest provides a habitat for a wide range of wildlife, and on this walk you may see roe deer, red squirrels, frogs, toads and foxes.

Overhead you may be lucky enough to spot buzzards, peregrines and many other species of bird life. One species you do have a good chance of seeing, depending on the time of the year, is the osprey. A breeding pair of ospreys has been nesting close to Bassenthwaite Lake since 2001, the species previously

▼ River Eden

having been persecuted to extinction in England more than 150 years ago. The huge nest, built by the Forestry Commission and the Lake District National Park Authority, is located in Dodd Wood and is subject to a round-the-clock guard once the female lays her eggs. Ospreys have a wingspan of nearly five feet, and are rich brown in colour with a white head and underside. They're fish eaters and you are most likely to see one hovering over the lake, its sharp eyes scanning the water for a fish, before streaking down unerringly to snag its prey.

Ospreys winter in Africa, but return to the Lake District in the spring to breed. The lower viewing point in Dodd Wood is staffed from April through to the end of August, from 10am to 5pm. High-powered telescopes and binoculars are available during the breeding period. Cameras are also trained on the nest, so that visitors can view live footage of the birds on a video screen at the Whinlatter Visitor Centre.

Cumbria's conifer plantations were planted during the early part of the 20th century. Woodland resources were severely depleted by the end of World War I, particularly by trench warfare, so there was a need to rebuild and maintain a strategic timber reserve. The Forestry Act came into force in September 1919, and the new commission's first planting in the Lake District was at Hospital Plantation, Whinlatter, in the same year.

The village of Braithwaite, which has several pubs, can be found nearby.

GET INDUSTRIAL
Force Crag Mine
nationaltrust.org.uk
Whinlatter Pass, CA12 5UP
This was the last working metal mine in Cumbria but closed in 1991. The National Trust run guided tours of the former mine buildings on five days each year.

ENTERTAIN THE FAMILY
Whinlatter Forest Visitor Centre
forestry.gov.uk
Whinlatter Forest Park, CA12 5TW
01768 778469 | Open daily, 10–4
This must be the best free family day out in the Lake District. England's only true Mountain Forest has stunning views, fantastic walks, exhilarating mountain biking and rare wildlife. Wild Play is a 1,968-foot children's trail through the woods with climbing frames, a log swing, Archimedes Screws, pulleys and much, much more.

WALK THE HIGH ROPES
Go Ape!
goape.co.uk
Whinlatter Pass, CA12 5TW
0845 643 9215 | See website for availability (pre-booking advised)
For a day out with a bit of adventure Go Ape! This is the highest course in the country,

at 1,180 feet above sea level. It's so high you can see all the way to Scotland. Get a thrill from riding a zip slide through the skies over water and through a real mountain forest. This is monkey business at its most untamed.

EAT AND DRINK

Coledale Inn

coledale-inn.co.uk
Braithwaite, CA12 5TN
017687 78272

Originally a woollen mill, the Coledale Inn dates from around 1824 and had stints as a pencil mill, a guesthouse and a private house before becoming an inn. The interior is attractively decked out with Victorian prints, furnishings and antiques, while footpaths, leading off from the large gardens, make it ideal for exploring the nearby fells. Two homely bars serve a selection of local ales while traditional lunch and dinner menus are served in the dining room.

The Cottage in the Wood ◉◉

thecottageinthewood.co.uk
Whinlatter Forest, CA12 5TW
017687 78409

Right at the heart of the Whinlatter Forest, this 17th-century former coaching inn sits in one of the most beautiful and tranquil parts of the national park, yet is only a short drive away from bustling Keswick. The Mountain View restaurant has just been refurbished, not that many diners will be looking at the decor with the atmospheric views of the Skiddaw range and forest drawing their gaze through the full-length windows. The setting is perfect Lake District and the food matches the setting – quality Cumbrian ingredients in imaginative menus, including a special 'Taste of Cumbria' menu. Not cheap, but a good choice for a special occasion.

The Royal Oak

royaloak-braithwaite.co.uk
Braithwaite, CA12 5SY
017687 78533

Surrounded by high fells and beautiful scenery, the Royal Oak is right in the centre of the village and is the perfect base for walkers. The interior is all oak beams and log fires, and the menu offers hearty pub food and local ales.

Siskins Café

forestry.gov.uk
Whinlatter Forest Visitor Centre, CA12 5TW | 017687 78469

High on the Whinlatter Pass, Siskins Café is a great place to start and finish your exploration of the surrounding woodland. From the balcony you can watch the never-ending stream of birds on strategically placed feeders, in the trees in front of you. The food is good too.

▶ Whitehaven

Your first stop in Whitehaven should be The Beacon, on West Strand, which will give you an insight into the history of the town and harbour with its audio-visual presentations and displays.

In the middle of the 18th century, Whitehaven was the third largest port in Britain after London and Bristol, shipping coal to Ireland and the Continent and importing tobacco from America. It was developed during the 17th century by three generations of the Lowther family, who became the Earls of Lonsdale, but in 1633, it was a miserable fishing hamlet, until the Lowthers built a harbour and a new town, which became a mining centre with shafts excavated far out beneath the sea.

Today, the handsome Georgian and Victorian buildings that you can still see testify to the town's prosperity. Whitehaven has a small fishing fleet and its harbour is a conservation area, with several monuments to its past mining history, which finally died out in 1986. At night, the bridge across the marina is lit up to dramatic effect. The town has two churches that are worth seeking out. St Begh's dates from around 1868 and is visually

▲ Whitehaven Harbour

quite striking, as it was built from white stone with a red-stone dressing. St James' is slightly older, from 1753, with Italian ceiling designs and a very atmospheric and moving Memorial Chapel.

Book lovers should note that Whitehaven has the largest antiquarian bookshop in Cumbria, and one of the largest in northern Britain, Michael Moon's Antiquarian Bookshop in Lowther Street.

VISIT THE MUSEUMS
The Beacon
thebeacon-whitehaven.co.uk
West Strand, CA28 7LY
01946 592302 | Closed for refurbishment until 22 May 2014. See website for opening times
The Beacon tells the story of this fascinating corner of the Western Lake District using interactive displays and activities. Experience the lifestyle differences between rich and poor, the hardships of working life and the dangers of disease. You can play hopscotch and bar skittles, while discovering how folks had fun in days gone by.

Look out for the early industries, such as salt making, farming and fishing; join the crew aboard the *Maria Lowther* ship, survive shipwrecks with the Rocket Brigade and relive the decline and revival of

The Rum Story
rumstory.co.uk
27 Lowther Street, CA28 7DN
01946 592933 | Open daily
10–4.30. Closed 1 week in Jan
You won't want to miss this fascinating museum in the original shop, courtyards, cellars and bonded warehouses of the Jefferson family, who have the distinction of being the oldest rum trading family in Britain. The exhibitions take you back in time to the early days of the rum trade, its links with the slave trade, sugar plantations, the Royal Navy, barrel-making and more. You can explore a tropical rainforest, an African village, a slave ship and a cooper's workshop.

Whitehaven Harbour. On the top floor is the Weather Gallery, full of high-tech equipment that monitors and records the weather and you can also enjoy panoramic views of the town and coast.

On the headland above The Beacon is the winding gear and engine house of the Haig Colliery Mining Museum.

Haig Colliery Mining Museum
haigpit.wordpress.com
Solway Road, Kells, CA28 9BG
01946 599949 | Open daily 10–4
Haig was the town's last deep pit, bringing up coal from several miles under the sea. Now you can discover the many tragic stories of the town's mining past, in which more than 1,200 men, women and children died.

SEE A LOCAL CHURCH
Church of St James
High Street, opposite Queen Street, CA28 7PZ
Built in 1752, St James' has an outstanding Georgian interior and fittings; it is like being inside a vast piece of pottery decorated by Josiah Wedgwood. In the west end porch are fine Georgian staircases leading to the three-sided gallery, which is supported by columns. Look for the roundels of decorative plasterwork on the ceiling, depicting the Annunciation and the Ascension. The apse has a top-lit dome and a striking central painting of the *Transfiguration* by Giulio Cesare Procaccini (1548–1626). A memorial chapel is dedicated to the dead of both World Wars and to local people killed in

mining accidents. It features a large piece of coal and uses a miner's lamp as the sanctuary lamp. All of the ground-floor windows are stained glass and include work by the renowned Victorian firms Shrigley and Hunt and William Wailes, as well as a modern window (1976) by L C Evetts.

GO SHOPPING
Michael Moon's Antiquarian Bookshop
moonsbookshop.co.uk
19 Lowther Street, CA28 7AL
01946 599010
If you love books, you could lose yourself for hours in this amazing bookshop. There are 13 rooms full of 100,000 books, covering every subject known to man, on its mile of shelving, with room for at least a hundred contented book browsers.

CATCH A PERFORMANCE
Rosehill Theatre
rosehilltheatre.co.uk
Moresby, CA28 6SE | 01946 692422
Oliver Messel (1904-1978), the stage, costume and film designer, designed this gorgeous little theatre. It opened on the hills above Whitehaven in 1959 and was described as a 'rose-red silk lined jewel box'. It is still one of Britain's most intimate theatres and here you'll find a diverse range of arts and entertainment from music, theatre, film, talks, comedy, shows for young people and more. Check the website for the current programme.

EXPLORE BY BIKE
Coast-to-Coast (C2C) Cycle Route
c2c-guide.co.uk
Britain's most popular long-distance cycle route follows a web of well-chosen minor roads, disused railway lines, off-road tracks and specially constructed cycle paths. As long as you are reasonably fit, you can complete at least part of this 140-mile-long route which links Whitehaven and Workington to Sunderland. Although there are some seriously hard climbs – the highest point being over 2,000 feet – the route is designed for everyone, from families to club riders. There are a number of off-road sections, but you always have the option of taking the surfaced alternative. The route starts in the former coal mining and industrial lands of West Cumbria, travels through the stunning scenery of the northern Lake District and heads into Keswick before passing through Penrith and the lush Eden Valley with its sandstone villages. It then starts the climb up to Hartside and onto the Northern Pennines. Meandering through old lead-mining villages, such as Nenthead and Rookhope, the route heads down into the Durham Dales before entering the old steel town of Consett on the edge of the Pennines. From here, it's an easy ride through one of Britain's old industrial heartlands to the North Sea and Sunderland.

The Reivers Cycle Route

reivers-route.co.uk

The Reivers Route is also known as the 'Return C2C' as it takes you from the end of the west–to–east route, 173 miles all the way back to the start of the C2C. Part of the National Cycle Network, the route winds its way through some of the wildest and most untouched countryside in Britain. Starting at the mouth of the River Tyne, the route finishes here on the Cumbrian coast. Along the way, you follow the shores of Kielder Water, take a brief foray into Scotland and cross the rugged countryside of the Northumberland National Park. Then, after the Borders and Carlisle, you head down through the Lake District to Cockermouth and Bassenthwaite. There are alternative options you can take along the way.

Haven Cycles

havencycles-c2cservices.co.uk

Preston Street, CA28 9DL

01946 63263

You can hire a range of bikes here: mens' and womens' hybrids, and mountain bikes including child sizes. Each cycle comes with a free rear pannier rack, mudguards, stand, gel seat, speed computer, bottle holder, lock, tool kit, puncture outfit, pump, spare tube and helmet.

PLAY A ROUND

Whitehaven Golf Club

whitehavengolfclub.com

Red Lonning, CA28 8UD

01946 591144

This relatively new course has nine ponds, three woodland areas, American-designed holes and, of course, glorious Lakeland views. They pride themselves on being welcoming and family friendly here.

EAT AND DRINK

Harbour Gallery and Café

thebeacon-whitehaven.co.uk

The Beacon, West Strand, CA28 7LY

01946 592302

After exploring Whitehaven's historic waterfront, unwind in the peaceful Harbour Gallery Café, with freshly made sandwiches, snacks or an excellent cream tea; surrounded by the artwork of local and community groups.

The Waterfront Restaurant and Bar

waterfrontwhitehaven.co.uk

West Strand, CA28 7LR

01946 328184

You'll find a warm welcome here and good service. The food is traditional, cooked from locally sourced ingredients and of very high quality. Some 95 per cent of their fish is locally caught, sourced from Donnan's on the harbourside. The meat here comes from a Lakeland butcher and they even bake their own bread. Whether you opt for lunch, afternoon tea or dinner à la carte you won't be disappointed.

▶ Windermere & Bowness-on-Windermere

To many visitors, a visit to the Lakes implies nothing more strenuous than mooching around the shops of Windermere and Bowness, and perhaps a relaxing boat trip on the lake. These twin towns – almost joined into one these days – attract a disproportionate number of holidaymakers. If you do want to shop, you'll find lots of quirky and interesting shops here and a buzz of activity. On the other hand, if you're looking for the National Park's ethos of 'quiet recreation', you should look elsewhere. Be aware, traffic congestion is a perennial problem, particularly in the summer months and on bank holidays.

The popularity of Windermere and Bowness is largely historical. Windermere is as far into the heart of the Lake District as the railway ever went. William Wordsworth lamented the coming of the railway; he foresaw that his beloved Lakeland would be spoiled by an influx of visitors. Certainly the railway opened up the Lakeland landscape to working people, instead of just well-heeled travellers with time on their hands. Wordsworth was right, of course – the Lake District did change.

▼ Lake Windermere with Ambleside in the distance

On the other hand, millions of people are now able to enjoy its unrivalled scenery.

It may seem a bit odd that it is Windermere, rather than Bowness, at the water's edge, which takes its name from the lake. But in fact, before the coming of the railway in 1847, Windermere was called Birthwaite; the station was called Windermere to attract visitors.

At Bowness Bay, the water of England's longest lake laps gently on the beach and sleek clinker-built dinghies can be hired by the hour. If you don't feel so energetic, you can enjoy a lake-long cruise, via Waterhead and Lakeside, on the cruise ships *Tern*, *Teal* and *Swan*. *Tern* is more than 100 years old and was once steam-powered. Since 2005, when the National Park Authority's 10mph water speed limit took effect, Windermere has become a more peaceful lake.

Opposite Bowness Bay is Belle Isle, the largest of Windermere's islands. You can still see the round house built there in 1774, when notions of the 'romantic' and 'picturesque' were at their height. The design was much mocked at the time; Wordsworth called it 'a pepperpot'. Before that, there was a manor house on the island, which was besieged by troops of Roundheads, while the Royalist owner was busy fighting in Carlisle, and archaeological finds reveal that Belle Isle was occupied during Roman times. It was bought in 1781 as a present for Mrs Isabella Curwen, and renamed in the lady's honour. While the National Trust owns most of Windermere's little islands, Belle Isle is still privately owned.

A couple of minutes' walk from the lake, at the bottom of Bowness Hill, is The Old Laundry Theatre, which caters for visitors and locals alike. As well as a theatre, there is a regular programme of exhibitions and events. Here, too, you'll find the World of Beatrix Potter, which uses the latest technology to bring the stories of Peter Rabbit, Jemima Puddleduck and many other characters to life.

Just a mile and a half from the centre of Bowness is a house of exquisite beauty. Completed in 1900 for the Manchester brewing mogul Sir Edward Holt, Blackwell (see page 70) was designed by Mackay Hugh Baillie Scott as an astounding expression of the Arts and Crafts Movement. Today it has been restored after decades of neglect and astonishingly almost all of the distinctive decorative features have remained intact.

A further two and a half miles north, along the Ambleside road brings you to Brockhole, a fine house in gardens that shelve down to the lake shore. Built for a Manchester

▲ Lake Windermere

businessman, the house has, since the late 1960s, been the National Park Visitor Centre. Brockhole is an excellent first stop, if you are new to the Lake District. There are gardens, displays, exhibitions, an adventure playground and a full calendar of events.

The eastern shore of Windermere is, for much of its length, in private hands. Mill owners who prospered from the trade in wool and cotton eagerly bought up plots of land to create tranquil oases with views of the lake. So the drive along the lake on the A592 can be disappointing since there are few public access points to the water's edge. However you will find plenty of lakeside walking on the less-populated western shore, much of which belongs to the National Trust.

For an elevated view of the lake, take a path to the left of the Windermere Hotel, at the top of the town. Within a few minutes you will be able to enjoy a glorious view of the lake and the southern Lakeland fells from the vantage point of Orrest Head. Another excellent viewpoint is the rounded hill called Gummer's How, which you can approach via a minor road just north of Newby Bridge. From the top – half-an-hour's walk from the car park – you will be able to see almost the length of Windermere, with the yachts and motor-boats looking like tiny toys.

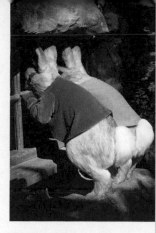

▶ The World of Beatrix Potter

hop-skip-jump.com
The Old Laundry, LA23 3BX | 01539
488444 | Open Apr–Sep daily 10–5.30,
Oct–Mar 10–4.30 (Closes at 3 on 24
& 31 Dec, at 4 on 26 Dec & 1 Jan)
If you're a Beatrix Potter fan, then
The World of Beatrix Potter will
transport you straight back to your
childhood, and for children it is just
like stepping into the books and meeting old friends. It
begins with a four-minute film presentation introducing Beatrix
Potter and her stories. As you go through the exhibition you'll
see 3D scenes from the stories, atmospheric lighting and real
sounds and smells straight from the books – you can smell the
laundry in Mrs Tiggy-Winkle's kitchen and the tomatoes in Mr
McGregor's greenhouse. You can walk through Jemima's
woodland glade and through the trees to see Mr Tod. You can
wander through the Peter Rabbit Garden, with the Cos lettuces
that Benjamin Bunny nibbled and the gooseberry bush where
Peter got caught in a net as he tried to escape Mr McGregor.
Using computer projection, you can take a journey to the places
that inspired Beatrix Potter. And don't miss the interactive
timeline, which tells the fascinating story of the author's life.

Lake District Visitor Centre at Brockhole

brockhole.co.uk

LA23 1LJ | 015394 46601 | Open all year daily

You couldn't do better than to start your visit to the Lake District at this interesting and informative establishment designed to help you get the most out of the area. Set in 32 acres of grounds, landscaped by Thomas Mawson, on the shore of the lake, it became England's first National Park Visitor Centre in 1969. You'll find something for everyone and all the information on the Lake District you could want. It has permanent and temporary exhibitions, lake cruises, an adventure playground, an indoor play area and an extensive events programme. The kids will love Tree Top Trek – an outdoor high-ropes experience – where they can swing, climb, balance and fly their way through 250-year-old oak trees, discovering views previously reserved for the squirrels and bats. Contact the Centre for a copy of their free events guide. Canoe and sailing tuition is available in school holidays and you can hire boats in summer, weekends and school holidays.

▼ Lake District National Park Visitor Centre, Brockhole

TAKE IN SOME HISTORY
Townend
see page 219

ENTERTAIN THE FAMILY
The World of Beatrix Potter
see page 245

GO ROUND THE GARDENS
Holehird Gardens
holehirdgardens.org.uk
Lakeland Horticultural Society,
Patterdale Road, LA23 1NP | 015394
46008 | Gardens open all year daily
dawn–dusk, reception desk: Apr–Oct
10–5

If you're a gardener you will
love the Lakeland Horticultural
Society's 17-acre garden,
maintained completely by
volunteer members of the LHS.
You'll find plenty of like-minded
gardeners to chat to in this
splendid hillside site with
stream gardens and rocky
outcrops looking to Windermere
and the Langdale Pikes. The
garden includes specimen trees
and flowering shrubs for all
seasons. Among the highlights
are autumn heather and
shrubs, spring bulbs and
alpines. There are also national
collections of astilbe,
hydrangea and polystichum,
as well as fine herbaceous
borders, herbs and climbers.
The Lakeland Horticultural
Society was founded in1969,
and there are a number of LHS
events throughout the year.

SEE A LOCAL CHURCH
Church of St Martin
Junction of Church Street and
St Martin's Parade, LA23 3DG
Although built onto a 13th-
century church, most of what
you can see today dates from
the 1870 restoration. Look out
for the different roof beams,
where the chancel was
extended to the east. The tower
was heightened and all the
seating renewed. Most of the
fine murals, including two large
wall paintings in the chancel,
date from this time as well. The
1870 restoration also skilfully
restored the 15th-century
stained-glass east window,
containing glass, which
survived the vandalism of
Cromwell's soldiers. Looking
towards this great window from
the font is another stunning
feature: eight black-letter
inscriptions from the 16th
century, high up on the beams
between the arches.

TAKE A BOAT TRIP
Windermere Lake Cruises
windermere-lakecruises.co.uk
Bowness LA23 3HQ, Ambleside
LA22 0EY, Lakeside LA12 8AS
015394 43360

A cruise on Windermere]is a
must. No matter where you
start your journey, be it
Bowness, Ambleside or
Lakeside, the voyage gives you
magnificent views of mountain
scenery, secluded bays and
wooded islands. You can break
your journey at any of the stops
and there is a range of ticket
options. The Freedom of the
Lake ticket from any pier is
good value, allowing you to hop
on and off as many times as you
want for a period of 24 hours.

Or in summer take the 75-minute cruise to watch the sun set over Lake Windermere. There are lots of activities that you can combine with a cruise on the lake to make a great day out. In summer, you can take a trip on the Lakeside & Haverthwaite Steam Railway (see page 146). At any time you can visit the Lakeland Motor Museum (see page 63) or the Aquarium at Lakeside (see page 176) or of course you can cruise and walk. You will find tickets to suit, whatever you want to do. Check the website for special events.

CATCH A PERFORMANCE
The Old Laundry Theatre
oldlaundrytheatre.co.uk
Crag Brow, LA23 3BX | 01539
488444 | Open Aug–Dec only
In this interesting Edwardian laundry building, only three minutes' walk from Lake Windermere, you'll find an intimate theatre presenting exciting and stimulating performances ranging from touring theatre companies to comedy to all sorts of music and film.

EXPLORE BY BIKE
Country Lanes
countrylaneslakedistrict.co.uk
Windermere Railway Station
LA23 1AH | 015394 44544
You can hire all sorts of bikes here: trek bikes, road, hybrid and tandems; child bikes, trailers and tag-a-longs are available too. Safety equipment and accessories are supplied as well. Or you could take one of their self-guided tours, with accommodation, meals, baggage transfers, routes and mechanical back-up all included.

PLAY A ROUND
Windermere Golf Club
windermeregolfclub.co.uk
Clearbarrow, LA23 3NB
015394 43123
Just two miles from Windermere, this is not a long course but it makes up for its lack of distance with heather, tight undulating fairways and some of the finest views in the country. The sixth hole has a nerve-racking but exhilarating blind shot over a rocky face to a humpy fairway with a lake to avoid on the second shot.

EAT AND DRINK
The Angel Inn
theangelinnbowness.com
Helm Road, LA23 3BU
015394 44080
Just five minutes' walk from Lake Windermere, in the centre of Bowness-on-Windermere, this family-owned and run gastro-pub offers plenty of city-chic style. Unusual local ales vie with international beers at the bar, and good food based on local produce is available throughout the day from a choice of menus. Sandwiches and light lunches, starters, nibbles and salads, cheese plates or main courses and a children's menu are all available. The terrace offers fantastic views.

Beech Hill Hotel ◉

beechhillhotel.co.uk
Newby Bridge Road, LA23 3LR
015394 42137

On the shore of Lake Windermere, Beech Hill Hotel offers wonderful views over the waters to the green fells beyond. You can enjoy the pleasant vista as you eat your meal in the restaurant, a large and smartly kitted-out room, where the menus offer an appealing range of dishes, completely in touch with contemporary tastes.

Cedar Manor Hotel & Restaurant ◉◉

cedarmanor.co.uk
Ambleside Road, LA23 1AX
015394 43192

This one-time gentleman's residence lies on the outskirts of Windermere in mature walled gardens, where you can see the 200-year-old cedar that gives the place its name. Dinners in the candlelit restaurant with its high-backed leather chairs and crisp linen are a soothing affair. They serve quality, award-winning food in their two AA Rosette restaurant and they have also won awards for top service and warm, friendly atmosphere.

Gilpin Hotel & Lake House ◉◉◉

thegilpin.co.uk
Crook Road, LA23 3NE
015394 88818

The Cunliffe family has associations with this lovely house going back to the beginning of the 20th century. They now run it as a country house hotel, where they always strive to provide the very best levels of hospitality. Gilpin is surrounded by 22 acres of magnificent Lakeland countryside, with soaring trees and beautiful gardens, and the hotel itself is stylishly decorated without an iota of chintz. The original features of the house, built in 1901, remain but the impression within is of modern luxury and comfort. The food is contemporary, but clearly focused at the same time. There are plenty of creative ideas and preparations on show and the ingredients are second to none. There's a wine suggestion for every dish, even on the light lunch menu, and the staff run the show with charm and professionalism.

Holbeck Ghyll Country House Hotel ◉◉◉

holbeckghyll.com
Holbeck Lane, LA23 1LU
015394 32375

Holbeck Ghyll has an outstanding location, even by Lake District standards. As you draw near along the driveway, the panorama unfurls over Lake Windermere to some of Lakeland's best-known peaks – Scafell Pike, Coniston Old Man and the Langdale Pikes. The house is far enough from the madding crowds to offer tranquillity, while its baronial oak-panelled walls, stained glass, artworks and rugs on burnished wood floors give you a taste of the good things in life. You can enjoy those fabulous Lakeland views in the opulence of the dining room and the service lives up to the surroundings. The food is contemporary, seasonal and accomplished and sourced from a well-established supply line of local growers and producers.

Miller Howe Hotel ◉◉

millerhowe.com
Rayrigg Road, LA23 1EY
015394 42536

Miller Howe is something of a Lakeland icon. Dining here is an indulgent experience, with its plush decor and romantic views of the lake. If you want to sample a range of the delicious food on offer, try the tasting menu. Or make the more difficult choice from the dishes on the à la carte.

The Samling ◉◉◉

thesamlinghotel.co.uk
Ambleside Road, LA23 1LR
015394 31922

This winsomely attractive, white-fronted country house, set amid 67 acres of grounds, overlooks Lake Windermere. The Samling was awarded a Michelin Star in 2014 and holds three AA Rosettes, as well as winning the 'Best Dining Hotel in the World' in the Boutique Hotel Awards in 2013. You can dine in either of the two rooms, one on either side of the house. The decor is quietly understated, with bare wood floors, plain painted walls and a fine prospect over the lake.

Storrs Hall Hotel ◉◉

englishlakes.co.uk
Storrs Park, LA23 3LG
015394 47111

This Grade II listed Georgian mansion sits in 17 acres of grounds by Lake Windermere, with a sensational view over gardens and the lake. Inside, there's an old-school approach, with game and traditional local produce figuring strongly on the menu. The service, of course, is excellent too.

▶ PLACES NEARBY

Church of St Kentigern

Crosthwaite, Church Lane
CA12 5RA

This enormous church is dedicated to St Kentigern (St Mungo), who came to Keswick in AD 553. The present church was built in 1181 and still has many interesting elements dating from the 12th to the 16th century. The elaborately carved font dates from 1395 and the bowl is 16th century. Look too for the uniquely English consecration crosses of 1523 (nine inside the church, and three outside near the window openings), marking the spots where holy water was sprinkled.

The Punchbowl Inn at Crosthwaite ◉◉

the-punchbowl.co.uk
Crosthwaite, Lyth Valley, LA8 8HR
015395 68237

If you want a relaxed atmosphere, good food and drink and friendly service, this award-winning pub fits the bill.

You can also eat or relax with a pint and a daily paper in front of an open fire in one of the two rooms off the bar.

Hare & Hounds Country Inn

hareandhoundsbowlandbridge.co.uk
Bowland Bridge, LA11 6NN
015395 68333

Slightly off the beaten track, but convenient for Bowness and Windermere, this traditional country inn with flagstone floors, exposed oak beams and ancient pews is the place to retreat from the tourist hurly-burly. Very much at the heart of the community, in the pretty little hamlet of Bowland Bridge, this 17th-century coaching inn even hosts the Post Office on Tuesday and Thursday afternoons. You'll find good local food and their signature real ale – Hare of the Dog beer – brewed for the pub by Tirril Brewery. Time your visit for the late May annual beer festival.

Staveley

The village of Staveley is off the A591 between Kendal and Windermere. It mainly comprises grey slate buildings, which lie between the Rivers Kent and Gowan. Only the tower of its 14th-century church remains. St James was built in 1865 and it's worth going in to see the stained-glass east window designed by Sir Edward Burne-Jones and made by William Morris and Co.

Eagle & Child Inn

eaglechildinn.co.uk
Kendal Road, Staveley, LA8 9LP
01539 821320

The name of this friendly inn refers to a legend of a baby found in an eagle's nest during the time of King Alfred. The rivers Kent and Gowan meet at the pub's gardens with its picnic tables for outdoor eating and local-ale drinking. You'll find classic Cumbrian dishes, which use ingredients from village suppliers and a number of vegetarian options too.

Hawkshead Brewery

hawksheadbrewery.co.uk
Mill Yard, Staveley, LA8 9LR
01539 825260

This is the biggest of the Cumbrian independents, family owned and run with the aim of brewing 'traditional beers with a modern twist'.

The Brown Horse Inn

thebrownhorseinn.co.uk
Winster, LA23 3NR | 015394 43443

This 1850s inn is full of original features. Despite all the time-worn charm, the decor has a modern edge on account of a refurbishment. The inn is virtually self-sufficient; the vegetables and free-range meat come from the owners' surrounding land, and ales are brewed on site. The innovative cooking is a contemporary take on traditional fare.

▸ Overleaf: The view over Lake Windermere

▸ Workington

Workington is an ancient market and industrial town at the mouth of the River Derwent. Some parts of the town, north of the River Derwent, date back to Roman times. Workington became a major industrial town and port in the 18th century with the expansion of the local iron ore and coal industries and Henry Bessemer introduced his revolutionary steel making process here. In recent years, the steel industry and coal mining has declined and the town has diversified into other forms of industry.

VISIT THE MUSEUM
Helena Thompson Museum
helenathompson.org.uk
Park End Road, CA14 4DE
01900 64040

Miss Helena Thompson was a local philanthropist, who bequeathed her house to the people of Workington in 1940. You can see displays of pottery, silver, glass and furniture dating from Georgian times, as well as find out about the social and industrial history of Workington. Helena had a special interest in the history of costume and needlework, and collected many examples of women's and children's dresses in the styles fashionable from the late 18th century to the beginning of the 20th century. You can see a selection of these too, along with jewellery and accessories.

CATCH A PERFORMANCE
Carnegie Theatre and Arts Centre
carnegietheatre.co.uk
Finkle Street, CA14 2BD
01900 602122

The historic Carnegie Theatre and Arts Centre started life as the Carnegie Library and Lecture Hall, built by Workington Town Council with £7,500 donated by the philanthropist Andrew Carnegie. It opened to the public in 1904 and the Lecture Hall was subsequently let as a Variety and Kinema venue to earn sufficient income to pay the librarian and buy books for the library.

In 1911, the Council extended the centre into the adjoining house to provide an adequate variety stage. It operated as a Cinema until 1958. In 1973 the Library Service moved out and the Town Council converted the former library into an Arts Centre. You will now find a regular programme of events including opera, classical and popular music, as well as theatre and dance. There are also classes and courses in dance, music and drama for all ages. Check the website for details.

EXPLORE BY BIKE
Coast-to-Coast (C2C) Cycle Route
see page 238

PLAY A ROUND
Workington Golf Club
workingtongolfclub.com
Branthwaite Road, CA14 4SS
01900 603460
You will be made very welcome at this undulating meadowland course, designed by James Braid. It has natural hazards created by a small beck and trees, and good views of the Solway Firth and the Lakeland Hills as you go round.

EAT AND DRINK
The Old Ginn House
oldginnhouse.co.uk
Great Clifton, CA14 1TS
01900 64616
When this was a farm, ginning was the process by which horses were used to turn a grindstone that crushed grain. It took place in the rounded area known today as the Ginn Room, which is now the main bar. These days you'll find Jennings and Coniston beers here, while the dining areas – all butter yellow, bright check curtains and terracotta tiles – have a Mediterranean feel. From the menu and specials you can choose cosmopolitan or traditional dishes.

Yewbarrow House
yewbarrowhouse.co.uk
Grange-over-Sands, LA11 6BE
01539 532469 | Open Jun–Sep selected Sun or by appointment
If you're a keen or even moderately interested gardener, don't miss this spectacular garden set high above sea level and with glorious coastal views. The use of local slate and limestone to create snaking paths, dividing walls and structural features gives the 4.5-acre garden of Yewbarrow House a fitting sense of place. The old Victorian garden has been transformed from a near-wilderness of brambles, unkempt trees and shrubs to a garden and woodland with year-round colour, a variety of moods and a number of surprises.

On an exposed, sloping site you might be surprised to see exotic plants thriving so far from their native warmer climes. And yet here at Yewbarrow House, where frost rarely penetrates the ground, there are olive trees that bear fruitful if modest crops; mimosa that sparkles like sunlight against the neutral background of a ruined stone bridge; and myriad exciting plants that are native to Mexico, Hawaii, Africa, Australia and New Zealand.

Much of the garden is decorative and inspirational, but the Victorian Kitchen Garden also has work to do, providing fruit, vegetables and herbs not just 'for the house', as in days gone by, but for the owner's three neighbouring hotels. It is entirely organic and everything is planted using the crop rotation system. There is also a large cutting garden with row upon row of flowers that, like the produce, are sent to the sister hotels.

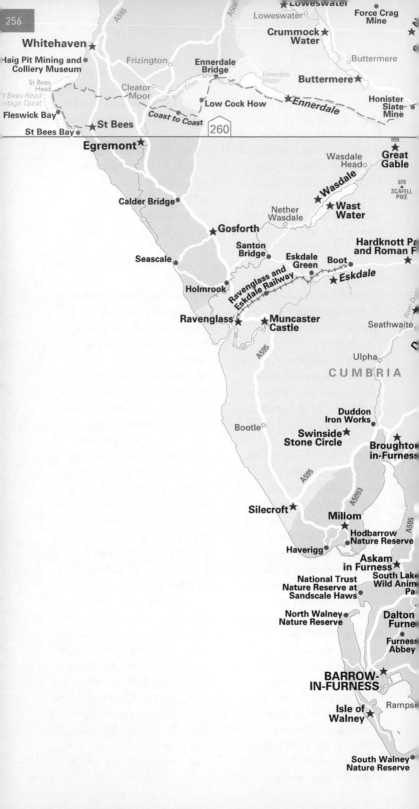

Loweswater

Loweswater

Force Crag
Mine

Crummock ★
Water

Buttermere

Whitehaven ★

Haig Pit Mining and
Colliery Museum ●

Frizington ○

Ennerdale
Bridge

Ennerdale Water

Buttermere ★

St Bees
Head

Cleator
Moor

River Ehen

Low Cock How

Ennerdale

Honister
Slate
Mine

St Bees Head
Heritage Coast

Coast to Coast

Fleswick Bay ●

★ St Bees

Coast to Coast

260

St Bees Bay ●

Egremont ★

Wasdale
Head ○

Great
Gable

899

Calder Bridge ●

Wasdale

978
▲
SCAFELL
PIKE

Nether
Wasdale ○

★ Wast
Water

Gosforth

Santon
Bridge ●

Eskdale
Green

Boot ●

Hardknott Pa
and Roman F

Seascale ●

Ravenglass and
Eskdale Railway

★ Eskdale

Holmrook ●

Ravenglass ★

★ Muncaster
Castle

Seathwaite

River Duddon

A595

Ulpha ○

CUMBRIA

Duddon
Iron Works ●

Bootle ○

Swinside ★
Stone Circle

Broughton-
in-Furness

A595

A5093

Silecroft ★

Millom
★

A595

Hodbarrow
Nature Reserve

Haverigg ●

Askam ★
in Furness

South Lak
Wild Anim
Pa

National Trust
Nature Reserve at
Sandscale Haws ●

North Walney ●
Nature Reserve

Dalton
Furne ●

Furness
Abbey ●

BARROW-
IN-FURNESS ★

Ramps

Isle of ★
Walney

South Walney ●
Nature Reserve

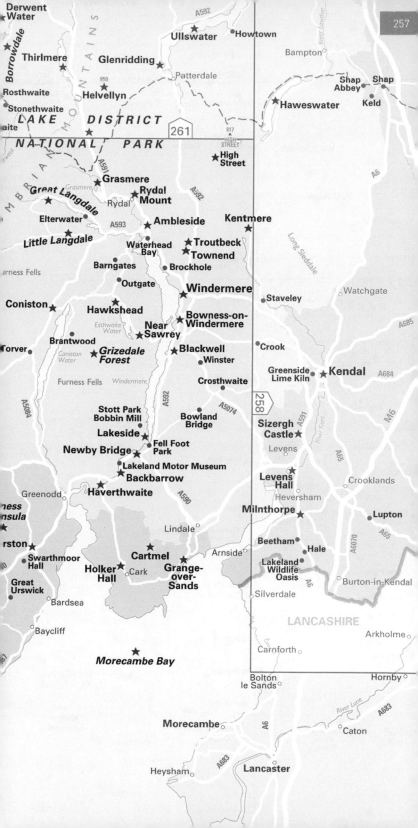

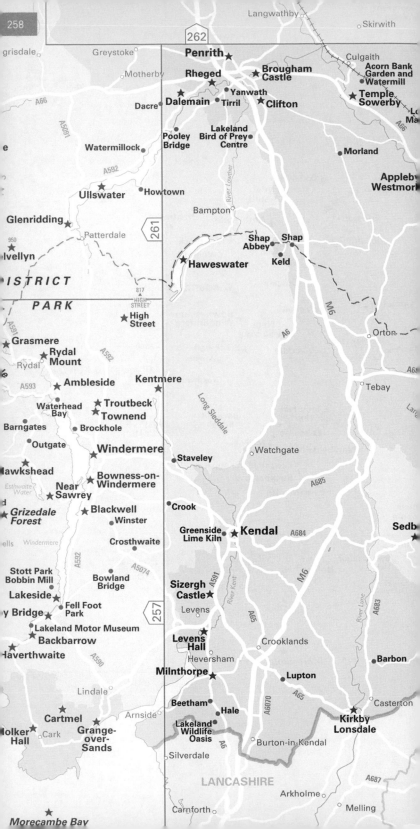

262

Penrith ★
Rheged ★
Brougham Castle ★
Culgaith

Acorn Bank Garden and Watermill
Motherby
Yanwath
Dalemain ★ Tirril
Clifton ★
Temple Sowerby ★
Dacre

Greystoke
grisdale
Langwathby
Skirwith

A66
A5091
Watermillock
Pooley Bridge ●
Lakeland Bird of Prey Centre ●
Morland ●
A592

Appleby Westmor

Ullswater ★ Howtown ●
Bampton ○

River Lowther

Glenridding ★
Patterdale ○
261
Shap Abbey ●
Shap ★
Keld ●
Haweswater ★

lvellyn ★
950

ISTRICT

817

PARK
HIGH STREET
M6

High Street ★
A6

Orton ○

Grasmere ★
Rydal
Rydal Mount ★
Tebay ○

A593
Ambleside ★
Kentmere ★
Long Sleddale

A6

Waterhead Bay ●
Troutbeck ★
Townend ★
Watchgate ○
A685

Barngates ●
Brockhole ●
Outgate ●
Windermere ★
Staveley ●

lawkshead ★
Bowness-on-Windermere ★
Esthwaite Water
Near Sawrey ★
Blackwell ★
Crook ●

Grizedale Forest
Winster ●
ells
Windermere
Crosthwaite ●

Greenside Lime Kiln ●
Kendal ★
A684
Sedb ★

A5074
Stott Park Bobbin Mill
Bowland Bridge ●
A591
M6

Lakeside ★
Fell Foot Park ●
257
Sizergh Castle ★
Levens ○
River Kent
A683

y Bridge
Lakeland Motor Museum
Backbarrow
Crooklands ○
River Lune

laverthwaite ★
A590
Levens Hall ★
Heversham ○
Barbon ●

Lindale ○
Milnthorpe ★
A65
Lupton ●
A6070

Cartmel ★
Arnside ○
Casterton ○
Beetham ●
Hale ●
Kirkby Lonsdale ★

lolker Hall ★
Cark ○
Grange-over-Sands ★
Lakeland Wildlife Oasis ●
Burton-in-Kendal ○
A687

Silverdale ○

LANCASHIRE

Morecambe Bay ★
Carnforth ○
Arkholme ○
Melling ○

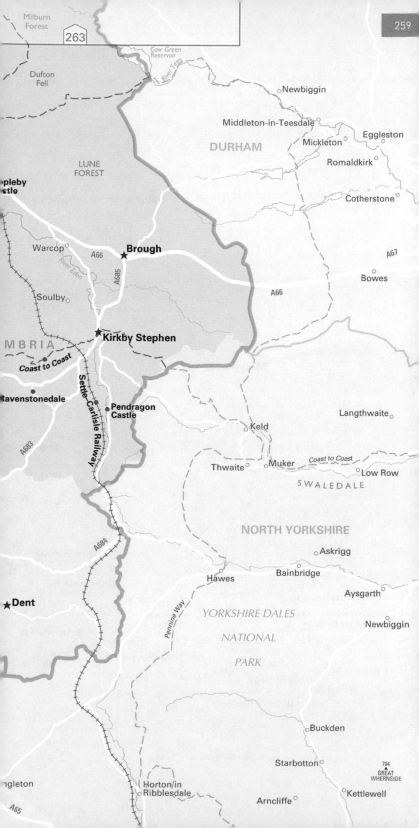

Kirkbean○

Mainsriddle○

Solway Firth

Grune Point

Moricambe Bay

Silloth★

Abbey Town○

Beckfoot Beach●

A596

Westnewton○

Allonby●

Allonby Bay

Prospect○

Aspatria○

River Ellen

Bothel○

As

Maryport★

○Dearham

A594

A595

Flimby○

○Standingstone

Cockermouth★

Bassenthwa La

A596

River Derwent

Brigham○

A595

Workington★

A66

★**Loweswater** Lorton Vale

Whin F

Branthwaite○

A597

A5086

★**Loweswater**

Loweswater○

Force Mir

Crummock★ **Water**

Whitehaven★

Frizington○

Ennerdale Bridge★

○Butter

Haig Pit Mining and Colliery Museum●

A595

St Bees Head

St Bees Head: Heritage Coast

Cleator○ Moor

Ennerdale Water

Buttermere★

River Ehen

Fleswick Bay●

Low Cock How●

Coast to Coast

★**Ennerdale**

Ho

St Bees Bay●

★**St Bees**

Egremont★

256

Wasdale Head○

Wasdale

Calder Bridge●

Nether Wasdale○

★**Wast Water**

★**Gosforth**

Hard and I

Santon Bridge●

Seascale○

Eskdale Green

Boot

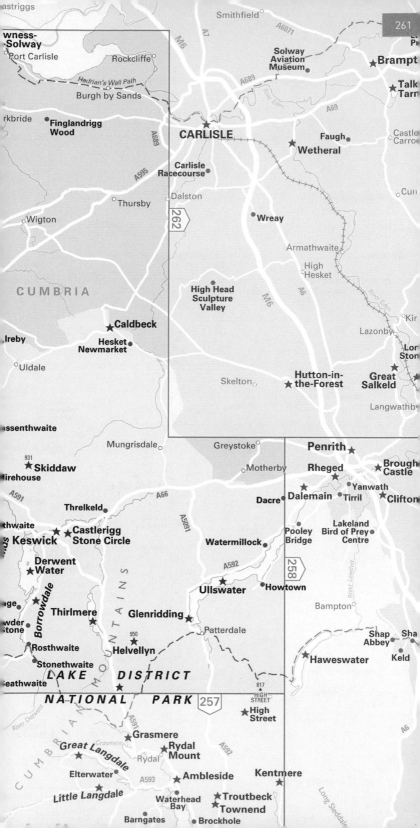

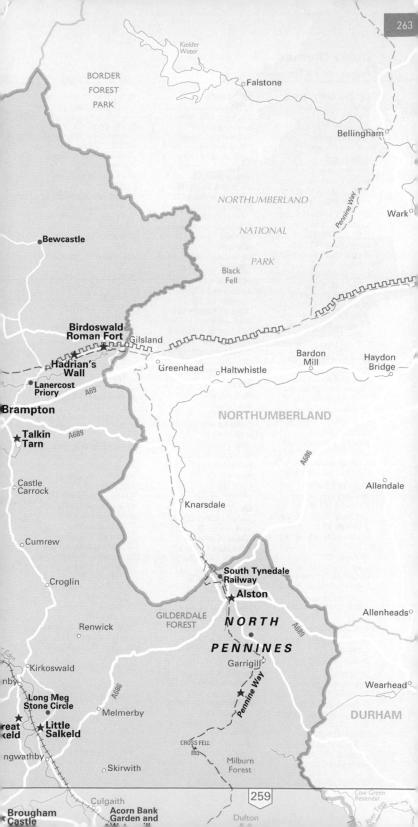

Kielder Water

Falstone

BORDER
FOREST
PARK

Bellingham

NORTHUMBERLAND

Wark

Pennine Way

Bewcastle

NATIONAL

PARK

Black
Fell

Birdoswald
Roman Fort   Gilsland

Greenhead   Haltwhistle

Bardon
Mill

Haydon
Bridge

Hadrian's
Wall

Lanercost
Priory

A69

Brampton

NORTHUMBERLAND

A689

★ **Talkin**
Tarn

A686

Allendale

Castle
Carrock

Knarsdale

Cumrew

South Tynedale
Railway

Croglin

★ **Alston**

Allenheads

GILDERDALE
FOREST

N O R T H

Renwick

A689

P E N N I N E S

Eden

Garrigill

nby

Kirkoswald

A686

Wearhead

Long Meg
Stone Circle

Melmerby

★ **Pennine Way**

★
eat
eld

★ **Little**
Salkeld

Pennine Way

DURHAM

ngwathby

CROSS FELL
893

Skirwith

Milburn
Forest

Cow Green
Reservoir

Culgaith

Brougham
Castle

Acorn Bank
Garden and

Dufton

River Tee

Index themed

Page numbers in **bold** refer to main text entries

Index, places

Page numbers in **bold** refer to main entries; page numbers in *italics* refer to town plans

The Automobile Association wishes to thank the following photographers and organisations for their assistance in the preparation of this book.

Abbreviations for the picture credits are as follows – (t) top; (m) middle; (b) bottom; (l) left; (r) right; (c) centre; (AA) AA World Travel Library.

Trade Cover: Anna Stowe Landscapes UK/Alamy
SS Cover: AA/T Mackie

4tl AA/E Bowness; 4tr–5tl AA/T Mackie; 4b AA/T Mackie; 5bl AA/A Mockford & N Bonetti; 5r AA; 8–9 AA/T Mackie; 11 AA/T Mackie; 12t AA/T Mackie; 12b AA/A Mockford & N Bonetti; 13t Courtesy of Theatre by the Lake; 13m Courtesy of the Brantwood Trust; 13b John Morrison/Alamy; 14t AA/R Coulam; 14m itdarbs/Alamy; 14b AA/E Bowness; 15t Courtesy of The World of Beatrix Potter; 15b The National Trust Photolibrary/Alamy; 16t AA/A Mockford & N Bonetti; 16m Photodisc; 16b AA/T Mackie; 17 AA/S Day; 19 AA/S Day; 20 AA/T Mackie; 22 AA/J Smith; 23 Photodisc; 24 Andrew Darrington/Alamy; 25 AA/T Mackie; 26 AA/A Mockford & N Bonetti; 29 AA/J Smith; 30 AA/A Mockford & N Bonetti; 32 AA/E Bowness; 33 AA/A Mockford & N Bonetti; 34 AA/A Mockford & N Bonetti; 36 AA/J Tims; 38 Andrew Page/Alamy; 39 numb/Alamy; 40 AA/E Bowness; 41 Courtesy of Jennings Brewery; 42 AA/J Tims; 45 AA/A Mockford & N Bonetti; 47 Courtesy of The World of Beatrix Potter/Steven Barber; 48 Mark Richardson/Alamy; 50 AA/A Burton; 52–3 AA/T Mackie; 56 AA/E Bowness; 57 AA/E Bowness; 60 AA/E Bowness; 68–9 AA/A Mockford & N Bonetti; 72 Clearview/Alamy; 73 AA/A Mockford & N Bonetti; 74 AA/A Mockford & N Bonetti; 79 AA/P Sharpe; 81 AA/P Sharpe; 82–3 AA/T Mackie; 85 AA/E Bowness; 87 Stan Pritchard/Alamy; 88 AA; 90 AA/E Bowness; 91 AA/R Coulam; 93 UK City Images/Alamy; 97 AA/E Bowness; 100–1 AA/S Day; 102 AA/C Lees; 105 AA/A Mockford & N Bonetti; 106 AA/S Day; 107 Courtesy of the Brantwood Trust; 109 AA/P Sharpe, 110 John Davidson Photos/Alamy; 112 AA/T Mackie; 115t AA/J Tims; 115b AA/P Kenward; 116–7 AA/D Tarn; 118–9 AA/T Mackie; 120–1 AA/A Mockford & N Bonetti; 123 AA/A Mockford & N Bonetti; 126–7 AA/J Sparks; 131 Paul White – North West England/Alamy; 132–3 AA/S Day; 137 AA/E Bowness; 140 AA/T Mackie; 141 AA/R Coulam; 142 AA/R Coulam; 143 AA/R Coulam; 144–5 AA/S Day; 146 AA/S Day; 151 Stewart Smith/Alamy; 152 AA/P Sharpe; 154–5 AA/P Bennett; 156 AA/E Bowness; 157 AA/P Bennett; 162 David Lyons/Alamy; 163t AA/E Bowness; 163b AA/A Mockford & N Bonetti; 164 Courtesy of Theatre by the Lake; 165 Barrie Neil/Alamy; 166–167 AA/T Mackie; 168 AA/T Mackie; 169 AA/D Tarn; 174 AA/S Day; 175 AA/A Mockford & N Bonetti; 178–9 AA/T Mackie; 181 AA/E Bowness; 185 AA/E Bowness; 188–9 Paul White Aerial views/Alamy; 190–1 AA/T Mackie; 193t WorldPhotos/Alamy; 193b AA/E Bowness; 194 AA/T Mackie; 195 AA/P Sharpe; 196 Arcaid Images/Alamy; 200–1 NDP/Alamy; 206–7 AA/E Bowness; 208 AA/A Mockford & N Bonetti; 211 AA/J Sparks; 214 AA/E Bowness; 215 AA/A Mockford & N Bonetti; 216–7 AA/T Mackie; 218 AA/E Bowness; 220–1 AA/A Mockford & N Bonetti; 223 AA/T Mackie; 226 AA/E Bowness; 230–1 AA/A Baker; 232 AA/R Coulam; 236–7 AA/T Mackie; 240–1 AA/A Mockford & N Bonetti; 242 AA/A Mockford & N Bonetti; 244 AA/P Sharpe; 245t Courtesy of The World of Beatrix Potter; 245b Courtesy of The World of Beatrix Potter/Ben Barden Photography Ltd; 246 John Morrison/Alamy; 252–3 Adam Burton/Alamy; 272 AA

Every effort has been made to trace the copyright holders, and we apologise in advance for any unintentional omissions or errors. We would be pleased to apply any corrections in any following edition of this publication.

Series editor: Rebecca Needes
Author: Hugh Taylor and
Moira McCrossan
Copy editor: Sandy Draper
Proofreader: Sheila Hawkins

Indexer: Marie Lorimer
Designer: Liz Baldin
Digital imaging & repro: Ian Little
Art director: James Tims

Additional writing by other AA contributors. *Lore of the Land* feature by Ruth Binney. Some content may appear in other AA books and publications.

Has something changed? Email us at travelguides@theaa.com.

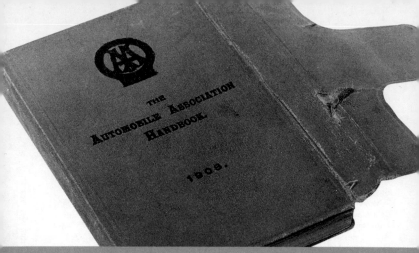

'WE KNOW BRITAIN'

The AA was founded in 1905 as a body initially intended to help motorists avoid police speed traps. As motoring became more popular, so did we, and our activities have continued to expand into a great variety of areas.

The first edition of the AA Members' Handbook appeared in 1908. Due to the difficulty many motorists were having finding reasonable meals and accommodation while on the road, the AA introduced a new scheme to include listings for 'about one thousand of the leading hotels' in the second edition in 1909. As a result the AA has been recommending and assessing establishments for over a century, and each year our professional inspectors anonymously visit and rate thousands of hotels, restaurants, guest accommodations and campsites. We are relied upon for our trustworthy and objective star, Rosette and Pennant ratings systems, which you will see used in this guide to denote AA-inspected restaurants and campsites.

In 1912 we published our first handwritten routes and our atlas of town plans, and in 1925 our classic touring guide, *The AA Road Book of England and Wales* appeared. Together, our accurate mapping and in-depth knowledge of places to visit were to set the benchmark for British travel publishing.

Since the 1990s we have dramatically expanded our publishing activities, producing high quality atlases, maps, walking and travel guides for the UK and the rest of the world. In this new series of regional travel guides we are drawing on over a hundred years of experience to bring you the very best of Britain.